Religion and Families

This is the first multidisciplinary text to address the growing scholarly connection between religion and family life. The latest literature from family studies, psychology, sociology, and religion is reviewed along with narratives drawn from interviews with 200 racially, religiously, and regionally diverse families that bring the concepts to life. Written in a thought-provoking, accessible, and sometimes humorous style by two of the leading researchers in the field, the book reflects the authors' firsthand experience in teaching today's students about religion's impact on families. Prior to writing the book, the authors read the sacred texts of many faiths, interviewed religious leaders, and attended religious services for a wide array of faiths. The result is an accurate and engaging account of why and how families are impacted by their religion. The pedagogical features of the text include boldfaced key terms defined in the glossary, text boxes, chapter conclusions, summary points, and review questions.

Religion and Families:

- Examines several denominations within Christianity, Judaism, and Islam.
- Reviews findings from racially and ethnically diverse families, as well as from traditional and diverse family forms, and examines gender and life-course issues.
- Addresses the impact of one's religious involvement on longevity, divorce rates, and parenting styles.
- Considers demographic, family-, couple-, and individual-level data that relate to prayer and other sacred practices.
- Presents a balanced treatment of the latest research and a new model for studying family and religion.
- Explores the "whys," "hows," and processes at work in the religion-family connection.

Intended as a text for undergraduate courses in family and religion, the psychology or sociology of the family, the psychology or sociology of religion, pastoral/biblical counseling, or family and youth ministry, taught in human development and family studies, psychology, sociology, religion, social work, pastoral counseling, and sometimes philosophy. This text will also appeal to family therapists and counselors.

Loren D. Marks is a professor in the School of Family Life at Brigham Young University and co-director of the *American Families of Faith* research project.

David C. Dollahite is a professor in the School of Family Life at Brigham Young University and co-director of the *American Families of Faith* research project.

Textbooks in Family Studies Series

The *Textbooks in Family Studies Series* is an interdisciplinary series that offers cutting-edge textbooks in family studies and family psychology. Volumes can be complete textbooks and/or supplementary texts for the undergraduate and/or graduate markets. Both authored and edited volumes are welcome. Please contact the series editor, Robert Milardo, at rhd360@maine.edu for details in preparing a proposal that should include the goal of the book, the table of contents, an overview of competing texts, the intended market including course name(s) and level, and suggested reviewers.

These are the books currently in the series:

Father-Daughter Relationships: Contemporary Research and Issues
written by Linda Nielsen (2012)

Stepfamilies: A Global Perspective on Research, Policy and Practice
written by Jan Pryor (2014)

Serving Military Families: Theories, Research, and Application, Second Edition
written by Karen Rose Blaisure, Tara Saathoff-Wells, Angela Pereira, Shelley MacDermid Wadsworth, and Amy Laura Dombro (2016)

Evidence-based Approaches to Relationship and Marriage Education
edited by James J. Ponzetti, Jr. (2016)

Evidence-based Parenting Education: A Global Perspective
edited by James J. Ponzetti, Jr. (2016)

Evidence-based Approaches to Sexuality Education: A Global Perspective
edited by James J. Ponzetti, Jr. (2016)

Religion and Families

An Introduction

LOREN D. MARKS
DAVID C. DOLLAHITE

Routledge
Taylor & Francis Group
NEW YORK AND LONDON

First published 2017
by Routledge
711 Third Avenue, New York, NY 10017

and by Routledge
2 Park Square, Milton Park, Abingdon, Oxon, OX14 4RN

Routledge is an imprint of the Taylor & Francis Group, an informa business

Library of Congress Cataloging-in-Publication Data
Names: Marks, Loren Dean, author. | Dollahite, David C. (David Curtis), author.
Title: Religion and families : an introduction / Loren D. Marks, David C. Dollahite.
Description: New York, NY : Routledge is an imprint of the Taylor & Francis Group, an Informa Business, [2017] | Series: Texbooks in family studies | Includes bibliographical references and index.
Identifiers: LCCN 2016019571 | ISBN 9781848725454 (hardback : alk. paper) | ISBN 9781848725461 (pbk. : alk. paper) | ISBN 9781315814599 (ebk)
Subjects: LCSH: Families—Religious life. | Marriage—Religious aspects. | Parenting—Religious life. | Religion.
Classification: LCC BL625.6 .M37 2017 | DDC 201/.7—dc23
LC record available at https://lccn.loc.gov/2016019571

ISBN: 978-1-84872-545-4 (hbk)
ISBN: 978-1-84872-546-1 (pbk)
ISBN: 978-1-315-81459-9 (ebk)

Typeset in Avenir and Dante
by ApexCovantage, LLC

To our parents
Renee & Larry Marks
Elizabeth & Melvin Dollahite

Contents

Foreword

For far too long we have been without a comprehensive, evidence-based textbook on religion and families. Loren Marks and David Dollahite have expertly crafted a book that deftly addresses important issues of faith and religious practices and their connection to family outcomes. In the 13 chapters that make up *Religion and Families*, the authors address core matters of religious beliefs and practices and their connection to individual and family well-being, to the character and consequence of parent-child relationships, and to the influence of faith communities. They provide us with an innovative model of how these core issues are connected and where we should look to improve our understanding of family relationships and what helps them flourish. Wisely the authors consider potentially controversial issues such as the possibility of religious beliefs as source of harm in marriage and parental relationships. They add discussion of a broad range of beliefs in a variety of faiths, for instance by addressing issues of faith among Jews and Muslims, and in this way consider issues of diversity in religious beliefs and practices with their consequent outcomes for families. They end the book with a chapter on forgiveness, which in many ways becomes a signature of one of the book's many strengths, a clear focus on important questions, both moral and empirical, and how the social science of family relationships adds to our understanding. In considering these issues we become better, more informed students and, perhaps, more informed citizens and family members.

Professors Marks and Dollahite are well qualified to write a book on religion and families. As young men they both spent time doing volunteer community work with families in inner cities. Both have families of their own and considerable personal experience in partnerships and parenting—a combined

50-plus years of marriage, 12 children, and 3 grandchildren at this writing. They are accomplished teachers and scholars, having taught at universities for several decades, and they have made important contributions to family scholarship and continue to do so. At the same time, they are great storytellers, and I appreciate their talent in combining their own personal experience with a wealth of material taken from their more formal study of families. Students will likely find the book readable and engaging.

Professors Marks and Dollahite state in their introductory chapter that "although we will not be dispensing many answers, we will be asking a number of questions that we believe are worth asking." Again, they wisely take the time to systematically present important ethical questions that confront students and families. At this time, in a world that is often tortured, I appreciate a strong core of ethics paired with and informed by an equally strong core of social science.

Robert M. Milardo, Ph.D.
Professor Emeritus of Family Relations
University of Maine
Series Editor

Preface

Series editor Dr. Robert Milardo has stated, "Our purpose [in the Routledge/Taylor & Francis *Textbooks in Family Studies Series*] is to pair leading scholars with core topics in the field of family studies that are surprisingly underrepresented." Dr. Milardo's identification of the topic of religion in families as "surprisingly underrepresented" is on the mark.

As university professors, we have taught a combined total of nearly 200 courses on families from the 1980s to the present. In most of those classes, the connection between religion and families is addressed. In some of these courses, including Dollahite's Family Life in World Religions class, this connection is central. And yet we have not encountered an undergraduate textbook specifically focused on religion and families. It is time.

Over the past two decades, as researchers, we have strived to better understand the connections between religion and family life. We have read the sacred texts of many faiths, visited with and interviewed religious leaders representing each of the Abrahamic faiths, and attended and participated in religious services for a wide array of faiths. All of this has been done in an effort to more accurately and respectfully understand the whys, hows, and processes at work in the religion-family connection. Most significantly, we have had the privilege of interviewing about 200 diverse families in their own homes in connection with our *American Families of Faith* project. These families shared their stories, experiences, and challenges with us. We will share some of their insights and narratives throughout the book in an effort to engage you as a reader.

Even though the book will be primarily for family studies, it is also multidisciplinary in that it deals with aspects of psychology, sociology, and religion. Thus we believe this book can serve as a primary text or a supplemental reader for courses in family and religion, the psychology or sociology of the family, the psychology or sociology of religion, pastoral/biblical counseling, family and youth ministry, human development, and family studies, as well as courses in social work, clinical psychology, and family therapy.

Learning Tools

Our goal was to write a book that resembles our classroom delivery styles—to try to keep students engaged. As such, scattered throughout this book we pose some of life's BIG questions and invite you to consider these questions in relation to religion and relationships. The book also features thoughts and experiences drawn from our database of qualitative interviews with 200 diverse religious families (including youth and young adults) to provide an engaging experience for undergraduate students. The tone is intended to be, alternatively, both thought provoking and lighthearted.

In addition, thought-provoking quotes from prominent thinkers as well as our students are sprinkled liberally throughout the book in textboxes. Boldfaced key terms defined in the glossary, chapter conclusions, summary points, and review questions provide valuable study tools at exam time. The goal of these elements is to promote deeper exploration among readers of the ideas presented and to facilitate class discussion.

Content Highlights

Chapter 1: Why Religion Matters to You Right Now and in Your Future Family

We explain why the religion-family connection matters to us on both the professional and personal levels. We also explain why the period of emerging adulthood matters and why we have dedicated our professional lives to working with people in this phase of life. We discuss the BIG (Being, Identity, and God) questions of life and argue that there is no richer opportunity to wrestle with and address these questions than during emerging adulthood.

Chapter 2: What in the World Is Religion?

We examine different definitions of **religion** from various figures including Sigmund Freud, Karl Marx, William James, and Harold Bloom. We also address what we call the BAD-RAP definitions of religion. We alternately accept and reject some elements of these definitions and offer our own research-informed definition of religion that includes the three dimensions of religious beliefs, religious practices, and religious communities.

Chapter 3: Does Religion Matter to Families?

Using our three-dimensional model of religion (that includes religious beliefs, religious practices, and religious communities), we look at research from an array of scholars and disciplines that indicates individual-level and family-level connections between religion and relationships. A majority of these connections appear to be encouraging and healthy, but some raise concern and indicate problems.

Chapter 4: Why Does Religion Matter in Marriage?

Using our three-dimensional model of religion, we look at the religion-marriage connection. In addition to presenting research from several leading researchers, we discuss issues including inter-faith marriage, marital conflict, challenges in marriage, the marital transition from "me" to "we," and the importance of being "equally yoked."

Chapter 5: The Influence of Religious Beliefs in Marriage

This chapter moves beyond research-based correlations to examine the deeper connections and reasons why religious beliefs can harm or help marriage. In-depth interview data from several studies are presented that address and explore pro-marriage beliefs, anti-divorce beliefs, religious beliefs as a source of harm in marriage, and the importance of shared faith in God as a marital support.

Chapter 6: Parenting in Faith—What Research Has Found

Based on the research of several leading researchers from various disciplines, we explore how religion can harm or help parent-child relationships. Findings related to both the mother-child and father-child relationships are compared and contrasted across the three dimensions of religious beliefs, religious practices, and religious communities.

Chapter 7: Parenting and American Families of Faith

In-depth, interview data from our *American Families of Faith* project is presented to provide a deeper exploration of the processes at work as religion influences parent-child relationships. Related themes include the importance of parents "practicing what they preach" and the vital role of parent-child conversations (with parents listening, not lecturing). Stories from some of our former students are shared to maintain a focus on real-life applicability.

Chapter 8: Muslim Families in the United States

Using demographic data, we present an overview of Islam in the United States. Then, with in-depth qualitative data from the *American Families of Faith* project, we offer an in-depth look into the challenges of being Muslim, the practice of *hijab* (covering), and insiders' perspectives on Muslim practices in the home, including the month-long fast of Ramadan.

Chapter 9: Jewish Families in the United States

Using demographic data, we present an overview of Judaism in the United States. Then, with in-depth qualitative data from the *American Families of Faith* project, we offer an in-depth look into the challenges of being Jewish, the importance of the synagogue and Jewish community, and insiders' perspectives on Jewish practices in the home, including rituals associated with *Shabbat* (Sabbath observance).

Chapter 10: Religion and Diverse Family Forms

Most religion and family research focuses on traditional, marriage-based families. High-quality data are scarce regarding religion in diverse family forms, including step, single-parent, and same-sex families. The *Does the Shape of Families Shape Faith?* project on families of divorce is a notable exception and is highlighted in this chapter. With this project's authors, we discuss how experiencing divorce influences faith—and explore how faith communities, parents, and children influence and are influenced by each other.

Chapter 11: How Religion Influences Coping with Stress and Challenges in Families

We review the work of leading religion and coping scholars including Kenneth Pargament, Annette Mahoney, and Harold Koenig. The role of religion in general (and prayer in particular) in dealing with death, loss, disability, and other profound challenges is addressed. We offer several supportive examples from our *American Families of Faith* interview data.

Chapter 12: Forgiveness, Faith, and Families

Few family processes that intersect and overlap with religion have received as much careful empirical attention as forgiveness. We present key findings from many of the leading researchers in this area, including how forgiveness can be helpful and harmful. We offer additional illustrative examples from our *American Families of Faith* interview data.

Chapter 13: What We Have Learned and What We Hope You Will Take with You

We review the central themes (and most important ideas) from the book and make a final effort to convey the importance of religion to some individuals and families. We highlight the importance of those working and serving in the helping professions (secular or religious) developing a healthy and sensitive awareness of why and how religion matters to those they serve, teach, and love.

Acknowledgments

We are honored by the invitation from the *Textbooks in Family Studies Series* editor Robert Milardo and Debra Riegert of Routledge / Taylor & Francis to convey, in a student-friendly way, the exciting and complex findings that are emerging in the topical area of religion and families. We would also like to thank the reviewers who provided invaluable insight: Matthew Murdoch, Carleton University (Canada); Joanne Roberts, Hardin Simmons University; Walter Schumm, Kansas State University; Joe Wilmoth, Mississippi State University; and one anonymous reviewer.

We are grateful to a number of institutions and individuals for substantive assistance in our ability to create this volume. Firstly, we are grateful to the institutions that have provided material and intellectual assistance to our American Families of Faith project. These include support from the University of Delaware, Louisiana State University, the Kathryn Norwood and Claude Fussell Alumni Professorship (LSU), a Kappa Omicron Nu National Alumni Research Grant, and the Jack Shand Research Award (from the Society for the Scientific Study of Religion) provided to Loren. Support also includes grants from the Eliza R. Snow Fellowship and other research support provided by the College of Family, Home, and Social Sciences and the School of Family Life at BYU provided to Dave. Dave is also grateful to the Center for Research on Families at the University of Massachusetts at Amherst for supporting a sabbatical research leave in 2002 that allowed him to interview families in New England, the Dominican University of California where Dave was a visiting scholar in 2004 and was able to interview families in California, and to the Center on Adolescence at Stanford University for supporting a sabbatical leave there in 2012 where he was able to develop ideas reflected in this book.

We are grateful to our student, Ashley Tuft, for helping us create the Chapter Summary Points and Review Questions at the end of each chapter, and our student, Essen Skabelund, who read through the final draft of page proofs and helped us find and correct errors. For their untiring patience and professionalism in editing, copyediting, typesetting, and other crucial aspects of producing this book, we are very grateful to Georgette Enriquez, Rachel Severinovsky, and Seth Townley at Taylor & Francis as well as Katherine Wetzel at Apex CoVantage. We deeply appreciate Mel Thorne and Kaylee Brown for their expert assistance in producing the author and subject indices.

—Loren Marks and David Dollahite

About the Authors

Loren D. Marks is a professor in the School of Family Life at Brigham Young University. From 2008–2015 he held the Kathryn Norwood and Claude Fussell Alumni Professorship and served as director of Louisiana State University's Child and Family Studies program (from 2011–2015) before moving to BYU in 2015.

His research efforts have centered on religion and family relationships, and he has published more than 80 articles or chapters, as well as the book *Sacred Matters: Religion and Spirituality in Families* (Routledge) with Wes Burr and Randy Day. His research on families has received national media attention from outlets including the *New York Times*, the *Washington Times*, the *Boston Globe*, and the *Wall Street Journal*.

Loren received his Ph.D. from the University of Delaware (2002). He was honored with college-level teaching awards in 2005, 2009, 2013, and 2015 and was twice nominated by LSU as a national Carnegie Professor of the Year—in 2011 and 2014. Loren and his wife, Sandra Martindale Marks, married in 1995 and are the parents of five dynamic children—Mishonne, Logan, Haley Renee, Denton, and Aliyah.

He is co-director (with Dr. David Dollahite) of the *American Families of Faith* project that includes 200 Christian, Jewish, and Muslim families from all eight regions of the United States. Findings from this ongoing project have resulted in over 50 scholarly articles/chapters. This volume, *Religion and Families*, is the culmination of 20 years of collaborative work between Dave and Loren.

David C. Dollahite is a professor of Family Life at Brigham Young University where he teaches classes and conducts research on the links between religion and family life. He is co-director (with Dr. Loren Marks) of the *American Families of Faith* project. He received the Eliza R. Snow Fellowship for his research on religion and family relationships and was an associate director in the School of Family Life.

He has been a visiting scholar at the Stanford University Center on Adolescence, the University of Massachusetts-Amherst, and Dominican University of California and was the Jawaharlal Nehru Visiting Scholar at Maharaja Sayajirao University of Baroda, India.

Professor Dollahite obtained a bachelor's degree in family life and a master's degree in marriage and family therapy from BYU (1985) and a doctorate in family studies from the University of Minnesota (1989).

He has published over 100 scholarly articles and chapters and has edited or co-edited four books including *Generative Fathering* (Sage, 1998) and three volumes on religion and family life: *Successful Marriages and Families* (BYU Studies, 2012), *Helping and Healing Our Families* (Deseret Book, 2005), and *Strengthening Our Families* (Bookcraft, 2000).

David and his wife, Mary Kimball Dollahite, J.D., have been married since August of 1983 and are the lucky parents of seven terrific kids—Rachel, Erica, Camilla, Kathryn, Spencer, Jonathan, and Luke—and are grandparents of David, Edward, and Eliza Lambourne (children of Rachel and Collin Lambourne).

1 Why Religion Matters to You Right Now and in Your Future Family

Why does this book on *Religion and Families* matter enough that you should take the time to read, ponder, and consider the central issues we want to discuss with you? In this initial chapter, we will briefly offer you several reasons why the religion and family connection matters to you now and in your future family. We are not trying to get preachy on you, but we do have some fascinating discoveries to share. Who knows, some of them may even influence your life. They have certainly influenced ours.

In this opening chapter, we hope to pique your curiosity, but we will spend the remainder of the book offering you a deeper and more probing view of the ideas and connections we can only introduce here. We sincerely hope you will not only read but also carefully consider the best and most meaningful ideas we present.

Why Does the Religion-Family Connection Matter to Us on a Personal Level?

Before we explain why the connection between religion and families matters to you, we would like to briefly explain how and why this connection has come to matter to us both personally and professionally. As a college freshman, Loren was playing basketball (and occasionally studying) at a state school in Oregon. After his freshman year, something happened. He decided to do some volunteer missionary work, spending a large share of his time in inner-city Milwaukee, Wisconsin. His 24 months there were spent carefully observing, interacting with, and learning from a variety of (predominantly

African-American) families from several faiths and living in an array of life situations. A take-home message for Loren, as a young man from rural Oregon, was that there were two factors that seemed to elevate the lives of those with whom he worked. Those factors were: (a) authentic engagement in a religious faith, and (b) a motivated college education. These are points to which we will later return.

At 18 years of age, Dave was a carefree California boy whose religion of choice was tennis. His "saints" were tennis stars Bjorn Borg and Stan Smith, not Peter and Paul. However, Dave was introduced to, read, and pondered some sacred religious texts that influenced him deeply enough that he went through a religious conversion of both belief and action. After a year of intense religious study, he made the decision to do some voluntary mission work in the Boston, Massachusetts area. This was both a life-enriching and life-changing experience for him. From closely observing thousands of individuals in hundreds of families, he learned that how people approached their deepest beliefs strongly influenced their most valued relationships. He also learned that those families that put their faith at the center of their family lives seemed better able to deal with a number of challenges than families with little or no faith involvement.

Why Does Emerging Adulthood Matter to Us?

If you will pardon the personal notes, the vitally important point is that, for both of us, the college years and "emerging adulthood" (as this stage is currently called in the social sciences) were transformative. We began these years absorbed in non-religious and non-academic interests—basketball and tennis—but we both experienced times of reflection and uneasiness and, at times, a search for something "more" and a desire to figure out *who we really were*. We both went through changes and the intensification of hope, faith, and a desire to connect with and serve others. Those changes impacted our subsequent academic interests and foci—we both emerged from our voluntary missionary and outreach service with a desire to study families. Our volunteer religious service also significantly influenced our decisions regarding whom and how to marry, as well as our philosophies of life and how to best pursue happiness. Today, we are both in long-term marriages. Loren and Sandra have been married since 1995 and have five children. Dave and Mary have been married since 1983 and have seven children and three grandchildren.

We also share an abiding interest in and love for emerging adults. We have taught a combined total of nearly 200 college courses on family life to young adults and are both convinced that (professionally speaking) we have the best job in the world. Additionally, roughly five combined decades of our lives have been spent in voluntary involvement with youth and emerging adults in community and faith community settings away from our university campuses. Emerging adults matter deeply to us, which leads us to an additional point.

If you have taken an introductory-level psychology or human development class, you are likely aware that one of the few points of consensus among leading psychologists is that "during the first six years, the template for life is set down" (Doherty, 2001, p. 43). We agree with this well-established perspective, but we are additionally convinced that during the stage of emerging adulthood, we make several central decisions that relate to religion, family, and identity—and that some of these decisions echo and resound throughout the remainder our lives. If the first six years of life are when the blueprint or template for life is sketched, it is often during the college years that early but vitally important aspects of *building* take place. This conviction represents one primary motive for accepting the invitation to write this book for you.

Why Does the Religion-Family Connection Matter to Us on a Professional Level?

As we have explained, we have a personal interest in the religion and family connection as well as a deep, personal investment in emerging adults. However, what led us to care enough about the connection between religion and families to write this book? We would like to answer that question in a way that will frame the remainder of this text.

In 1995, Dave was a young professor and Loren was an undergraduate student in family studies. One day after class, Dave extended an invitation to Loren to work with him on a research project that was examining families with children who had special needs. Loren gratefully accepted the invitation.

As we studied these families with a special needs child, we learned that (particularly when a child is born with a profound disease or disability) the eventual divorce rate and likelihood of the father moving out of the family picture were discouragingly high. After some consideration, we decided that rather than focus on the reasons many fathers left these difficult situations, we might be able to learn something of significance by interviewing fathers who *stayed*. With the help of a kind woman who served as a director of a services center for children with special needs and their families, we began interviewing fathers who had remained closely supportive of their wife and child(ren) in the face of heartbreaking challenges. We asked these fathers several questions about the source of their strength—and we received several recurring answers. Those answers, across several research articles we eventually wrote, included: (a) God, (b) their wife and marriage, (c) spiritual beliefs, (d) religious practices including prayer, and (e) their faith community (Dollahite, 1998, 2003; Dollahite, Marks, & Olson, 1998, 2002; Marks & Dollahite, 2001). There was an agnostic father or two who did not frame their ongoing commitment in terms of the Divine, but most of the dads (if we talked with them long enough) allowed us to step onto what we have now come to call "the sacred ground" of their inner world (Marks, 2004). One father, Luke,[1] whose son had severe mental and physical delays and was not likely to ever walk, was one example. Luke shared with us a sacred "vision" he had that kept him going. He said:

> After this life is over, we will meet the Savior, and my son, Robert, will be there, and he will be perfectly normal and alert and the child of God that I hoped he would be. He will look at me and say, "Thank you for taking care of me, for doing the things that you did." I think about the long-term perspective after this life when we meet the Savior, and he looks at you and says, "You did a good job as a father," and when Robert will say to me that I did good.
>
> (Marks & Palkovitz, 2007, p. 221)

This vision was especially powerful to Luke because Robert, his son, could not speak.

Another father Loren interviewed was unforgettable. We will call him Brad. Brad and his wife had a son with some special needs. Then, several years after the birth of their son, they had triplet daughters who were born severely premature. One of the triplets died shortly after birth. The other two survived but had significant developmental delays in addition to visual and hearing problems. Our home-based interview was extended due to frequent and chaotic interruptions from a series of mild "emergencies" involving the girls, then age two. (Brad had given his wife a rare "night off" with her friends). Brad cared for his girls with a patience and easiness of manner that seemed to evenly counter the visible chaos of an exceptionally challenging parenting situation. At the conclusion of the interview, Loren (unable to restrain himself) blurted, "I know you are a man of faith, but don't you ever shake your clenched fists at the heavens and say, '*Why, God? Why!?*'"

Brad looked at a point off in the distance that only he could see and said, "I did once."

"Well, do you feel like you got a response?"

"Eventually."

"Please, tell me what it was . . ."

Again, Brad looked at the distant point visible only to him. And then he softly replied, "God told me that I will *live* into the answer."

Please think about that response for a while. Then think about it a little longer. We have been thinking about it for almost 20 years.

> There are times when God asks nothing of his children except silence, patience, and tears.
>
> —Charles Seymour Robinson

Why do we study and write about the religion and family connection? One initial answer is that because of parents like Luke and Brad we found ourselves in a situation where we had to do so. We asked these parents what mattered most to them and to their families, and they told us. As social scientists we were bound to report what we found. However, if that is what started us down the road of inquiry, it is not a sufficient explanation for why we continued down the religion and family road for two additional decades and conducted in-depth interviews with another 200 families around the United States. A more complete and honest answer may be that we continue to ask questions because, like Brad, we too are struggling and striving "to *live* into our own answers." This book is a continuation of that quest for the right questions . . . and maybe some answers.

Not an Answer Book but a Question Book

This book is not an answer book. It does, however, provide insight into the lives of diverse families from various faiths as they wrestle to find and "live into" answers that provide hope and meaning. We hope that this book will be different from any you have previously read and that you will learn much that will be of worth to you. Although we will not be dispensing many answers, we will be asking a number of questions that we believe are worth asking. The answering is left to you.

Among the most important questions we will ask are those that the Greek philosophers, including Aristotle, called "the Terrifying Questions"—terrifying in that they can be frightening *and* terribly difficult to answer. Perhaps the most central of all of the Terrifying Questions is: "When I die, is it all over, or is there something more?"

Our objectives in this book are unique in a couple of ways. First, we want to delve much deeper than most books or textbooks—indeed, life does not get much deeper than the Terrifying Questions. A second objective is to have some fun. We believe the two can be mutually inclusive. If we can think deeply together *and* laugh warmly together, we all win. In the text and text-boxes scattered throughout this book, we will invite you to think and sometimes just to laugh.

The BIG Questions

With all due respect to Aristotle, we prefer to rename the "terrifying" questions of life as the **BIG questions**.[2] The BIG questions have to do with existential mysteries about human origins and destinies; questions about ultimate concerns such as the meaning of existence and the purpose of life; questions about one's life calling or mission (what Catholics often call questions about vocation); and questions about close relationships such as marriage and family life. Again, for those who are young adults, we think these questions are not necessarily terrifying—they are exciting, challenging, and essential. What better time in life to contemplate the very issues that matter most? We call these issues that are worthy of careful contemplation the BIG questions because they tend to pertain to matters of **B**eing, **I**ntimacy, and **G**od.

Being questions deal with ultimate origins and destinations and the meaning and purpose of existence, life, and death along with matters of identity (e.g., Who am I?). Being questions explore the nature of self and others and one's place in the world. From a faith perspective, the fundamental questions of being include such questions as:

Should I remain as I am or strive to become what I am meant to be?
What is the nature of my soul?
Where did I come from?
What is my purpose in life?
What is my destiny?
How can I become what I am supposed to become?
How will I balance various aspects of my "self"?

> Always be your self, but be your better self.
>
> —Karl G. Maeser

Intimacy questions deal with relationships with others, especially close relationships, and particularly those among family members. From a faith perspective, the central questions relating to intimacy might include questions such as:

To whom do I belong?
Who are "my people"?
With whom should I share my deepest self?
To whom shall I give my heart?
How can I best love the person to whom I have committed myself?
Do I want to marry?
Do I want to have children?
What qualities do I want my partner and/or co-parent to have?
What is my responsibility to my future children and grandchildren?

God questions deal with the existence and nature of God and the nature of the relationship one has (or does not have) with the Divine. God questions also have to do with matters of transcendence, **spirituality**, devotion, morality, and "eternal" issues about life after death. From a faith perspective, some of the big God questions include:

Do I believe in God or only in what is currently visible and knowable by the senses?
What is the nature of God?
What is the meaning of existence?
What does God expect of me?
How can I please God in this life?
Where will I go after death?
What is the mission/calling/vocation God has for me?
How can I commune or connect with God?
How should I serve God and others?

In the following section and throughout this book we refer to some of these BIG questions and invite you to consider these kinds of questions and other big questions you have in relation to religion and relationships.

Why Should Any of This Matter to *You*?

The title of this chapter promised to address "Why Religion Matters to You Right Now and in Your Future Family." We have shared with you a little about how we became personally involved in studying the religion and family connection, as well as why we are uniquely interested in emerging adults and the important decisions that lie in front of you. Now it is time for us to begin delivering on our promise to explain why the religion and family connection matters to *you*.

In a landmark study of religion, youth, and emerging adults, more than 3,300 youth were followed across time (Smith & Denton, 2005). About two-thirds were tracked and surveyed all the way into their emerging adulthood years, and 230 were also interviewed in-depth (Smith & Snell, 2009). The researchers, Christian Smith and Patricia Snell, share the following statement from an emerging adult named Amanda, who explains that the biggest challenge for those her age is "*deciding who we are*, the growing up process of separating from our parents and *deciding for ourselves what we want to be and do*" (p. 26, emphasis added).

Question 1: Who Am I?

One of the BIG questions is "Who am I?" Of course, this is a question that *you* must answer. In fact, according to the psychologist Erik Erikson, it is *the* question of adolescence (and perhaps of emerging adulthood as well)—it is a question so central that Erikson called it a **crisis** (Erikson & Erikson, 1997). Crisis, in this context, does not mean a disaster, it means "the decisive moment; a turning point; a crucial time" (*Webster's New Collegiate Dictionary*).

One reason the religion and family connection matters to you now is that decisions regarding faith impact our identity and our responses to the "Who am I?" question. Next, we share two personal statements from individuals in research studies on family stress and coping. Both statements reflect clear but different resolutions to the "Who am I?" question. The first respondent, Kate, had weathered the historic natural disaster of Hurricane Katrina in 2005. In response to a question regarding whether God or religion had been helpful during her time of need, she stated:

> No, [religious beliefs] did not [help me cope]. I'm mature enough to know [better]. . . . I think I've had enough experience that I can see the thing as it is and live with it. You have to live with it in your own way.
>
> (Tausch et al., 2011, p. 247)

Kate self-identified as resilient, pragmatic, mature, and an atheist (as she indicated elsewhere). A participant from a second study, Joseph, presented another perspective. He said of himself:

> If [my relationship with God] wasn't there, I wouldn't know who I was. I would be ungrounded, I wouldn't be me without Christ in me. . . . The whole way I construct my understanding of who I am is based in my relationship to God . . . In relation to Him, *I'm His child*. I've been adopted. I'm His heir, I'm His brother, I'm His friend, I'm His servant, I'm His helper.
>
> (Marks, 2002, p. 93)

In contrast to Kate, Joseph's sense of self was reportedly rooted in his relationship to his God.

Both of these adults answered the question "Who am I?" Their answers are different but clear. Why does this matter to you? It matters because across the lifespan, from adolescence to emerging adulthood to older adulthood, a large body of research indicates that high levels of involvement and engagement in religion are generally correlated with healthy patterns and outcomes. These outcomes, however, seem to be strongly associated with those who are "devoted" to their faith, not just those who attend occasionally or sporadically (Smith & Denton, 2005; Smith & Snell, 2009). Conversely, there are some emerging data that indicate that those who are "actively non-religious" also seem to do quite well on a number of measures. If these findings hold out across time, it may be that the ambiguous persons and families in the middle who are not really "in" or "out" of religion may miss out on both sets of "benefits." Indeed, recent longitudinal research indicates that both the "not at all religious" category and the "very religious" categories have both increased significantly since 1970, while the "moderately religious" category has declined substantially (Bengtson, Putney, & Harris, 2013, p. 61)—findings that have been supported in other recent research as well (Pew, 2012; Wuthnow, 2007).

Question 2: Where Am I Going?

Another of the BIG questions that relates to "Who am I?" is the question, "Where am I going?" Though this question has a variety of applications, emerging adulthood is a time when this question is posed in a very pragmatic and relentless way—and in ways that relate to matters of faith and family. For now, let's examine the "Where am I going?" question through the following poem.

Driver

Driving nowhere but I'm late,
No time to self-evaluate.

Fuel light's blinking says I'm low
But I've got to go, go, go.

Infernal light! I hate that flash!
I grab a bottle and smash the dash.

No more nagging irritation,
No stopping at the service station.

I put my foot down on the gas,
Heading nowhere, moving fast.

—anonymous

How does the question "Where am I going?" relate to deeper issues of faith and family? Economist and Nobel laureate Gary Becker has emphasized the power and influence of the *horizon*. We will offer our own adapted explanation. This is important, but it will take a moment and about three steps to explain. In a book section entitled "On the Event Horizon," Harvard psychologist Daniel Gilbert shares the following story, borrowed from Turnbull's (1961) field study entitled *The Forest People*. Turnbull reported:

> About fifty years ago a Pygmy named Kenge took his first trip out of the dense, tropical forests of Africa and onto the open plains in the company of an anthropologist. Buffalo appeared in the distance—small black flecks against a bleached shy—and the Pygmy surveyed them curiously. Finally, he turned to the anthropologist and asked what kind of insects they were. [The anthropologist reported that,] "When I told Kenge that the insects were buffalo, he roared with laughter and told me not to tell such stupid lies."
>
> (Gilbert, 2006, p. 115)

Gilbert then goes on to explain that "because Kenge had lived his entire life in a dense jungle that offered no views of the horizon," Kenge had severely distorted perceptions (p. 115).

Similarly, our Point 1 is: *Without an expansive vision of the horizon, our perceptions are likely to be severely flawed.* Gilbert later adds that although you and I "rarely mistake a distant buffalo for a nearby insect . . . we tend to make the same mistake that Pygmies do" when the horizon is one of time instead of space (p. 118). Indeed, whether we fully realize it or not, each of us have a **time horizon** in our lives—including assumptions about how much time we have until we reach the edge of our own life's horizon.

Let's talk about this "time horizon" briefly. I (Loren) am named after and physically resemble my late maternal grandfather. Grandpa got married, had a large family, and lived a generative, productive, and healthy life before passing away in his early 80s, shortly after his 50th wedding anniversary. These facts helped establish a perceived time horizon for me when I was an emerging adult—a horizon that extended another 60-plus years in front of me. I went to college, got married, bought a house, pay into a retirement fund each month, and even floss my teeth because of the location of my (hopefully distant) time horizon.

Conversely, some qualitative research we have done on families living in volatile, dangerous, drug-laden, inner-city neighborhoods yields a very different kind of life horizon. Consider the following statement from a father we interviewed in a violent part of New Orleans:

> Let's just face it, a lot of these kids out here are getting killed because of the fact that there is no structure. [If they're not in church, they're in the "streets" and] now a lot of times they're dying.
>
> (Marks et al., 2005, p. 457)

During my (Loren's) volunteer experience in inner-city Milwaukee, I spoke with many young African-American men who would say things like, "Most of my boys have been shot or are locked up." How would life look to you if you doubted you would live long enough for your emerging adulthood to "emerge" into adulthood? Perceiving that your life horizon is likely to end at age 25 (instead of 85) can have a significant influence on your decisions in the present. In a situation where 25 is "the end of the road," many might ask themselves why they should bother with college or any serious commitments.

Having a life horizon of 85 years instead of 25 years likely changes the way we live today. However, does having an "eternal" life horizon also matter in measurable ways? Phrased differently, does believing in a life after death that may involve a divine judgment alter the way persons actually live in the present? Among those who believe *strongly*, the answer appears to be yes. Let's move to Point 2.

Point 2: *Perceptions matter profoundly*. The early 20th-century sociologist W.I. Thomas argued that *a situation perceived as real is real in its consequences* (Thomas, 1923)—an idea that came to be known as the **Thomas Theorem**. To state this idea in a more concrete manner, if you perceive that the interstate highway lane on your left is empty and you approach a slow-moving car directly from behind, you are likely to move over into that vacant lane in order to pass the dawdling vehicle. If you failed to perceive a semi-truck in your blind spot, the consequences may be severe. If you perceive the vacant lane accurately, you are likely to reach your destination safely and quickly. Either way, your perceptions stimulate actions that yield consequences.

What does this have to do with religion? A great deal, actually. About 20 years before the now famous Thomas Theorem that *a situation perceived as real is real in its consequences* was put to paper, William James, "the father of American psychology," noted the following in his (1902) work *The Varieties of Religious Experience*:

> Name it the mystical region, or the supernatural region. . . . Yet the unseen region in question is not merely ideal, for it produces effects in this world. . . . *That which produces effects within another reality must be termed a reality itself*, so I feel as if we had no philosophic excuse for calling the unseen or mystical world unreal. . . . *God is real since he produces real effects.*
>
> (pp. 399, 400, emphasis added)

Are these "real effects" William James discusses limited to miraculous events like the parting of the Red Sea, the transformation of water to wine, or you earning an *A* grade on a statistics exam? No, these "real effects" also include Islamicist extremists taking their own and others' lives in violent *jihad* . . . in exchange for a perceived hero's welcome in the heavens beyond. Additionally, a real effect is seen as a faithful Muslim pays her annual ***zakat*** of 2.5% of all her excess to the poor, for the sake of Allah. A real effect is seen when, as sociologist Christian Smith has noted, some teens and emerging adults postpone sex until marriage for religiously grounded reasons. In short, consistent with William James's argument, *real effects* result whenever beliefs in God or "the supernatural region" are strong enough to be converted into action and "effects in this world."

One more note on real effects. In our *American Families of Faith* project, we interview highly religious families in their homes. While questions like "Please tell us what you believe" and "On a scale of 1–10, how spiritual are you?" might be helpful, we have found that the following questions can offer important insight into lived religion:

1. *If you feel comfortable responding, approximately what percentage of your income do you spend or donate in direct and indirect ways that involve your faith community?*
2. *Approximately how many hours a week do you spend in faith-related activities? (Including worship services, faith-related meetings, prayer and meditation, scripture study, family worship, youth or children's organizations, service to other congregational members, etc.)*

These two questions cut to the heart of decisions and actions involving the precious resources of *money* and *time*. In some ways, it may seem base or irreverent to focus on "the bottom line" of money and time when we are examining something as sacred as God and family relationships. However, families who are willing to contribute substantial amounts of time and money are demonstrating an observable, measurable "manifestation of religious spirit" that we (as social science researchers) view as at least as valid and potent as professed belief. The religiously involved and contributing families in the *American Families of Faith* (AFF) project believe deeply enough to produce *real* effects.

Elsewhere in *The Varieties of Religious Experience*, William James argued that we can best understand the force of religion in individual and family life by studying and learning from those who are passionately devoted to their faith. Specifically, James wrote:

> We may learn most about a thing when we view it . . . in its most exaggerated form. This is as true of religious phenomena as of any other kind of fact. The only cases likely to be profitable enough to repay our attention will therefore be cases where the religious spirit is unmistakable. . . . Its fainter manifestations may tranquilly pass by.
>
> (James, 1902, p. 48)

Individuals and families who believe and "perceive" God in unmistakable ways have much to teach us—including lessons of both relational beauty and relational destruction. Again, as Point 2 states: *Perceptions matter profoundly*.

Point 3, drawn from the work of Burr, Marks, and Day (2012), is, "It is what we *do* as a result of [our perceptions], ideals, and beliefs about the sacred that determines whether the sacred is helpful or harmful in families." Phrased differently, it is the way that beliefs are *lived out* that gives them destructive or creative power. This is true on global and historical levels, but this also plays out on personal and familial levels. One African-American father we interviewed offered his conviction as such:

> It's not what you do in the [church] building, it's what you do outside the building . . . because we can clap the right "Hallelujah" and say the right words and everybody sees, but when no one that's in your church sees you, how are you acting then? Hmmm? . . . Are you living the . . . walk of faith . . . or are you living like the world's living? I can't say it any [plainer] than that. . . . Are you practicing what you preach?

The word may be mightier than the sword, but the word is not mightier than a visible example. One Muslim mother we interviewed, reflecting on her husband's example to their two children, explained:

> In terms of religion, it doesn't matter how much the father talks to the children [about religion], the children will learn from what the father *does*. . . . If my children see my husband . . . setting an example. I don't have to "teach" it. They are seeing it.

Point 4: The statement of this Muslim mother illustrates a fourth and final point about why this book matters to you. This point—a point that has recurred across our professional and personal study of human relationships—is this: *Our behavior is permission to others to behave similarly . . . but it is more than that. It is an invitation to do so.* We call this **the principle of lived invitation** and will refer to it throughout the book. In short, our decisions to act or not to act have ripple effects that extend well beyond our own lives. This reality will be implicitly and explicitly demonstrated throughout the book.

Conclusion

We began this chapter by suggesting why the combined topic of religion and families matters to us enough that we gladly agreed to write this book for you and other emerging adults. We then briefly overviewed some **B**eing, **I**ntimacy, and **G**od (BIG) questions: "Who am I?" "Where am I going?" and "What is my relationship to God?" We then proceeded to outline four points that begin to explain why the religion and family connection matters to you. Those four points are summarized here:

Point 1: *Without an expansive vision of the horizon, our perceptions are likely to be severely flawed.* This matters because when you wrestle with and think deeply about the BIG questions, your vision and perception of your personal "life horizon" are expanded, extended, and clarified.

Point 2: *Perceptions matter profoundly.* As William James teaches us, when we believe or perceive so deeply that these beliefs or perceptions become *real* to us, these beliefs and perceptions then begin to cause *real effects*. This matters because authentic, "unmistakable religious spirit" is transformed into observable action. (These actions, however, can range from devastatingly violent to beautifully helpful.)

Point 3: *It is what we do as a result of perceptions, ideals, and beliefs about the sacred that determines whether the sacred is helpful or harmful in families.* This matters because regardless of what we *claim* to believe, it is our action and behavior that most defines us individually . . . and our relationships with our family members.

Point 4: *Our behavior is permission to others to behave similarly . . . but it is more than that. It is an invitation to do so.* This matters because your perceptions, beliefs, and especially your actions relating to the sacred are much bigger than just the individual called "you." Your decisions influence the lives of countless others—providing all the more reason to truly ponder the BIG questions.

Thus ends our introduction of the first few reasons the religion-individual-family connection matters to you. Many more reasons are to follow in the chapters to come.

Chapter Summary Points

1. A key purpose of this textbook is to help readers explore and understand the connections between religion and families in the world around them, as well as in their own life.
2. Emerging adulthood is a time of decision-making, including decisions about religion, family, and identity.

3. As humans, we are invariably faced with the "BIG" questions (such as "Who am I?" and "Where am I going" and "What is the meaning of life?"). Many turn to religion for answers to these questions.
4. Our perceptions matter. They influence our time horizons, how we act, and whether the sacred will be helpful or harmful.
5. Our behavior is permission to others to behave similarly . . . but it is more than that. It is an invitation to do so.

Review Questions

1. According to most psychologists, during what time frame is the "template of life" established?
2. What developmental stage do the authors argue is the "building stage" of life?
3. What issues do the BIG questions address?
4. Look through the example BIG questions and think and about how you would answer these for yourself.
5. Why did Kenge the Pygmy think the buffalo was an insect? How does this relate to our perceptions of where we are going?
6. What is a time horizon, and why does it matter in personal, religious, and family life?
7. What do William James and the Thomas Theorem say about perceptions? What might this mean for those who believe deeply in God?

Notes

1. Except where otherwise noted, all names associated with narratives in this book have been changed to pseudonyms to protect the identity of the individual.
2. Bolded terms are defined in the glossary at the end of the book.

References

Bengtson, V. L., Putney, N. M., & Harris, J. (2013). *Families of faith*. New York: Oxford.

Burr, W. R., Marks, L. D., & Day, R. D. (2012). *Sacred matters: Religion and spirituality in families*. New York: Routledge.

Doherty, W. J. (2001). *Take back your kids*. New York: Sorin Books.

Dollahite, D. C. (1998). Fathering, faith, and spirituality. *The Journal of Men's Studies, 7*, 3–16.

Dollahite, D. C. (2003). Fathering for eternity: Generative spirituality in Latter-day Saint fathers of children with special needs. *Review of Religious Research, 44*, 339–351.

Dollahite, D. C., Marks, L. D., & Olson, M. M. (1998). Faithful fathering in trying times: Religious beliefs and practices of Latter-day Saint fathers of children with special needs. *The Journal of Men's Studies, 7*, 71–94.

Dollahite, D. C., Marks, L. D., & Olson, M. M. (2002). Fathering, faith, and family therapy: Generative narrative therapy with religious fathers. *Journal of Family Psychotherapy, 13*, 263–294.

Erikson, E. H., & Erikson, J. M. (1997). *The life cycle completed*. New York: Norton.

Gilbert, D. (2006). *Stumbling on happiness*. New York: Vintage.

James, W. (1902). *The varieties of religious experience: A study in human nature*. New York: Longmans, Green.

Marks, L. D. (2002). Illuminating the Interface between Families and Faith. Unpublished dissertation. University of Delaware.

Marks, L. D. (2004). Sacred practices in highly religious families: Christian, Jewish, Mormon, and Muslim perspectives. *Family Process, 43*, 217–231.

Marks, L. D., & Dollahite, D. C. (2001). Religion, relationships, and responsible fathering in Latter-day Saint families of children with special needs. *Journal of Social and Personal Relationships, 18*, 625–650.

Marks, L. D., Nesteruk, O., Swanson, M., Garrison, M. E. B., & Davis, T. (2005). Religion and health among African Americans: A qualitative examination. *Research on Aging, 27*, 447–474.

Marks, L. D., & Palkovitz, R. (2007). Fathers as spiritual guides. In S. E. Brotherson, & J. M. White (Eds.), *Why fathers count* (pp. 209–223). Harriman, TN: Men's Studies Press.

Pew (2012). The global religious landscape. Pew Research Center. Retrieved December 18, 2014, from http://www.pewforum.org/files/2014/01/global-religion-full.pdf.

Smith, C., & Denton, M. L. (2005). *Soul searching: The religious and spiritual lives of American teenagers*. New York: Oxford.

Smith, C., & Snell, P. (2009). *Souls in transitions: The religious and spiritual lives of emerging adults*. New York: Oxford.

Tausch, C., Marks, L. D., Brown, J. S., Cherry, K. E., Frias, T., McWilliams, Z., Melancon, M., & Sasser, D. (2011). Religion and coping in the aftermath of Hurricanes Katrina and Rita: Qualitative themes from the Louisiana Healthy Aging Study. *Journal of Religion, Spirituality, and Aging, 23*, 236–253.

Thomas, W. I. (1923). *The unadjusted girl: With cases and standpoint for behavior analysis*. Boston, MA: Little, Brown and Co.

Turnbull, C. (1961). *The forest people*. New York: Simon & Schuster.

Wuthnow, R. (2007). *America and the challenges of religious diversity*. Princeton, NJ: Princeton University Press.

2 What in the World Is Religion?

In the Tim Burton film *Big Fish*, Albert Finney's yarn-spinning character comments that wild parrots in the Congo will discuss most anything: politics, fashion, literature . . . but not religion. "Why not religion?" his son queries. "[Because] it's rude to talk about religion," snaps the father, "You never know who you gonna offend" (Marks, 2013).

As with the wild parrots in the Congo, religion is the taboo topic at gatherings for many families. Further, for a sizable portion of the last 100 years or more, social scientists followed the same rule—most chose to discuss and research virtually anything *but* religion (Marks, 2006a).

> Science without religion is lame, religion without science is blind.
> —Albert Einstein, *Jewish Wit and Wisdom*

In 2001, a pioneering scientist and researcher named Jeff Levin reflected that "there was a time . . . [circa 1985] when those of us actively investigating the linkages between religion and [mental, physical, and familial] health could have fit around a single conference table. A very small one" (2001, p. viii). Not long before, leading religion researchers such as the late David Larson were still referring to religion as "the anti-tenure topic"—the fast track *out* of a respectable academic job. In other words, for a considerable stretch of time, conducting research that examined the connections between religion and family was not only considered rude, it was professionally dangerous. In many ways, it still is.

Even so, in the years since Jeff Levin's "very small table" comment, a significant expansion has taken place. Specifically, more than a dozen social science journals have dedicated special issues to religion. It appears that a growing number of social science researchers are sufficiently fascinated by the religion and family connection that they have been willing to accept (or ignore) the dangers that have historically accompanied the topic. The careful discussion of connections between (a) religion and (b) mental, physical, and/or family health has spread from the setting of a very small conference table to requiring a conference. In this book, we invite you to listen to, and perhaps even participate in, the discussion that breaks the rules of the Congolese parrots. Let's talk about religion.

Defining "Religion"

As we begin our discussion, an important question to ask is: What in the world is religion? Before we present the conceptualization of religion that we will use throughout this book, we will take a look at some definitions offered by others who have presented their interpretations of this concept. By "in the world" we imply that the world is a large and complex place and that there are many definitions of religion. We will first discuss some of the various ways religion has been defined and then provide our own definition so that throughout the rest of the book we will be on the same page. We will begin, however, by explaining what religion is not.

Religion Is Not Spirituality

First, "religion" is not the same thing as "spirituality." A great deal of ink has been spent teasing out the difference between the two. One commonly agreed-upon difference is that spirituality tends to be broader and more inclusive than religion. We will not spend much additional ink except in briefly making three important points:

1. Much of social science is based on drawing and formulating comparisons between distinguishable groups (e. g., women/men, black/white, single/divorced/married). We typically need at least two distinguishable groups to draw comparisons.
2. U.S. surveys from a variety of pollsters have repeatedly reported that more than 90% of Americans consider themselves to be "spiritual"—in some polls, the rate has been as high as 96%–98%. In short, having "spirituality" is like having opinions—just about everybody seems to possess some. To frame it differently, being spiritual correlates at about a 0.90

level with having a pulse. Because nearly everyone considers themselves as spiritual, we are left with little or no comparison group.

3. Finally, spirituality is defined so broadly by different persons that it "can include walking in the woods, [watching a game of] football, listening to music, going to an art gallery, enjoying a sunset, or watching a butterfly emerge from a cocoon" (Burr, Marks, & Day, 2012).

Highly inclusive, broad, and wide-canvassing definitions like these make "spirituality" very difficult to accurately discuss, measure, and study. In this book, for the most part, we will stick with discussing religion—not because spirituality is unimportant but because it is so difficult to specifically identify.

"So, what is religion then?" you might ask. As we move into our first set of definitions, we note that "with few exceptions, the scientific and historical [scholars] of religion are themselves *not* persons of any religious faith and are not participating . . . in any religious community" (Adler, 1990, p. 42). This observation holds true for those offering some negative conceptualizations of religion we discuss in the next section—conceptualizations that we refer to as the BAD/RAP definitions of religion, as explained next.

Some BAD/RAP Definitions of Religion

For Karl Marx, the influential co-author of *The Communist Manifesto*, religion was the opiate of the masses. Sigmund Freud categorically defined religion as humankind's universal obsessional neurosis. In fact, Freud once referred to religion as an "intoxicant," a "poison," and "childishness to be overcome"—all on the same page (Freud, 1927, p. 88; Stark & Bainbridge, 1996). Later in the 20th century, prominent psychologist Albert Ellis (1980) repeatedly described religion as a form of psychopathology or mental illness.

> Religion is the sigh of the oppressed creature, the feeling of a heartless world. . . . It is the opium of the people.
>
> —Karl Marx
>
> How many evils has religion caused!
>
> —Lucretius
>
> If men are so wicked with religion, what would they be without it?
>
> —Benjamin Franklin

More recently, a group called New Atheists[1] led by persons including Richard Dawkins, Daniel Dennett, Sam Harris, and Christopher Hitchens have argued that religion is not only silly superstition and deserving of ridicule but also dangerous and thus deserving of strident attack (Prothero, 2010). They argue that evidence supporting the existence of God and miracles does not exist and that therefore basic religious claims are unsubstantiated by science.

The early criticisms of religion by Marx, Freud, Ellis, and others (that sometimes reached book length) typically were not grounded in empirical data. Even so, these critiques profoundly influenced and shaped the view of religion among many family professionals, mental health workers, and social science researchers for decades to come (down to and including the present). Indeed, social scientists in general and psychologists in particular are among the least religious groups in America (Stark & Finke, 2000). We refer to the influential definitions of religion by Marx, Freud, Ellis, and others as "**BAD/RAP** (**B**ogus **A**nd **D**angerous/**R**eligion **A**s **P**sychopathology) hypotheses" because religion is conceptualized by these authors as bogus (the "opiate of the masses"), dangerous ("a poison," "a childishness [to] overcome"), and as "psychopathology" (mental illness).

One lesson that can be drawn from this scenario is that where data are scarce, dogma can become doctrine—as evidenced by abundant negative references to religion that occurred in the third edition of the mental health handbook *Diagnostic and Statistical Manual for Mental Disorders* (*DSM-III*). In subsequent editions, most of these negative references have been removed or appropriately contextualized, largely due to the body of research that has emerged to challenge the BAD/RAP hypothesis. By the time you finish reading this book, you will have learned much about this research. However, before we move to a lengthy discussion of these studies, let's return to the question, "What is religion?" This time we will hear definitions that differ from the BAD/RAP hypothesis in that they are less condemning of religious belief and involvement.

Beyond BAD/RAP Definitions of Religion

MacArthur Fellow and renowned literary and religion critic Harold Bloom (1990) was not gentle in his assessment of supporters of what we call the BAD/RAP hypothesis. He stated:

> Freud's *The Future of an Illusion* [where he vehemently attacks religion] can be accounted as one of the great failures of religious criticism. Simply, he underestimated his opponent.
>
> (p. 34)

However, one definition of religion that moves beyond the BAD / RAP hypothesis is also from Sigmund Freud. Although he saw religion as "poison" and "childishness," Freud offered a supplemental statement indicating that the essence of religion was *the longing for the father.*

Freud's critic Harold Bloom would move in a different direction. He saw religion as inseparably connected with the existential wrestle with death. Bloom observed:

> Very few of us [in the United States] believe that death closes all, and perhaps no nation has ever rejected death with an intensity comparable to ours. Death, in literature, is the mother of beauty; death, in life, is the father of religion. . . . When death becomes the center, then religion begins.
>
> (pp. 257, 29)

Indeed, Bloom argued that religion is not Karl Marx's "opiate of the masses" but that it is *the poetry of the masses*—the path to meaning in the face of death. It is this same fixation, fascination, and wrestle with death that seems to prompt Shakespeare's Claudio in *Measure for Measure* to conclude:

> The weariest and most loathed worldly life that age, ache, penury, and imprisonment can lay on nature is a paradise to what we fear of death . . .
>
> (Act III, Scene I)

> Any man's death diminishes me, because I am involved in mankind. And therefore never send to know for whom the bell tolls; it tolls for thee.
>
> —John Donne

> When death comes to me it will find me busy, unless I am asleep. If I thought I was going to die tomorrow, I should nevertheless plant a tree today.
>
> —Stephen Girard

> They that love beyond the world, cannot be separated. Death cannot kill what never dies. Nor can Spirits ever be divided that love and live in the same Divine Principle; the Root and Record of their Friendship. Death is but crossing the world, as Friends do the Seas, they live in one another still.
>
> —William Penn, *Fruits of Solitude*, Pt. II

The wrestle involving the universal fear of death is, in some measure, what makes religion matter. Religion becomes poetry that matters when it strives to respond to what the Greek philosophers referred to as the Terrifying Questions and what we call the BIG questions about Being, Identity, and God: "Who am I?" "Why am I here?" "Where did I come from?" "When I die, is it all over?" and "Is there any Higher Power I can access?"

The late scholar Hugh Nibley, although holding a different worldview than Bloom, agreed with him on the defining purpose of religion. Nibley (1992) summarized:

> There is only one question, the sole question for religion, the only reason for religion existing at all. Religion alone is supposed to answer it, and if religion can't, then religion can't do anything—let us forget religion. . . . The real question, of course, is, *Is this [life] all there is?* This is what everybody wants to know.
>
> (p. 338, emphasis added)

> Some people need one thing, but we green youths need another, we need first of all to resolve the everlasting questions, that is what concerns us. All of [the youth are] talking now only about the eternal questions. . . . [They meet at a] local tavern. . . . Well, then, what are they going to argue about, seizing this moment in the tavern? About none other than the universal questions: is there a God, is there immortality? And for those who do not believe in God, well, they will talk about socialism and anarchism, about transforming the whole of mankind . . . but it's the same damned thing, the questions are all the same, only from the other end.
>
> —Fyodor Dostoevsky, *The Brothers Karamazov*

From our perspective as social scientists, when religion is framed as the poetic struggle with death and the other BIG questions—and when the ways in which individuals, couples, and families seek to *answer* the BIG questions become powerful enough to influence their thinking, their speaking, their choices, and their actions—then religion becomes a force that is unwise to ignore. Indeed, if we are to truly understand and help families, particularly families who hold their religion central and sacred, it is (at very least) incomplete to be oblivious to their faith. This point may hold particularly true for those who are wrestling with existential crises such as disability, disease, or death.

In his classic work, *The Varieties of Religious Experience*, William James (1902) defined religion as "the feelings, acts, and experiences of individual men in their solitude . . . in relation to . . . the divine" (p. 42). James's definition can be quite useful to social scientists. In this book, we will widen our focus from James's "individual in solitude" to include the individual in a family and faith community context. Despite our adaptation of his focus, however, we appreciate James's pragmatic definition of religion—one that is concrete and behavior based with emphasis on "acts and experiences." Indeed, although the beliefs, doctrines, and ideas in a religion are very important, perhaps *the* fundamental question for social-behavioral scientists is, "When all is said and done, does the belief actually change *behavior*?"

As we discussed in the previous chapter, William James argued that the best way to learn about how religion influences individuals (or couples or families) is to examine those who hold their religion as "unmistakably" important. It is in families where the fire of faith burns intensely that the "effects [of] the religious spirit" are most likely to be observable. On this note, James emphasized, "God is real since he produces real effects" (p. 400). We paraphrase this idea as follows:

> *When religion becomes sufficiently important to an individual, couple, or family that decisions, actions, and destinations are changed, then we must pay attention to religion.*

Based on research drawn from a variety of fields, a major purpose of this book is to carefully examine individual, couple, and family outcomes that have been associated with religious involvement. Please note that we avoid William James's word "effects." The research we will discuss does not establish indisputable cause-and-effect relationships. For example, later in the book we will discuss some high-quality studies that indicate that religious persons who attend worship services regularly tend to live substantially longer lives than those who do not attend—but it is still not a scientific fact that church attendance *causes* longer life (Marks et al., 2005). These differences may result from closely related factors such as the lower use of alcohol and tobacco among frequent church attenders, or from increased levels of social support, or (most likely) from a combination of several factors (Hummer et al, 1999; Marks et al., 2005).

To be good scientists, we must be careful not to overstate what we claim to know. It may be that truth is diminished by adding to it. The tendency toward dogmatic overstatement was a serious obstacle to high-quality empirical research on religion and individual, couple, and family well-being during much of the 20th century and must be avoided in the future. We now pause for a brief illustrative historical lesson that illustrates this reality.

The (Partial) Rejection of the BAD/RAP Hypothesis of Religion

In the late 1960s, sociologist Rodney Stark decided to empirically test elements of what we refer to as the BAD / RAP hypothesis of religion. Stark did so in a study eventually published in 1971 under the title "Psychopathology and Religious Commitment." Stark did find a significant connection between psychopathology (mental illness) and religious commitment, but it was in the opposite direction of Freud's widely held view. In Stark's study, those with higher levels of religious commitment reported *lower* levels of psychopathology (mental illness). The study was modest in size and scope, but it was important because of the study's implicit message that Freud's widely accepted anti-religion statements regarding mental illness had, ironically, been prematurely accepted on faith.

Stark went on to become a leading American sociologist of religion, producing many rigorous studies that helped displace Freud's anti-religion dogma with high-quality data. Conversely, Stark also produced work documenting that many atrocities throughout history were directly or indirectly linked with religion, a point not lost on other towering intellects that preceded Stark (see the textbox that follows).

> Measured by our Christianity of to-day, bad as it is, hypocritical as it is, empty and hollow as it is, [where] neither the Deity nor his Son is a Christian. . . . ours is a terrible religion. The fleets of the world could swim in spacious comfort in the innocent blood it has spilled.
>
> —Mark Twain (in his posthumous *Autobiography*)
>
> Millions of innocent men, women and children, since the introduction of Christianity, have been burned, tortured, fined and imprisoned, yet we have not advanced one inch toward uniformity. What has been the effect of coercion? To make one-half of the world fools and the other half hypocrites.
>
> —Thomas Jefferson, *Notes on Virginia*

From our perspective, Stark's work in 1971 and thereafter provided a key and groundbreaking transition by promoting a sense of empirically based fair play in defining how religion should be framed and studied in the social sciences. Indeed, religion is a power that has both enriched and destroyed human lives—and both realities must be acknowledged if we are to claim a pursuit of truth worthy of the name (Prothero, 2010). We now move to a brief discussion of a definitional issue that is very important in understanding the limitations of the research that has been done on individuals, couples, and families since Stark's (1971) study.

Operational Definitions of Religion: How Should We "Measure" Religion?

The issue we will now consider is operational definition, also called operationalization. Perhaps the most basic way to explain operational definition is with a brief discussion of indicators (Neumann, 1997). For example, if a woman wanted to operationally define her physical appearance with only two indicators, she might select height and weight. However, if she were allowed to operationally define her physical appearance using a dozen indicators, she could additionally include measurements for her neck, arm length, chest, waist, and inseam; she could include eye, hair, and skin color; she could include a body fat/density analysis; and she could select a high-quality photograph as an indicator. Clearly, the second operational definition of physical appearance (with more than 10 indicators) would be more complete and valid.

What does this have to do with the scientific study of religion? Quite a bit, as it turns out. A central challenge in the scientific study of religion has been *how* to operationally define religion. Just how should an inquiring mind "measure" religion? In the absence of a "Faith-O-Meter" that gives us a precise and valid measurement of a person's level of religiosity, what indicators should a scientist use?

Until about 20 years ago, operational definitions of religion were frequently based on *one* of three different indicators: (a) denomination or reported affiliation with a faith community; (b) frequency of church attendance; or (c) self-reported values (Marks, 2005). Subsequently, in many 20th-century studies on religion and family, religion was measured with minimal breadth and depth (Mahoney, 2010; Mahoney et al., 2001; Marks, 2005, 2006b). A similar problem recurred in psychology-based studies of religion, prompting psychologists Miller and Thoresen (2003) to note that the "measurement of spiritual/religious constructs . . . has usually been poor in quality" (p. 26). Just as height is a helpful but inadequate operational definition of physical appearance, a one- or two-indicator study addressing "religion" does not typically convey a clear picture of all we wish to know. On this note, in a detailed review of the studies linking religion with marriage and parenting during the 1980s and

1990s, leading religion and family scholar Annette Mahoney and colleagues (2001) found that 83% of the studies used only *one* or *two* items to assess family members' religiosity. The research from the first decade of the 21st century improved only marginally—79% of marital and 76% of parenting research studies (still) used only one or two items to measure religion variables (Mahoney, 2010).

On one hand, these limitations encourage a healthy skepticism in reading most empirical studies on religion. On the other hand, it is noteworthy that even when religion has been measured in a very limited way (for example, by only using the indicator of church attendance), these indicators *still* appear to be statistically significant in hundreds of studies. These recurring findings indicate connections between religion and individual, marital, and family well-being, even if researchers cannot yet satisfactorily measure, much less explain, all of the processes at work (Koenig, McCullough, & Larson, 2001; Koenig, King, & Carson, 2012; Marks, 2005).

Gratefully, more recent work seems to reflect efforts to better operationally define and measure religion by using a higher quantity of valid indicators to create a more detailed and accurate picture. One important improvement that has been made in some recent religion and family studies has been to use indicators from more than one member of the family, as discussed next.

Inviting More Than One Family Member to Sit for the Family Portrait

Imagine that an artist is commissioned to paint a portrait of a family of five. She arrives on site to paint, but only the mother of the family is available to pose. This artist's predicament has much in common with the plight of many social scientists. Even after we finally decide on the indicators that we are going to observe to help us paint an accurate and colorful family portrait, we are stuck with Mom and only Mom. We love Mom. We love the Moms who brought us into the world, and we love the Moms to whom we are married, but if the social scientist who shows up to capture our blended portrait of religion and family only uses Mom to paint the picture (and social scientists typically do this), then we are leaving everyone else out—or simply guessing at what their portion of the portrait would look like.

The sociologist and family studies scholar Gerald Handel (1996) has argued that most "family" research is not truly family research because it tends to focus exclusively on one relationship (usually the mother-child *or* marital relationship). He further notes that most family research is limited to indicator data that was collected from only *one* family member. As mentioned earlier, Annette Mahoney (2010) has noted a similar pattern in social science research on religion. A similar limitation is that in-depth, interview-based, qualitative research on religion and family experience has typically been limited to specific, same-gendered groups (for example, Davidman's [1991] and Kaufman's [1991] interviews with Orthodox Jewish women or our interviews with Latter-day Saint fathers [Dollahite, 2003; Dollahite, Marks, & Olson, 1998, 2002; Marks & Dollahite, 2001]). The constraints of having a single "posing" model from which to paint a family portrait are regrettable, especially given that women and men tend to view religion, family, and other related issues from different perspectives and in different ways. Children, of course, have their own perspectives as well, and these perspectives are also typically overlooked.

With reference to the limited (one participant per family) approach to collecting indicator data, Handel (1996) has argued, "No [single] member of any family is a sufficient source of information for that family" (p. 346). We agree with Handel, and over the years we have tried to improve and have moved from interviewing (1) fathers only (in our early work), to (2) mothers and fathers, to (3) mothers, fathers, and children from the same family, when possible (Marks & Dollahite, 2011). When researchers allow this kind of family participation in defining, explaining, and even narrating their religion-family experience, the result is likely to produce a richer, truer, and more colorful portrait with three-dimensional qualities. It is to a three-dimensional vision of religion that we now turn.

A Three-Dimensional Definition of Religion

This definition of religion will be the last, for which you are undoubtedly grateful. This definition is our own, and it is the one we will use throughout the rest of the book. A fair question might be, "If you were going to use your definition all along, then why did you have to drag me through the BAD/RAP recap, Bloom's and Nibley's obsessions with death, and William James's definition that is over 110 years old?" A partial answer is that we believe that an awareness of previous definitions' limitations will help you see the advantages of the definition we employ. We are using our definition because we believe it will provide the most useful tool to convey to you what the field has learned about the religion and family connection. We all also think that each of the definitions we have presented contains elements of truth. Even the

BAD/RAP folks are at least partly right; there *are* "sick-souled" expressions of religion that harm individuals and families—as William James, Rodney Stark, and others have empirically and historically documented. However, it is also apparent that there are "healthy-souled" expressions of religion that are linked with positive outcomes for individuals, marriages, and families. Further, some of these benefits are likely traceable to the coping mechanisms and meaning making that religions offer in the face of pain, challenge, profound loss, and death—as Bloom and Nibley noted.

In sum, we are saying that every definition we have shared with you has something to offer. Studying the religion and family connection is not as simple as memorizing the "right" definition and discarding all others. The religion and family connection is a fascinating but complex topic that can be difficult to wrap your mind around. Nearly 20 years ago, as we started reading through the mountain of religion and family studies that had been published to help us better conduct our own budding research in this area, the myriad ideas around us seemed to form what Dave later called a confusing mountain of "conceptual spaghetti" (Snarey & Dollahite, 2001). After a lot of thought, we decided on a three-dimensional approach to defining religion. Our three dimensions of religion are religious *beliefs*, religious *practices*, and religious *community*. Let us briefly explain each of these dimensions:

Dimension 1: ***Religious beliefs*** are personal, internal beliefs, framings, meanings, and perspectives that are sacred in nature. (For example, "I know that God loves me"; "Marriage is ordained of God"; "God will hold me accountable for how I treat my family members.")

Dimension 2: ***Religious practices*** include outward, observable expressions of faith such as prayer, scripture study, rituals, traditions, or less overtly sacred practices or abstentions that are religiously grounded. (Examples might include praying, studying the Torah, fasting during Ramadan, and refraining from sex before marriage for religious reasons.)

Dimension 3: ***Religious community*** includes support, involvement, and relationships grounded in one's congregation or religious group.

There are admittedly some areas of overlap and ambiguity among these three dimensions, but these dimensions jointly comprise a three-part definition of religion that is valuable because it helps us clearly answer the question, "*What is religion?*" Our three-dimensional answer and definition is not perfect, but it is relatively simple and clear. It helps us see that religion includes (1) the sacred things we believe, (2) how we practice what we believe, and (3) those with whom we worship, believe, and practice. In addition to being simple, this definition is pragmatic in that it allows us to categorize religion and family research in ways that will allow us to figure out what we know and what we do not know. For example, if a study claims that religious people have better well-being (and many studies make this assertion), we can ask, "To which dimension of religion is the study referring?" Does the study use religious beliefs as an indicator? If so, what beliefs? Does the study use religious practices as an indicator? If so, what type of practices (e. g., prayer, Bible study)? Does the study use faith community as an indicator? If so, how is faith community operationalized (e.g., Are the questions addressing denomination, frequency of church attendance, or sense of social support)?

Some previous work has shown how these three dimensions of religion relate to individual-level development, including biological, psychological, and social development (Dollahite, Marks, & Goodman, 2004; Marks, 2005). Koenig and colleagues' (2001) *Handbook of Religion and Health* addressed more than 1,200 studies and 400 reviews, and more recent work goes even further (Koenig, King, & Carson, 2012). In our discussion with you, we include the overview in the following textbox, and we will later highlight a few individual-level findings that are so potent they have direct, family-level implications. For now, however, we will pass over most of the hundreds of studies relating to religion and individual-level health in order to focus on *family* relationships and issues.

Figure 2.1 shows the relationship between the three dimensions of religion and different ties within the family. We briefly discuss those connections in the following. First, we will briefly discuss arrows A, B, and C, which connect the three dimensions of religion with one another. *Arrow A* links the dimension of religion practices with the dimension of religious beliefs. This connection is significant because religious practices (sacred actions) and abstinences (activities that are *avoided*) are often influenced by religious beliefs. For example, some religious persons entirely avoid the use of alcohol, tobacco, and illegal drugs—based largely on the belief that "bodies are temples." Conversely, religious beliefs are often strengthened by religious practices. For example, some religious persons report feeling a sense of deeply meaningful connection and closeness with God during prayer or other sacred rituals. As a result, these practices seem to strengthen their belief in the Divine (Marks, 2004). As we have written elsewhere, neither sacred beliefs nor practices seem complete without the animating influence of the other (Marks & Dollahite, 2012).

Ten chapters in the landmark *Handbook of Religion and Health* were dedicated to the review and discussion of religion and mental health. Ten key conclusions include:

1. More than 80% of related studies found a positive association between religiousness and greater hope or optimism about the future.
2. Fifteen of 16 studies reported statistically significant associations between greater religious involvement and a greater sense of purpose/meaning in life.
3. Sixteen of the 29 studies on religion and self-esteem reported greater self-esteem among the more religiously involved while only 1 study found a negative relationship (12 studies had no findings or mixed findings).
4. Eight of the 17 studies on coping with bereavement reported better adaptation among the more religious while only 1 found a negative relationship (8 studies reported no findings or mixed findings).
5. Sixty of the 93 cross-sectional or prospective studies on the religion-depression linkage reported lower depression among the religiously involved while only 4 reported greater depression among the more religious (29 studies had no findings or mixed findings).
6. Fifty-seven of the 68 studies that examine suicide rates and religious involvement found less suicide among the more religious while 11 studies yielded no findings or mixed results.
7. Eighty-six percent of clinical trial studies found less anxiety and fear among the more religiously involved.
8. Seventy-six of 86 studies reported significantly lower alcohol use or abuse among more religious subjects while only 2 studies showed higher abuse (8 studies yielded no findings or mixed results).
9. Forty-eight of 52 studies found significantly lower drug abuse among the more religious.
10. Twenty-eight of 36 studies found significantly lower crime and delinquency rates among the more religious while only 1 study reported negative findings (7 studies reported no findings or mixed findings).

—adapted from Koenig et al. (2001) and Marks (2006b)

Arrow B links the dimensions of religious beliefs and religious community. This connection represents the reality that the sacred religious beliefs an individual or couple hold can powerfully influence what congregation an individual or couple becomes involved in or whether they become involved in a faith community at all.

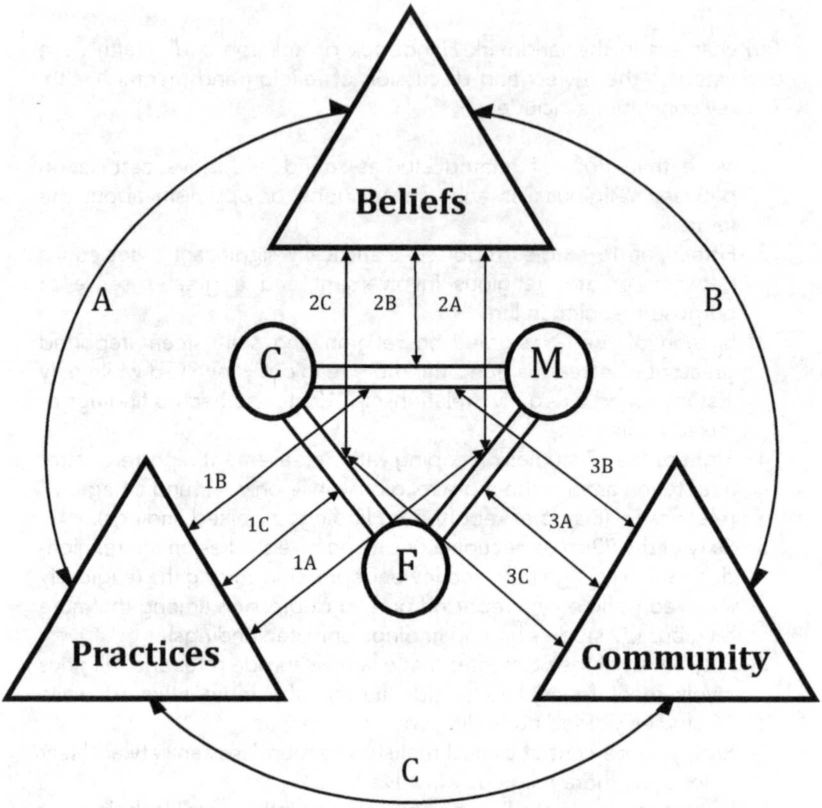

Figure 2.1 Research Connections Between Religious Beliefs, Practices, and Communities and Mother-Child, Father-Child, and Marital Relationships
Source: Adapted from Marks (2006).

Conversely, once an individual, couple, or family is involved in a faith community, the efforts of most religious congregations involve indoctrinating their members with specific beliefs. The 20th-century philosopher of science Giorgio de Santillana posited that religion is like language in that an individual can only "speak" one at a time and that the power of lived religion comes from a specifically and deeply held set of biases. In illustration, we have a friend and fellow religion and family scholar who reported that, during emerging adulthood, he strived to be a Jewish-Buddhist-Catholic because he resonated with elements of all three world faiths. For him, the effort was short-lived, frustrating, and unsuccessful. While it is possible to study or even master three languages, it is quite another thing to speak all three simultaneously. Our friend decided to strive to "speak" and live one religion the best he could.

Arrow B represents the reality that beliefs influence (specific) community involvement and that specific faith communities tend to promote specific beliefs. We now turn to Arrow C. *Arrow C* represents the connection between the dimensions of religious community and religious practices. In most world faiths, specific religious practices are promoted by faith communities. Some of these practices are individual, some are marital, and some are familial. However, some religious practices are inherently communal and serve to both symbolically and literally unite a faith community. Examples of this include the Catholic Mass, the Islamic call to prayer, and the Jewish holy day of **Yom Kippur** (Day of Atonement). As with the *A* and *B* connections, there is a mutually reinforcing connection captured by *C*—shared religious practices serve to build and strengthen a faith community while the faith community offers, promotes, and integrates certain religious practices into worship and community life in a way that fosters a sense of belonging (Marks & Dollahite, 2012).

Conclusion

In chapter 2, we have presented several different views of religion from an array of past scholars from a variety of disciplines. Each has something to offer, including the anti-religion, BAD/RAP hypothesis. However, most of these definitions or views have been presented without much balance and without empirical testing and support. Our three-dimensional view of religion includes and integrates religious beliefs, practices, and faith community and rests on a foundation of empirical support that provides a more balanced and scientifically grounded view. In the next chapter, the polite parrots of the Congo will again be disappointed in us as we examine the taboo topic of how religion influences family relationships.

Chapter Summary Points

1. The BAD/RAP hypothesis portrayed religion as harmful to mental health, and this view dominated the social sciences for most of the 20th century.

2. Many theories have arisen to explain the purpose of religion, including religion as a form of psychopathology (BAD/RAP), as an obsession with death, and as a way to answer the BIG questions.
3. William James's definition—that includes "acts," behaviors, and outcomes—is useful because it directs scientists to move beyond beliefs to examine observable outcomes.
4. Rodney Stark's (1971) finding that religious involvement related to lower levels of mental illness opened a new and more empirical chapter in the study of religion and well-being.
5. An overview of current research shows that religion has frequently been correlated with positive outcomes, although there are negative as well as positive evidences.
6. The research addressing religion and family has many limitations, including a lack of depth, difficulty in measuring religion with validity, and limited participation in "family" research (often mothers only).
7. A three-dimensional definition/conceptualization of religion (beliefs, practices, and community) can be helpful in better understanding how religion influences individual, marital, and family well-being.

Review Questions

1. What is the commonly accepted difference between religion and spirituality?
2. What does BAD/RAP mean? Which historical figures promoted universally negative views of religion?
3. What reason did Bloom and Nibley give for the purpose of religion?
4. How is William James's definition of religion valuable to social scientists who are studying religion?
5. After having read a few of the theories about religion, what do *you* believe is the purpose of religion?
6. What are some of the limitations of social science research on religion and family?
7. What are the three dimensions the authors chose to define religion?

Note

1. For an introduction to New Atheism see http://en.wikipedia.org/wiki/New_Atheism.

References

Adler, M. J. (1990). *Truth in religion: The plurality of religions and the unity of truth*. New York: Macmillan / Collier.

Bloom, H. (1990). *The American religion: The emergence of the post-Christian nation*. New York: Simon & Schuster.

Burr, W. R., Marks, L. D., & Day, R. (2012). *Sacred matters: Religion and spirituality in families*. New York: Routledge.

Davidman, L. (1991). *Tradition in a rootless world: Women turn to Orthodox Judaism*. Berkeley, CA: University of California.

Dollahite, D. C. (2003). Fathering for eternity: Generative spirituality in Latter-day Saint fathers of children with special needs. *Review of Religious Research, 44*, 339–351.

Dollahite, D. C., Marks, L. D., & Goodman, M. (2004). Families and religious beliefs, practices, and communities: Linkages in a diverse and dynamic cultural context. In M. J. Coleman & L. H. Ganong (Eds.), *The handbook of contemporary families: Considering the past, contemplating the future* (pp. 411–431). Thousand Oaks, CA: Sage.

Dollahite, D. C., Marks, L. D., & Olson, M. M. (1998). Faithful fathering in trying times: Religious beliefs and practices of Latter-day Saint fathers of children with special needs. *The Journal of Men's Studies, 7*, 71–93.

Dollahite, D. C., Marks, L. D., & Olson, M. M. (2002). Fathering, faith, and family therapy: Generative narrative therapy with religious fathers. *Journal of Family Psychotherapy, 13*, 263–294.

Ellis, A. (1980). *A case against religion: A psychotherapist's view and the case against religiosity*. New York: American Atheist Press.

Freud, S. (1927). *The future of an illusion*. Garden City, NY: Doubleday.

Handel, G. (1996). Family worlds and qualitative family research: Emergence and prospects of whole-family methodology. *Marriage and Family Review, 24*, 335–348.

Hummer, R., Rogers, R., Nam, C., & Ellison, C. G. (1999). Religious involvement and U.S. adult mortality. *Demography, 36*, 273–285.

James, W. (1902 / 1997). *The varieties of religious experience*. New York: Penguin.

Kaufman, D. R. (1991). *Rachel's daughters*. New Brunswick, NJ: Rutgers University.

Koenig, H. G., King, D. E., & Carson, V. B. (2012). *Handbook of religion and health (2nd ed.)*. New York: Oxford University Press.

Koenig, H. G., McCullough, M. E., & Larson, D. B. (2001). *Handbook of religion and health*. New York: Oxford University Press.

Levin, J. (2001). Foreword. In H. G. Koenig, M. E. McCullough, & D. B. Larson (Eds.), *Handbook of religion and health* (pp. vii–viii). New York: Oxford University Press.

Mahoney, A. (2010). Religion in the home 1999 to 2009: A relational spirituality perspective. *Journal of Marriage and Family, 72*, 805–827.

Mahoney, A., Pargament, K. I., Tarakeshwar, N., & Swank, A. B. (2001). Religion in the home in the 1980s and 90s: A meta-analytic review and conceptual analyses of links between religion, marriage and parenting. *Journal of Family Psychology, 15*, 559–596.

Marks, L. D. (2004). Sacred practices in highly religious families: Christian, Jewish, Mormon, and Muslim perspectives. *Family Process, 43*, 217–231.

Marks, L. D. (2005). Religion and bio-psycho-social health: A review and conceptual model. *Journal of Religion and Health, 44*, 173–186.

Marks, L. D. (2006a). Mental health, religious belief, and "the terrifying question." *Journal of Child and Family Studies, 15*(2), 135–141.

Marks, L. D. (2006b). Religion and family relational health: An overview and conceptual model. *Journal of Religion and Health, 45*, 603–618.

Marks, L. D. (2013). Wrestling with *Sacred Matters*: A new theory in family studies. *NCFR Report, 57*, F17–F18.

Marks, L. D., & Dollahite, D. C. (2001). Religion, relationships, and responsible fathering in Latter-day Saint families of children with special needs. *Journal of Social and Personal Relationships, 18*, 625–650.

Marks, L. D., & Dollahite, D. C. (2011). Mining the meanings and pulling out the processes from psychology of religion's correlation mountain. *Psychology of Religion and Spirituality, 3*, 181–193.

Marks, L. D., & Dollahite, D. C. (2012). "Don't forget home": The importance of sacred ritual in families. In J. Hoffman (Ed.), *Understanding religious ritual: Theoretical approaches and innovations* (pp. 186–203). New York: Routledge.

Marks, L. D., Nesteruk, O., Swanson, M., Garrison, M. E. B., & Davis, T. (2005). Religion and health among African Americans: A qualitative examination. *Research on Aging, 27*, 447–474.

Miller, W. R., & Thoresen, C. E. (2003). Spirituality, religion, and health: An emerging research field. *American Psychologist, 58*, 24–35.

Neumann, W. L. (1997). *Social research methods (3rd ed.)*. Boston: Allyn & Bacon.

Nibley, H. (1992). *Temple and cosmos*. Salt Lake City, UT: Deseret Book.

Prothero, S. (2010). *God is not one*. New York: HarperOne.

Snarey, J. R., & Dollahite, D. C. (2001). Varieties of religion–family linkages. *Journal of Family Psychology, 15*, 646–651.

Stark, R. (1971). Psychopathology and religious commitment. *Review of Religious Research, 12*, 165–176.

Stark, R., & Bainbridge, W. S. (1996). *A theory of religion*. New Brunswick, NJ: Rutgers.

Stark, R., & Finke, R. (2000). *Acts of faith: Explaining the human side of religion*. Berkeley, CA: University of California Press.

3 Does Religion Matter to Families?

In chapter 2, we discussed one important issue: *What is religion?* In our effort to define religion, we proposed a three-dimensional approach that includes examining and considering beliefs, practices, and community.

In the last chapter, we did not spend much space on the religion and mental health connection, but we did document that the BAD/RAP, or "religious people are nuts," hypothesis has not stood up well to empirical testing. With these findings noted, we have known plenty of religious people who *are* crazy. However, the science of the last 40 years indicates that we need to be very careful about drawing a causal arrow between church attendance and psychopathology because there are also a fair number of folks with severe psychological problems who do *not* attend worship services. Our point is that assertions regarding religion need to be sound, careful, and empirically based.

Dogma, according to *Merriam-Webster*, refers to "a belief or set of beliefs that is accepted by the members of a group without being questioned or doubted." The "believing" group is often religious, but (as we have briefly outlined in the preceding chapters) the dogmatic group can be social scientists. Although no individual is entirely without biases or dogma, in this book we strive to rely on established empirical data. We rely heavily on the work of social scientists who have produced multiple, high-quality, data-driven studies on religion and family life. Our footnotes and references provide an audit trail for those wanting to learn more. We also draw from our own previous empirical and conceptual work. With a few noted exceptions (for example, personal narratives from college students) the works upon which this book is based have been subjected to the scrutiny and peer review of scholarly experts. The findings that are highlighted have, in many cases, been replicated in multiple studies. It is important to us that you be aware of our aim to privilege data over dogma. The central points in this book are not drawn primarily from our own thinking, but from recurring findings from social scientists who are trying to answer important religion and family questions from a variety of different perspectives and angles.

In this chapter, using a conceptual model, we overview empirical research that indicates connections between marriage, divorce, and parent-child relationships. This chapter will also set the table for deeper discussions regarding the whys and hows behind religion-family connections that will take place in future chapters. Our initial question in the present chapter, however, is *Does religion matter to families?*

As we move to an in-depth discussion of the religion and families conceptual model, let's carefully review and consider just three (of the more than a dozen) recurring correlations between religious involvement and individual well-being that also impact the lives of others in the same family as the individual (i.e., a spouse, child, grandchild of the individual).

Religious Practices and Well-Being: Individual-Level and Family-Level Connections

Remember that in our three-dimensional model of religion, the dimension of religious practices includes not only religiously based practices like prayer and the study of sacred texts, but also abstinences or things people do *not* do for religiously based reasons, such as avoiding sexual activity or *not* using alcohol and/or illegal drugs. As Harold Koenig and his colleagues have reminded us, "There are nearly a hundred studies suggesting that religion may be a deterrent to alcohol or drug abuse in children, adolescents, and adult populations." Further, for those who start down the path to substance abuse, research indicates "more successful rehabilitation among the more religious" (Koenig, McCullough, & Larson, 2001, pp. 179–180). One Christian father who had flirted with drugs earlier in his life reflected during his interview with us:

> I don't know where I'd be without [God]. Well, I do know where I'd be without Him . . . I'd probably be dead or insane or addicted. . . . I'd be a

> mess. . . . If [my relationship with God] wasn't there, I wouldn't know who I was. I would be ungrounded.

Another narrative from our interviews that harmonizes with Koenig's report of "more successful rehabilitation among the more religious" is the following from a father of five children:

> I've done been to rehabs, to AA and NA meetings, I tried everything you can basically try to quit. Now I'm not saying that these places don't have [a] good foundation because they do. But for me, I found something that was true to me and what I needed [in my church]. It took me a long, long, long road to find it. I mean to really soul search and find it. It took a long time, but I did . . . the church that I go to now.

These two fathers attribute their success in overcoming addiction to God and to active church involvement. Many others we have interviewed avoided drugs altogether for similar sacred reasons.

The avoidance of alcohol and drug abuse is associated with longer life, better mental and physical health, and fewer hangover-filled mornings, but this life pattern of "staying clean" is also associated with lower criminality, higher employability, and greater employment stability (Stark & Finke, 2000). Each of these drug-related issues impact an individual's "marriageability" and likelihood of long-term marital success stability (Wilcox & Wolfinger, 2016). In short, addictions are a family issue, not just an individual issue.

Let us ride this train of thought to one more station. Careful estimates from the 1980s stated that approximately 65% of child abuse and wife beating were related to alcohol and drug abuse (Gallagher, 1987). However, estimates have increased in more recent decades to 80% (Kroll & Taylor, 2003). To frame this in "real world" terms, if 20 women and children need medical attention due to severe domestic beatings in your city's hospitals this coming weekend, 16 of them would likely not be there if it were not for alcohol/drug abuse (see Figure 3.1).

The striking interrelationship between alcohol/drug abuse and domestic violence is a sobering thought—at least it should be. Thus we see at least two ways (i.e., better employment and less domestic violence due to the absence of alcohol/drug abuse) in which individual-level, religiously based practices and abstinences can indeed have consequences that impact family relationships.

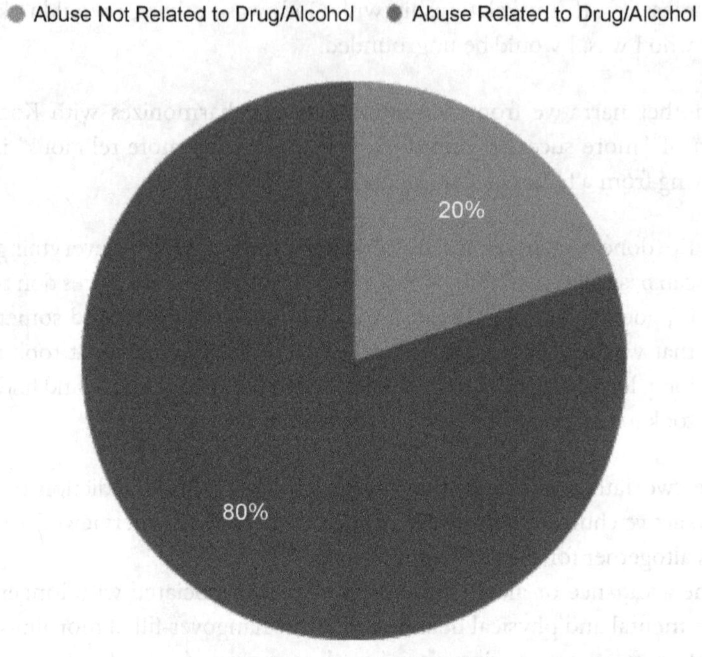

Figure 3.1 Percentage of Domestic Physical Abuse Related to Drug/Alcohol Abuse

Religious Beliefs and Well-Being: Individual-Level and Family-Level Connections

The connection between lower rates of alcohol and drug abuse among those who hold religious beliefs is not the only connection we should consider. Additional review work indicates that

> Of the more than two hundred total studies focused on both faith and mental health, roughly 80 percent indicate greater hope or optimism, greater well-being, a greater sense of purpose/meaning in life, lower depression, less anxiety and fear, and less negative coping among those who are religious.
>
> (Marks, Dollahite, & Freeman, 2011, p. 192; see also Koenig et al., 2001; Koenig, King, & Carson, 2012)

What are the *family*-level implications of the connections between (a) (healthy) religious beliefs and (b) positive coping and mental health? One of many relevant answers is that parental mental health is often a significant benefit to children, who appear to reap secondary benefits (Koenig et al., 2012). In other words, having mentally healthy parents significantly *decreases* the likelihood of mental illness in the children. One of the more striking lived experiences we have encountered during our *American Families of Faith* interviews involved at least two of the issues we have addressed in this section: (a) drug abuse and (b) using faith to cope with parental challenges. Sheila,[1] an African-American mother of two adopted children, watched her cousin leave the church her extended family attended and then saw her cousin become involved in "the street life" and commence a pattern of drug abuse and addiction that ultimately led to Sheila and her husband, Rashaad, adopting the cousin's two children as infants. Sheila discussed her parental stressors and her religious beliefs as follows:

> When I come into a situation that I can't handle physically, then . . . I rely on God. . . . It's hard being a mother with girls. . . . Our daughters are adopted, I got them from my cousin, we've had them since they were babies. . . . Some of the actions of my oldest are getting to a point where they irritate me because they remind me of her [biological] mother [who is still runnin' the streets] and I have to get over that. It's the God in me that lets me look at it [with patience]. . . . That's how the situation is going to be until I teach [our daughter] certain things. I feel that [my faith] makes me a better mother.

Sheila, in a moment of raw honesty, then explained:

> Sometimes I just don't want to be a Mommy. . . . I didn't have nine months to deal with, "Oh, it's coming." I mean I got two kids in one year and we were married for ten years without kids, just me and [Rashaad], doing whatever we wanted to do [before that]. Once I got them, that's when we really started getting into our religion. Faith makes me a better mom because I can look on [our] situation and [pray], "God, why did I make that decision?" and He brings it back to me, the personal reasons why things had to happen the way that they happened. [Yes, God helps me].[2]

Based on Sheila's self-report, her faith in God promotes perspective, patience, and reflection that help with her unusual and often challenging family situation. Does help from God actually help preserve Sheila's mental health? Science has difficulty answering such questions, but based on her in-depth interview, we were told that Sheila *perceives* Divine help, and William James

(1902/1997) and W.I. Thomas (1981) have both emphasized that *a situation perceived as real is real in its consequences*.

The family-level implications of mental health relate to more than just parenting. Benefits of mental health extend to (and probably from) healthy marriages as well (Waite & Gallagher, 2001; Wilcox et al., 2011). Like addiction, mental health is an individual-level issue with profound family-level consequences. We now move from the dimension of religious beliefs to faith community and well-being.

Faith Community and Well-Being: Individual-Level and Family-Level Connections

Two of the most pronounced individual-level benefits associated with frequent worship service attendance and faith community involvement are lower cancer rates and substantially increased life expectancy (Hummer et al., 1999; Marks et al., 2005). More specifically, significantly lower rates of cancer and increased life expectancy began to be identified several decades ago among some religious groups, most notably Seventh-Day Adventists and Latter-day Saints (Mormons). These particular religious groups were studied repeatedly because their dietary codes meshed well with American Cancer Society (ACS) recommendations.[3] A series of research studies performed by UCLA medical researcher James Enstrom from the 1970s into the late 1990s found a cancer rate among "actively involved" Latter-day Saints that was about 50% of the national rate. Findings by other researchers investigating Seventh-Day Adventists revealed similar findings, and a published review of studies on these two groups concluded that "certain religious groups, including Mormons and Seventh-Day Adventists, have cancer rates about one-half to two-thirds those of persons in the general population" (Koenig et al., 2001, p. 317). Latter-day Saints were also found to live, on average, between 4 and 11 years longer than comparison groups. With these significant differences in cancer rates and lifespan noted, we turn to the question: What about the 97% of the U.S. population who are *not* Seventh-Day Adventist or Latter-day Saint?

Based on additional research, a review in the *Handbook of Religion and Health* concludes that "religiously active persons of any denomination who live healthy life-styles . . . appear to have the same low cancer rate as Mormons" (Koenig et al., 2012, p. 303). Low cancer rates, then, are not necessarily exclusive to certain faiths. What about increased lifespan? Do those benefits extend to multiple faiths as well?

One research team, Hummer et al. (1999), used a nationally representative sample of 22,080 participants from the National Health Interview Survey to investigate the connection between faith community involvement and lifespan. The researchers compared: (1) participants who reported that they *never* attended religious services with (2) respondents who reported that they attended *more than once a week*. What were the findings? There was a 7.6 year increase in lifespan for the frequent church attenders. This research story, however, is not yet finished. In what we see as one of the more remarkable findings in modern social science, when Hummer's research team compared non-attending African-Americans with "more than once a week" African-American attenders, the difference in average lifespan between the two groups nearly doubled to 13.7 years (80.1 years versus 66.4 years).

In the social sciences, it is much easier to capture or describe differences than it is to accurately explain the reasons for discovered differences. While Hummer and his research team were able to rule out some potential sources of this difference, they were not able to offer definitive explanations for the 13.7-year increase in life.

A qualitative follow-up study explored possible reasons for the difference in African-American lifespan and reported several "insider" explanations. One of these explanations was that church involvement helps African-American teens and young adults "stay away from the street life," an important point given that too often, particularly in inner-city neighborhoods, "the ones who don't attend church are . . . dying at a young age" (Marks et al., 2005, p. 454). Similarly, two other researchers have noted that the black "church is there to help [youth] dodge both the real and figurative bullets of life in a major urban center" (Williams & Warner, 2001, p. 3; cf. Lehrer, 2009). Another research participant addressed several factors that may relate to longer (and shorter) lifespan:

> Lifestyle is one [reason religious people live longer]. . . . Obviously you're not out partying and doing other things that are not good for your health, but from a mental standpoint, I think your perspective on life changes, you deal with life's stresses better. You go through a little valley, but you can deal with [stress], because you have faith that you'll get through it. . . . Most people that have some kind of religious faith, when they go through things like that, they endure it . . . because of their faith. They actually believe that they'll endure the things and actually come out for their betterment. . . . They believe there's something better for them at the end of it. And I think that is what plays into the whole health issue. Your whole attitude toward life is different. You

> know, you tend to be less depressed, less stressed, you handle all those things in everyday life differently than the majority of people outside of [faith].
>
> (Marks et al., 2005, pp. 465–466)

In this response, this "insider observer" indicates that lifestyle, health, perspective on life, stress management, faith, belief in a positive outcome, attitude, less depression, and life management are all related to religious involvement—based on his life experience. We will see that research supports and confirms many of these assertions.

For many religious groups, the benefits that seem to accompany active faith community involvement include increased lifespan (Koenig et al., 2001; Koenig et al., 2012). Better health and longer life are relevant to the family because increased health and longevity provide additional opportunities for a higher quantity and quality of interaction between wives and husbands, parents and children, grandparents and grandchildren, and (in some cases) great-grandparents and their descendants.

Another documented correlation of faith community involvement is greater social support for consistent attenders. More specifically, involvement in a faith community has been linked with a greater number of social relationships and greater support from those relationships (Ellison & George, 1994; Koenig et al., 2012). These benefits are not only individual but are marital and familial as well. To offer one of several possible illustrations, economists who study **social capital** have documented that in a world where it is often who you know and not just what you know, a parent with an extensive network of trusted friends may be able to open doors of employment opportunity for children and grandchildren that might otherwise have remained locked. The faith community is a rich context for the establishment and maintenance of social capital for many families, not only across years but also across generations (Burr, Marks, & Day, 2012).

In the preceding three sections we see that while three-dimensional religious involvement can matter in measurable (and often beneficial) ways to individuals, these benefits are often not solely individual in nature—they are often familial as well. We address additional family benefits next.

Religion, Relationships, and Responsibility

An important point rarely made explicit in the research linking religious involvement with generally higher levels of personal, marital, and family well-being is that most American religions are highly marriage and family oriented. Therefore, some apparent "influences" of religion may be effects of self-selection bias (Marks, 2006). In other words, while it is possible that religious involvement might help make families strong, it is also possible that strong families are more likely to want to attend religious services together. Indeed, religious involvement can influence family . . . and family can influence religious involvement (for reviews, see Christiano, 2000; Dollahite, Marks, & Goodman, 2004; Mahoney, 2010; Mahoney et al., 2001; Marks et al., 2011). Even so, several scholars from a variety of academic disciplines have emphasized that one of the key positive functions of religious communities is to promote responsibility to our brothers and sisters in the human race and to promote responsibility and care for our families in particular.[4]

> Make no mistake about it, responsibilities toward other human beings are the greatest blessings God can send us.
>
> —Dorothy Dix

The role of religion in promoting responsibility to others and in moving beyond the self is both prosaic and profound. Loren's daughter Aliyah, as a baby, had a "onesie" shirt that declared in bold, colorful letters: "It's all about ME!" This worldview, as portrayed on the tummy of a toddling one-year-old, tends to produce smiles. However, when this same "It's all about ME" attitude is portrayed on the T-shirt or in the actions and attitudes of a 40-year-old, it is no longer adorable. In the words of the Overstreet brothers, "To the immature, other people are not real" (cf. Warner, 2001, p. 41). For many people of faith, their decisions related to religion and well-being are often much bigger than just the "ME" who is making those choices, and truly mature persons (of whatever age or degree of religiousness) demonstrate a sensitivity to and awareness of the reality of others. The following narratives from two fathers we have interviewed reflect this sensitivity. The first is from a father whose daughter, Megan, passed away at age six following an extended battle with leukemia. Tom Boyer, her father, recalled:

> [My wife and I] went to give blood at a blood drive [at our church], and our good friend Mr. Clyde was there giving blood. He'd visited Megan in the hospital a couple of times and prayed with her. We had gone through the line and I was just happy because I'd just gotten a penicillin shot and they wouldn't take my blood. Sandra (my wife)

> had given her blood and Mr. Clyde was there giving blood. Megan went over and held his hand while he had that blood drawn, because she knew what it was like to have needles poked in your skin and she felt for him. She couldn't do much but she could hold his hand and she did that. The impact that has on me just tells me that a little bit of loving concern for others goes a long way, not just in the life of either person in the interaction, but in the people who see that. It makes you want to go forth and do likewise.

Megan's actions recall the words of a former university administrator, Neal Maxwell, whose life included multiple battles with cancer. He observed that every time we experience a new kind of pain, it allows us to empathize with a new group of people.

Continuing on the theme of connection and relationship with others, a Christian father of four named Joseph concluded his interview with us by saying:

> There's something that . . . when as a *family* your hearts are pointed together toward the same thing, and it's God, then parenting and economics and space and food and disagreements and hassles and joys and celebrations and all that other stuff . . . it works different, it seems different, it feels different. . . . Our family are all oriented in the same way. Christ is king, He's center, He's what it's all about. . . . I don't know how to convey to you that . . . yes, our faith informs our relationships and everything about us.

A mother from another family seemed to capture a similar point when she said, "Faith is living outside yourself, living beyond yourself."

Research efforts over the past decade have indicated that many of the emerging "explanations" of why religion and faith matter are not only individual-level factors—these factors often spill over, influence, and inform our marriages, families, and other relationships.

Conclusion

In the present chapter, we have illustrated that there are positive connections between individual well-being and different dimensions of religion. These benefits—including lower cancer rates, lower alcohol and drug abuse rates, and greater life expectancy—also influence family members. Conversely, some damaging connections between religion and family relationships have also been reported. A central concern in most of the research, however, is that *depth* is not a characteristic of most religion-family studies. Indeed, research exploring the hows, whys, meanings, and processes behind these religion and family correlations (including both healthy and unhealthy connections) is needed. Additionally, future research needs to become more pluralistic and practical in at least three ways (Marks, 2006). Our recommendations include examinations that involve: (a) non-Christian world faiths (particularly Islam and Judaism, given their prevalence in the United States; see chapters 8 and 9); (b) a variety of family forms (see chapter 10); and (c) more families of color. As we have previously exhorted, "Careful, moderate, balanced scholarship in this area is needed to counter popular media that tend to accentuate extremes" (Marks, 2006, p. 615).

A scholarly dialogue on family issues that does not include thoughtful and challenging discussion of the influence of religion on family relationships is a poorer one. Conversely, our knowledge will be expanded as religion-family research moves beyond recurring correlations to examine the important whys, hows, meanings, and processes that are at work (Marks, 2006).

As a more detailed and accurate portrait of religion and families has developed, we are offered more and more insight as to how religion, marriages, and families connect with and influence each other. In the current picture, does religion appear to be good or bad for families? Our considered answer is yes. Religion can be a potent influence for bad or for good, depending on how family members believe, interpret, act out, and experience their religion (Burr et al., 2012).

A 2012 poll from the Pew Forum on Religion and Public life indicates that up to 20% of Americans do not claim any specific religious affiliation (Pew, 2012). About another 20% or more seem to have relatively loose ties with a religion (e.g., they are "affiliated" but rarely attend) (see Figure 3.2). However, 60% of Americans report that religion is important or very important in their lives (McCullough et al., 2000). Within this group that holds religion as important, "a substantial minority" reportedly hold religion as "the single most important influence in [life]" (Miller & Thoresen, 2003, p. 25). Individuals and families who have been studied in recent years report levels of religious involvement that range from "none" to "high"—and the *quality* of influence also seems to range widely (from very harmful to very helpful). We will continue to explore how and why religion can do considerable harm or good to marriages and families in the next chapter.

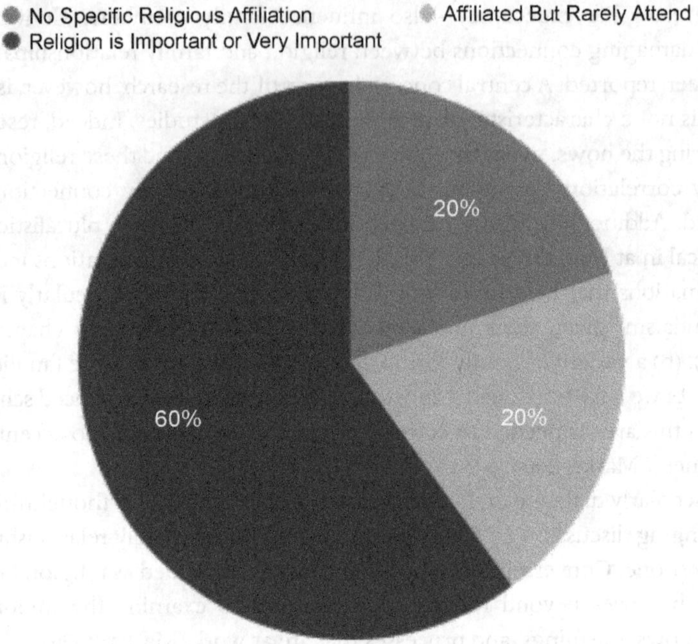

Figure 3.2 Religious Affiliation in the United States

Chapter Summary Points

1. Religious practices, beliefs, and involvement in faith communities are not just individual matters; they impact families.
2. Religious practices are typically correlated with decreased alcohol and substance abuse, improved addiction recovery outcomes, and decreases in alcohol-related domestic violence.
3. Religious beliefs are correlated with increased mental health and greater optimism.
4. Active involvement in a religious community has been correlated with benefits including lower rates of cancer, increased life expectancy, more social relationships, and greater social support.
5. Not all outcomes of religious activity on families are positive, but more research is needed to provide depth to the existing research.

Review Questions

1. How does the "religious practice" of avoiding alcohol and drugs impact families, according to the text?
2. Which of the three religious dimensions do the authors link with better mental health? Why do you think this link exists?
3. What were the benefits listed in this chapter related to being involved in a religious community?
4. According to the *Handbook of Religion and Health*, which denominations have especially low cancer rates? What are the likely reasons for this?
5. According to the text, what do scholars across multiple disciplines say is one key of the positive functions of religious communities?
6. What do you think the phrase "To the immature, other people are not real" means? What does this have to do with religion in families?
7. How do the authors respond to the question, "Is religion good or bad for families?"

Notes

1. Throughout the book, pseudonyms are used to protect the identity of the individuals involved. The stories, however, are related verbatim as told by the participants.
2. Unless otherwise noted, all narratives and data excerpts used in this book are drawn from the *American Families of Faith* data set compiled by the authors.
3. For example, the Latter-day Saint (Mormon) health code called the Word of Wisdom promotes high intake of fruits, vegetables, and grains (especially wheat). The Word of Wisdom also encourages the sparing use of meat and forbids the use of alcohol, tobacco, and "hot drinks" (defined as coffee and tea) (Dollahite & Marks, 2006).
4. These scholars include Agius & Chircop, 1998; Browning & Clairmont, 2009; Dollahite, 1998; Eberly, 1999; Marks & Dollahite, 2007; and Nock, 1998, to name a few.

References

Agius, E., & Chircop, L. (1998). *Caring for future generations: Jewish, Christian, and Islamic perspectives*. Westport, CT: Praeger.

Browning, D. S., & Clairmont, D. A. (Eds.) (2009). *American religions and the family: How faith traditions cope with modernization & democracy*. New York: Columbia.

Burr, W., Marks, L., & Day, R. (2012). *Sacred matters*. New York: Routledge.

Christiano, K. (2000). Religion and the family in modern American culture. In S. Houseknecht, & J. Pankhurst (Eds.), *Family, religion, and social change in diverse societies* (pp. 43–78). New York: Oxford.

Dollahite, D. C., & Marks, L. D. (2006). Family and community nurturing spirituality in Latter-day Saint children and youth. In K. Yust, A. N. Johnson, S. E. Sasso, & E. C. Roehlkepartain (Eds.), *Religious perspectives on spirituality in childhood and adolescence* (pp. 394–408). Lanham, MD: Rowman & Littlefield.

Dollahite, D. C., Marks, L. D., & Goodman, M. (2004). Religiosity and families: Relational and spiritual linkages in a diverse and dynamic cultural context. In M. Coleman, & L. H. Ganong (Eds.), *The handbook of contemporary families* (pp. 411–431). Thousand Oaks, CA: Sage.

Eberly, D. E. (Ed.) (1999). *The faith factor in fatherhood* (pp. 219–240). New York: Lexington.

Ellison, C. G., & George, L. K. (1994). Religious involvement, social ties, and social support in a southeastern community. *Journal for the Scientific Study of Religion, 33*, 46–61.

Gallagher, B. (1987). *The sociology of mental illness (2nd ed.)*. Upper Saddle River, NJ: Prentice Hall.

Hummer, R., Rogers, R., Nam, C., & Ellison, C. G. (1999). Religious involvement and U.S. adult mortality. *Demography, 36*, 273–285.

James, W. (1902/1997). *The varieties of religious experience: A study in human nature*. New York, NY: Longmans, Green.

Koenig, H. G., King, D. E., & Carson, V. B. (2012). *Handbook of religion and health (2nd ed.)*. New York: Oxford University Press.

Koenig, H. G., McCullough, M. E., & Larson, D. B. (2001). *Handbook of religion and health*. New York: Oxford University Press.

Kroll, B., & Taylor, A. (2003). *Parental substance misuse and child welfare*. London: Jessica Kingsley Publishers.

Lehrer, E. L. (2009). *Religion, economics, and demography: The effects of religion on education, work, and the family*. New York: Routledge.

Mahoney, A. (2010). Religion in families, 1999–2009: A relational spirituality framework. *Journal of Marriage and Family, 72*, 805–827.

Mahoney, A., Pargament, K. I., Tarakeshwar, N., & Swank, A. B. (2001). Religion in the home in the 1980s and 90s: A meta-analytic review and conceptual analyses of links between religion, marriage and parenting. *Journal of Family Psychology, 15*, 559–596.

Marks, L. D. (2006). Religion and family relational health: An overview and conceptual model. *Journal of Religion and Health, 45*, 603–618.

Marks, L. D., & Dollahite, D. C. (2007). Fathering and religious contexts: Why religion makes a difference to fathers and their children. In S. E. Brotherson, & J. M. White (Eds.), *Why fathers count* (pp. 335–351). Harriman, TN: Men's Studies Press.

Marks, L. D., Dollahite, D. C., & Freeman, J. J. (2011). Faith and prayer in family life. In T. W. Draper, A. J. Hawkins, & D. C. Dollahite (Eds.), *Strengthening our families (2nd ed.)* (pp. 185–195). Provo, UT: BYU.

Marks, L. D., Nesteruk, O., Swanson, M., Garrison, M. E. B., & Davis, T. (2005). Religion and health among African Americans: A qualitative examination. *Research on Aging, 27*, 447–474.

McCullough, M. E., Hoyt, W. T., Larson, D. B., Koenig, H. G., & Thoresen, C. (2000). Religious involvement and mortality: A meta-analytic review. *Health Psychology, 19*, 211–222.

Miller, W. R., & Thoresen, C. E. (2003). Spirituality, religion, and health: An emerging research field. *American Psychologist, 58*, 24–35.

Nock, S. J. (1998). *Marriage in men's lives*. New York: Oxford University Press.

Pew (2012, October 9). Pew research center: Religion and the unaffiliated. Retrieved from http://www.pewforum.org/2012/10/09/nones-on-the-rise-religion/.

Stark, R., & Finke, R. (2000). *Acts of faith: Explaining the human side of religion*. Berkeley, CA: University of California Press.

Thomas, W. I. (1981). *Social behavior and personality*. New York: Greenwood.

Waite, L. J., & Gallager, M. (2001). *The case for marriage*. New York: Doubleday.

Warner, C. T. (2001). *Bonds that make us free: Healing our relationships, coming to ourselves*. Salt Lake City, UT: Shadow Mountain.

Wilcox, W. B., Anderson, J. R., Doherty, W., Eggebeen, D., Ellison, C. G., Gilbert, N., Haskins, R., Lerman, R., Malone-Colon, L., Marks, L., Palkovitz, R., Popenoe, D., Regnerus, M., Stanley, S., Waite, L., & Wallerstein, J. (2011). *Why marriage matters: Thirty conclusions from the social sciences*. New York: Institute for American Values.

Wilcox, W. B., & Wolfinger, N. (2016). *Soul mates*. New York: Oxford.

Williams, R. S., & Warner, R. S. (2001). Creating urban evangelicalism: Youth ministry, moral boundaries, and social diversity. Youth and Religion Project. Retrieved from http://www.uic.edu/dept/soci/yrp/simple_pap3.html.

Why Does Religion Matter in Marriage?[1]

4

In chapter 2, we used a conceptual model to briefly overview several of the recurring connections that have been observed between the three dimensions of religion (beliefs, practices, and faith communities) and three different types of relationships within families (mother-child, father-child, and marital). In the present chapter, we will take a much closer look at research relating to the latter of these relationships, marriage. (Parent-child relationships will be treated in-depth in chapters 6 and 7). We will also examine the important consideration of challenges in marriage.

Challenges in Marriage: A Humorous View

> Marriage is wonderful. Without it husbands and wives would have to fight with strangers.
>
> —Morey Amsterdam, *Jewish Wit and Wisdom*

> Marriage always demands the greatest understanding of the art of insincerity possible between two human beings.
>
> —Vicki Baum, *Jewish Wit and Wisdom*

> Two dollars will buy all the happiness or all the misery in the world. At least, that used to be the price of a marriage license.
>
> —Eddie Cantor, *Jewish Wit and Wisdom*

> Women marry men hoping they will change. Men marry women hoping they will not. So each is inevitably disappointed.
>
> —Albert Einstein

> An archaeologist is the best husband a woman can have; the older she gets, the more interested he is in her.
> —Agatha Christie, 1891–1976, *Women's Wit and Wisdom*

A Conceptual Model of Family Relationships and the Three Dimensions of Religion

Our conceptual model, introduced in chapter 2, will be used as a visual aid over the next few chapters to illustrate how religion and family relationships intertwine. In the present chapter on why faith matters in marriage, we will examine and discuss Arrow 1A (the connection between religious practices and marriage relationships), as well as 2A (religious beliefs and marriage), and 3A (faith community and marriage). In later chapters on parenting and faith, we will discuss the connections between the three dimensions of religion and the mother-child and father-child relationships. Our discussions on the connections between religion and families will be based on previous research by a variety of researchers over the past five decades. However, we will draw heavily on one particular resource, discussed next.

The Conceptual Model and the *American Families of Faith* Research Project

As previously outlined, our conceptual model links three different dimensions of religion (religious beliefs, religious practices, and religious community) with various family relationships (see Figure 4.1). The model presents individuals (M = mother, F = father, C = child) in the context of a nuclear family, "reflecting the fact that most research on religion and families examines intact, nuclear families" (Dollahite, Marks, & Goodman, 2004; Marks, 2006, p. 605). Disappointingly, "little is known about religion in connection with other family forms" in spite of the fact that intact, two-parent families are decreasing while other diverse family forms are increasing in prevalence (Marks, 2006, p. 605). We will address diverse family forms at length in chapter 10.

Further, most available data are drawn from white, Christian, same-faith families. Much of our present knowledge is constrained by a lack of family, religious, or racial diversity. The *American Families of Faith* data set we draw from throughout this book includes in-depth interviews with 200 families and

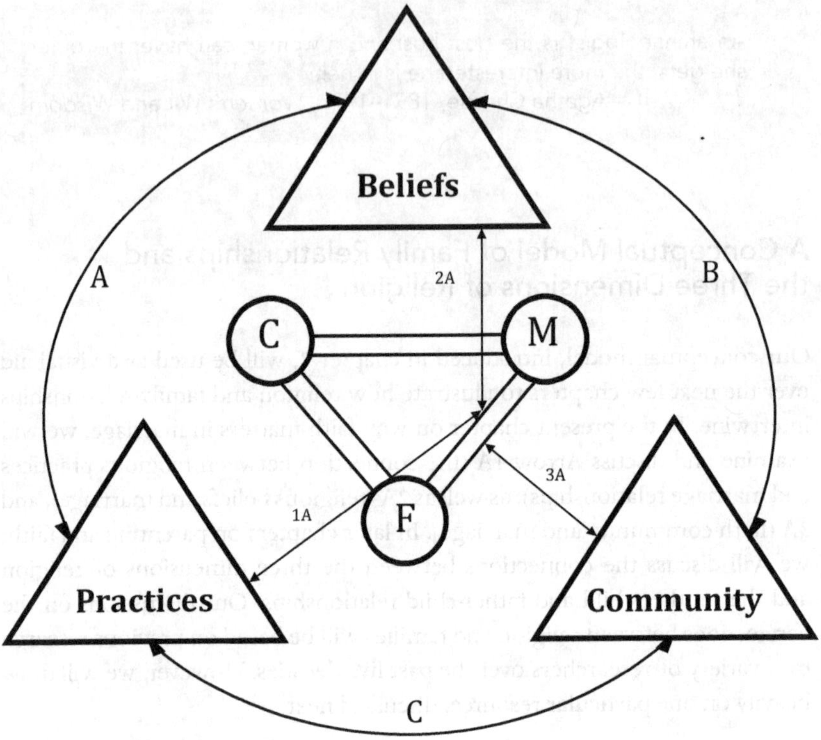

Figure 4.1 Research Connections between Religious Beliefs, Practices, and Communities and Marital Relationships

Source: Adapted from Marks (2006).

nearly 500 individuals (i.e., mothers, fathers, and children). The diversity of family forms in the families we interviewed includes (a) families based on marriage with children and (b) families based on remarriage with children. However, the religious and racial diversity represented is far wider. In terms of religion, families from the three world religions of Christianity, Islam, and Judaism were interviewed, and many different denominations or types were interviewed within each world religion.

In Christianity, we interviewed families from more than a dozen different denominations—and from a variety of traditions including Catholic, **Conservative Protestant** (e.g., Baptist, Pentecostal, non-denominational Christian), **Mainline Protestant** (e.g., Episcopalian, Methodist, Lutheran, Presbyterian), and **New Christian Religious Traditions** (e.g., Latter-day Saint, Jehovah's Witness, Seventh-Day Adventist). Within Islam, we interviewed families from the **Shia**, **Sunni**, and **Nation of Islam** traditions. In Judaism, we interviewed families from **Hasidic**, **Modern Orthodox**, **Conservative**, and **Reform** traditions.

In terms of racial diversity, approximately half of the families we interviewed represented an ethnic or racial minority. More specifically, the minority families we interviewed included those from African-American, Asian-American, Native American, Latino, Middle Eastern, East Indian, and Pacific Islander cultural backgrounds. About 50 (or 25%) of the families we interviewed were immigrants to the United States. The in-depth interviews with the more than 100 minority families we refer to in this book will provide a richer and more diverse array of perspectives on religion and families.

Religious Practices and the Marital Relationship: Arrow 1A

Key research connecting religious practices with the mother-father marital relationship includes a research study with a primarily Catholic sample. The study showed that shared, meaningful religious holiday rituals were associated with higher levels of marital satisfaction (Fiese & Tomcho, 2001). A study by Lee, Rice, and Gillespie (1997) also linked home-based family worship with higher marital satisfaction. These studies suggest that there is something important about practicing *shared* religious rituals as married couples. Perhaps when couples make time to create and maintain shared religious practices, it serves to cement their relational commitment. Or perhaps happier couples are more likely to continue with shared religious rituals than less happy couples. Most likely of all, perhaps there is a complex and sensitive two-way connection between religious rituals and relational happiness that requires additional in-depth research to fully understand.

In spite of the aforementioned benefits, Lee and colleagues (1997) also found that forced or "compulsory family worship may be more detrimental for children than no family worship at all . . . [illustrating the] need for research that moves beyond reported frequencies of religious behaviors [and practices] to an examination of the meanings and processes associated with the practices" (Marks, 2006, p. 606). Returning to our chapter 2 discussion on the importance of inviting more than one family member to "sit for the family portrait," we are reminded of the importance of asking *multiple* members of the family about the meanings they associate with religious practices.

In terms of other research on religiously based practices in the family, "research on Jewish families indicates that certain rituals, including the celebration of the Sabbath (i.e., the lighting of the candles, the *Shabbat* meal, and sacred prayers and blessings), can serve as family-strengthening practices" (Marks, 2006, p. 608; see also Hatch & Marks, 2014; Kaufman, 1991). A central purpose behind many of these rituals is "to prompt a deliberate turning from the mundane to the sacred" (Marks, 2006, p. 608; see also Eliade, 1959) and also to promote a renewal of relationships with one's spouse (and children). Several Jewish families in the *American Families of Faith* project have discussed the familial nature of home-based rituals. Participants from highly religious Muslim and Mormon families have highlighted marriage-strengthening practices as well (Dollahite & Marks, 2005; Marks, 2004). In chapters 8 and 9, we will share several real-life examples of these with you. We now shift our attention from religious practices to the connections between religious beliefs and marriage.

Religious Beliefs and the Marital Relationship: Arrow 2A

Correlations between religious beliefs and various aspects of marriage are complex and somewhat mixed (Dollahite et al., 2004; Koenig, McCullough, & Larson, 2001; Koenig, King, & Carson, 2012). Even so, there are some recurring connections. Arrow 2A, which links the dimension of religious beliefs with the father-mother (F-M) marital relationship, represents research correlating religiosity with several benefits including increased marital satisfaction, longer duration, and increased commitment and fidelity (Bahr & Chadwick, 1985; Marks, Dollahite, & Freeman, 2011; Thomas & Cornwall, 1990). Call and Heaton (1997) similarly found that several aspects of *shared* religious experience were related to **marital stability** (lower divorce rates). Three additional qualitative studies examining factors in "successful long-term marriages" (defined as satisfying marriages of 25, 30, or 35+ years, depending on the study) found that religious faith and/or beliefs were one of the top five facilitative factors reported by the participants, although these samples were small and not **generalizable** (Kaslow & Robinson, 1996; Robinson, 1994; Robinson & Blanton, 1993).

> Whoever lives true life will love true love.
>
> —Elizabeth Barrett Browning, *Aurora Leigh*, I
>
> Marriages may be made in heaven, but man is responsible for the maintenance work.
>
> —Bertrand Russell

Some reports linking religious belief with other aspects of marriage are negative, however. Sullivan (2001) found that religiosity seemed to promote marital satisfaction when husbands were in good mental health but also found that religiosity may contribute to relationship problems when the husband's mental health and psychological functioning were poor. Similarly, Arterburn and Felton (2001) present several clinical case studies where some religious beliefs they refer to as "toxic faith" were expressed in damaging and sometimes extreme behaviors and views that *harmed* marital and family relationships. Similarly, one study found that battered women were often highly religious and concluded that some specific beliefs (e.g., tolerance of abuse) seemed to contribute to the ongoing victimization of these women (Hathaway-Clark, 1980). In contrast, however, two other larger studies found no relationship between conservative Protestantism and domestic violence (Ellison & Anderson, 2001; Ellison, Bartkowski, & Anderson, 1999).

We concur with Burr, Marks, and Day's (2012) evidence-based proposition that religious beliefs can be helpful or harmful to marriages and families, depending on what individuals and families actually *do* as a result of their beliefs. We now shift our attention from religious beliefs to the connections between religious community and marriage.

Religious Community and the Marital Relationship: Arrow 3A

Research has repeatedly identified the local faith community or congregation as a means of social support for married couples and families who are actively involved. The *Handbook of Religion and Health* has established that 19 of the 20 studies on religion and social support (95%) reported at least one statistically significant relationship between a religious indicator and greater social support. Further, in their comprehensive review of the literature, Koenig and colleagues (2001) found that 79 of the 100 studies they reviewed indicated "at least one positive correlation between *religious involvement* and greater happiness, life satisfaction, morale, or positive affect" while only one study found a negative correlation (p. 101).

Let's examine the national picture of religious community involvement for a moment. According to the 2012 Pew Forum on Religion and Public life, about 80% of Americans claim a specific religious affiliation (Pew, 2012). This percentage is even higher among married couples, with more than 86% of married couples identifying with a specific religion. There is, however, significant variation in actual levels of involvement for those who claim an affiliation. For example, the Harris Poll #11 (2003) indicated that 90% of

American adults reported a belief in God (a figure very similar to the percentage of married couples claiming a religious affiliation, 86%), but the Harris Poll #59 (2003) found that only 36% of Americans actually *attend* a religious service once a month or more. Other research indicates that this percentage of monthly attenders is far higher among married couples than it is among singles—and that it is highest among married parents.

Taken together, these statistics indicate that although U.S. families attend religious services at rates that are a fraction of reported rates of religious belief or religious affiliation, religious attendance is nevertheless an important part of American marriage and family life for a sizable minority of those in the United States (Burr et al., 2012; Stark, 2012).

Limited Depth and Color in the Research on Religion and Family

As correlations between religious involvement and families have accumulated, an apparent limitation of this research, in addition to the paucity of detailed explanations, is the reality that most available studies have been based on Christian-only samples that also tend to be predominantly or exclusively white. Non-Christian and racial/ethnic minority families are conspicuously underrepresented in much of the available research (Dollahite et al., 2004; Marks et al., 2011). In short, then, the research on the religion and marriage connection lacks depth and color. In the *American Families of Faith* project, we strive to address both these needs.

In connection with the need for data regarding racially diverse couples, we intentionally oversampled minorities. More specifically, in our total sample of 200 families, just over half (101) are from racial and ethnic minorities—striving to avoid the monochromatic (all-white) tendencies of previous research. In terms of pursuing depth, as we asked the participants regarding the whys, hows, and processes that were at work in their families, we repeatedly asked couples for *real-life narratives*, for stories and experiences from their marriage and family life that captured and conveyed their experience in depth, richness, and living color. We share several of these narratives with you in the next two sections of this chapter on (a) inter-faith marriage and (b) challenges in marriage.

What Is Known About Inter-Faith Marriage?

A closer look at available research reveals that claiming a religious denomination seems to have relatively little influence on marriage; it seems to be *active* involvement and attendance in a faith community that matters. Indeed, the linkage of several marital benefits with *shared religious activity and involvement* is a prominent theme in the research. For example, shared religious involvement also appears to promote higher levels of marital adjustment and commitment (Bahr & Chadwick, 1985; Lambert & Dollahite, 2006; Mahoney et al., 2001).

Most of the research data linking involvement in a religious community with marital benefits are, however, based on *same-faith* marriages. In contrast to same-faith marriages, **inter-faith marriages** generally report more conflicts and less stability (Curtis & Ellison, 2002; Heaton & Pratt, 1990; Lehrer, 2009; Lehrer & Chiswick, 1993). For denominations that have been studied, the divorce rate among inter-faith marriages is higher than same-faith marriages—and among some denominations it is much higher. The finding that "same faith marriages are much more stable than interfaith marriages" has been documented for decades (Bahr, 1981, p. 260) and has been corroborated with large national samples by Evelyn Lehrer, a prominent sociologist of religion (Lehrer, 2009).

Let us be clear. Do all same-faith marriages produce happy families? No. You likely know of several exceptions. Do all inter-faith marriages result in conflict and divorce? No. Again, you may be aware of exceptions. Even so, across the board, inter-faith marriages are significantly more likely to end in divorce than within-faith marriages.

Conflict in Inter-Faith Marriage

There are several typical sources of marital conflict—marital researcher John Gottman lists the top six as "work stress, in-laws, money, sex, housework, [and] a new baby" (Gottman & Silver, 2004, p. 187). Research also indicates that in many inter-faith marriages, conflict over religion is often intertwined with several of the struggles and conflicts Gottman outlines—perhaps because different religions promote (and discourage or forbid) different practices and approaches to personal, married, and family life (Curtis & Ellison, 2002).

Like a rope that can be used to helpfully bind in some situations—or annoyingly chafe and burn at other times—religious commitments that reportedly help unify many same-faith marriages may produce tension, irritation, and conflict in marriages where commitment to a faith is *not* shared (Curtis & Ellison, 2002; Dollahite & Marks, 2006). This appears to be particularly true of **high-tension** or high-demand faiths that involve significant investments of time, energy, and money (Starke & Finke, 2000). For example, sociologist Evelyn Lehrer has found that within the first five years of marriage, Latter-day Saint (LDS, Mormon) inter-faith marriages are more than three times as likely to end in divorce than within-faith LDS-to-LDS marriages (i.e., 40% divorce rate for inter-faith marriages versus 13% for within-faith marriages; Lehrer, 2009; Lehrer & Chiswick, 1993). We have written on this disparity in other work and concluded that a leading explanation for the three-fold divorce differential between these families is that "the challenges and high demands of the LDS Church may be best met by married couples who *share a commitment to the faith*" (Dollahite & Marks, 2006, p. 405). Although this three-fold increase in divorce rate is one of the more extreme examples from the related research, the divorce rate in inter-faith marriages is higher than same-faith marriages for each of the major faiths that have been examined in demographic studies (Lehrer, 2009).

As additional in-depth, qualitative research has begun to reveal, a shared commitment to a faith can run much deeper than just checking the same denominational box on a survey form. In fact, it may even run deeper than shared attendance at worship services (although this is about as deep as most social science studies delved until the past decade or so). Yaxin Lu, a Chinese researcher who has worked on the *American Families of Faith* research project with us, spent several years examining the influence of faith on marriage and family for highly religious, immigrant Chinese converts to Christianity. In her published work on these families, Lu has reported that not only does sharing a religion and denomination matter—it is also reportedly important that the *level* of commitment to the faith be shared (Lu, Marks, & Apavaloiae, 2012; Lu, Marks, & Baumgartner, 2011; Lu et al., 2013). Multiple women and men in Lu's studies emphasized that they "not only chose to marry a Christian, but also sought a partner that *matched their personal level* of spiritual faith." For example, a Chinese husband named Pan stated:

> We met at a Christian college [after we both immigrated]. One value [I held] was simply [seeking] someone who . . . *understood the level of my faith*, not just a regular Christian, but someone who [could] understand the depth, the level, of my faith [in God].

Pan's wife, Wan, added:

> Since I was a teenager . . . [I] made up my mind that I had to marry someone . . . who is also a Christian. And I think I had really good teaching in my church too, so that I know, like Pan said, [not to marry] "just another Christian." I've seen other Christian boys or [other] Christian guys, they're not necessarily at [what for me is the right] level spiritually. *I think that [having a shared level of faith] is very important because I'm*

> *looking for someone that I can pray with, and really live a real Christian life [with].* Not just someone who just goes to church. So *it was very important to have the same [level of] Christian faith.*

Pan and Wan emphasized looking for the same level of spiritual faith in a mate so they could understand each other, pray together, and "really live a real Christian life" as a couple.

Zhou, an immigrant Christian wife from mainland China, expressed similar sentiments and shared her convictions in this way:

> I believe the words in the Bible: *marriage is established by God.* If both the husband and wife have the same faith and *the same level of faith,* if they both have [a] good relationship with God, they will have good marital and family relationships.

As with Wan and her husband, we see Zhou emphasize that "both the husband and wife have the same faith" as well as "the same *level* of faith."

A student in one of our college courses wrote on her observations of differences in the "level of religious devotion" in marriage and explained:[2]

> So far, every woman in my family who has gotten married has gotten a divorce (sometimes multiple). Those who are currently in a marriage are extremely unhappy and, at the rate they're going, [they] are on their way to repeating history. One common factor among each of these marriages is [big differences] in the level of religious devotion. My grandfather raised his six children in a very conservative, Southern Baptist home. As they grew up, each child found out what religion actually meant for them. My three aunts and my mom are the strongest, most faith-filled women I know. Their husbands, however, are/were the complete opposite. Each one of the women butted heads with their husbands on how to raise their children in terms of religion . . . [but I have realized] what I need to do to change this for my generation. . . . I will find a man who not only will [walk in faith with] me but who will [walk in faith with] my children. One who shares the same values and faith with me and consistently challenges me in my devotion. I refuse to settle for anything else and that will be a first for my family.

In a follow-up communication with this student, we asked how many divorces had taken place, and she indicated that the family was currently "on its way to [number] nine."

To restate, the importance of not only a *shared-faith* marriage (i.e., Christian-to-Christian), but also a **matched-level marriage** (i.e., a similar degree of commitment to the shared faith), is a concept that is emerging in the ongoing work related to *American Families of Faith*, as discussed next. The challenge with this is that, on average, across virtually all cultures and faiths, women tend to be more religious than men. As a result, a religious woman frequently will often feel pressed to settle for a man with somewhat lower levels of religious belief and commitment given the statistical fact that there are not as many highly religious men as women. As a result, the deeply personal question many highly religious women address is this: Settle for a less religious man or stay single?

Are You on the Same Page?

Whether activities that separate spouses are sacred or secular, too much time apart is not healthy. Marital therapist and researcher Bill Doherty refers to heavy involvement by only one spouse in any outside-the-marriage activity as a **time affair** (Doherty, 2000). We interviewed an African-American Baptist father named Alvin who similarly commented:

> [I]f you're doing your thing [and] I'm doing my thing, [then] never the two shall meet. Some people do that, they do their thing, [and the] other one [is] doing their thing [and] they very seldom are doing it together. That just leads to problems.
>
> (Marks et al., 2008)

According to Alvin, too much time apart "leads to problems."

Nesha was a remarried African-American Christian wife who related a portion of her own story that conveyed the deeper meaning of shared religious involvement in marriage for her. She reflected:

> I've been married before, and my first husband was not saved, and he wasn't interested [in my church]. [It] goes back to what the Lord said about being equally yoked. . . . I was at the church, but . . . as a nonbeliever [my ex-husband] thought I was giving too much time. Because of that, we weren't serving together, [and] we weren't going together . . . we would always feel some type of rift.
>
> (Marks, Dollahite, & Baumgartner, 2010)

Nesha later explained:

> [In my second marriage], to be able to go to church with my husband on Sunday morning, he and I sayin', "We are doin' it together." . . . To me, [that] strengthens the family. . . . It's really beneficial for me to be worshiping in the same church [with my husband]. The benefits are . . . very, very great, because [by doing it together] you are investing in the lives of your children [and in your marriage].

As we see from Nesha's accounts regarding her two marriages, faith may be a unifying force, or a dividing one in marriage, depending on whether the involvement is shared and how the faith is lived out (Burr et al., 2012). As Nesha noted in her closing line, from her perspective, "by worshiping in the same church" she and her current husband are uniting not only in their faith and in their marriage, they are also "investing in the lives of [our] children." The fact is that inter-faith marriage is often not only a marital issue, but an intergenerational one that can be exacerbated if and when children are born. Is the child going to be Catholic or Jewish? Will it be Catholic baptism by a priest or a naming ceremony by a rabbi? Will it be Catholic school or Jewish day school? In later childhood will it be catechism/confirmation or bar/bat mitzvah? And so on.

Additionally, particularly in families where religion and/or faith are of central importance, inter-faith marriage may influence and impact extended family members as well. One Jewish father we interviewed lamented:

> (Two of my brothers) married persons out[side] of the faith and I don't think they'll have much religion of any sort now. I don't think they'll have much Christianity or much Judaism. I see the family dynamics, the relationship between my parents and them. . . . I mean, my parents love them very much but it *hurt* my parents. When we're all together, although we love them all and we get along with them all, we see the differences. When we are all sitting around at the [ritual-filled] holidays they [the non-Jewish family members] just don't get it.

Inter-faith marriage is just one of several challenges that involve marriage and/or faith. Several other challenges were mentioned by the participants in the *American Families of Faith* project—enough, in fact, that we were motivated to alter our definition of what "strong marriage" means, as discussed in the next section.

> Having a healthy marriage is more than finding the right person, it's becoming the right person.
>
> —Lolly Pisoni, in Goddard & Marshall (2010), *The Marriage Garden*, p. 37

Challenges in Marriage: Do They Unite or Divide?

One important finding that emerged from our interviews with religious wives and husbands was that in spite of the fact that these women and men had built marriages and families that were viewed as exemplary by their clergy (who referred us to the couples), many wives and husbands were quick to point out that they had faced challenges from the day of their marriage forward and emphasized that an enduring marriage requires high levels of work and commitment. An African-American Baptist father named Joseph (who acknowledged several challenges in his marriage) extended a plea and challenge to "young people" near the end of our interview with him and his wife, Lisa. With passion, he exhorted:

> Marriage is sacred. Marriage is wonderful. [I want to tell young people] that there is nothing better. You . . . treasure your mate, and you get to know your mate. Don't be selfish, don't be in the world. Make God above all. God will glorify your marriage. . . . Be forgiving, be loving, [as a father and husband] be tender and be strong. Take care of your family. Love your family. Love your kids. Honor your wife. Don't be in the world.
>
> (Marks et al., 2010)

Many of our *American Families of Faith* participants offered similar counsel and, like Joseph, even invoked God in doing so. A few of the couples we interviewed reportedly had a pretty smooth go of it from the start, but most confessed several profound struggles, especially early on in their marriages. Next, we take a closer look at both situations.

Some of the couples we interviewed reported that their beliefs or core ideals, such as "Mak[ing] God above all" (Joseph) and adopting a "we-first" over "me-first" way of life, were there from the outset of their marriage. One Episcopal wife and mother, Janet, said:

> I feel secure in my relationship with Mike. I know he'll take care of me as Christ takes care of the church and [that he will] take care of the family. I never have [had] any doubts about that.

Most men, however, did not make the marital transition as seamlessly as Janet's husband Mike—nor did their wives have the security and reported lack of doubt that Janet expressed. For many others, the transition from (1) living as a self-focused individual to (2) becoming an other-focused marital partner was often a significant, if not monumental, step.

The Early Years of Marriage: "Growing Up" and Moving from "Me" to "We"

Although we interviewed relatively strong and happy families—couples who were viewed as **exemplars** of committed marriage and family life by their clergy and others—it was not uncommon for these couples to discuss the early years of marital life as extremely challenging. Clive, a Christian father from Louisiana, reported:

> I think there were moments [early in our marriage] that I was playing that role of a kid and she was [like my] Mama, 'cause I didn't want to grow up. But now I know I [had] to grow up. That [was] a real turning point for me. I can't tell you exactly when that "Aha" moment came for me. It gradually came and [in some ways it still] continues.
>
> (Marks et al., 2010, p. 26)

Many of the men we interviewed struggled in the effort to move from "me" to "we." A profound challenge for some was to overcome what they called "the bachelor mindset" (Marks et al., 2010). A Christian father named Terrence reflected:

> [I remember asking myself (about marriage)], "Can I really do this?" [And] asking God, "Really, can I do this?" 'Cause [my wife] will tell you, I still had the bachelor mindset. She was chasing me down in the street. Telling me when to come home. I mean, we went back and forth with that for five or six years. I mean, my thing was: "I'm a bachelor." I couldn't get [out of] that mindset that. . . . I'm independent. [I'd ask her], "What are you calling me for? Why do I got to come home? Why do I have to be there with you? Why do we have to eat together? I'm over here [with my boys]. I'm okay. I'm fine. I'll be home when I get ready." I couldn't connect [the marriage vows with the actions]. [Well], I'm [fully] married now.
>
> (Marks et al., 2010, p. 25)

Note that for Terrence, during his doubts and struggles he turned to his God and his faith—and even so, it took time before he was "fully married." After a similar reflection on his immaturity early in marriage, a wife named Vanessa said of her husband, Jake:

> [Over time, I have seen a lot of] maturity [and] spiritual growth [in him]. [Early on], he was extremely impulsive and selfish; very singularly absorbed. [He] just couldn't even see anything beyond what he wanted for himself. . . . That has changed.
>
> (Marks et al., 2010, p. 26)

For a Catholic husband named Fidel and his wife, Consuella, the early years were rocky as well. He reported:

> There are several years that were *very hard*, and I guess that is [like] any other couple, but I think one of the things that has kept us together is the fact that we are thinking on the same plane as far as what might be better for us as a couple.

Consuella and Fidel have kept their marriage alive—and reportedly did so by leaning on their shared beliefs. However, their marriage still did not smooth out until weathering "several years that were very hard." We have noted a distinct early marital pattern that emerged in several of the interviews we conducted with religious couples from various backgrounds:

> (a) boy meets girl; (b) boy loves girl but has difficulty leaving "the single life" behind; (c) the man faces a choice point; (d) the man turns to God and/or religious faith to help him overcome his selfishness; (e) the man commits himself to God and to wife and makes needed changes in order to make marriage work, *or* (f) the husband did not change and/or unity was not achieved and the marriage ended.

It should be noted that these steps were *not* mentioned in a majority of the marital interviews, but these steps (or variations on them) recurred frequently enough to be noted as a pattern.

The challenge of moving from the "me" to "we" mindset during the often selfish, early years of marriage was not limited to husbands. Christy, a Latter-day Saint wife, reflected:

> The first couple years of our marriage were *very hard*. I was raised in a house where everything revolved around my mother, and [my

> husband] was raised in a house where everything revolves around his father. So, coming into marriage, I think that we both had those [conflicting] expectations. I thought [life] was going to revolve around me, and he thought it was going to revolve around him. The first two years were a challenge. . . . I ended up in [a] marriage and basically it was a failure. I did not do things well and I did not do things right, and I can remember standing . . . at my kitchen sink one [day] when we'd been married for a couple of years, and I thought, "I'm so unhappy, but I can't leave," because divorce was never an option. So I said, "Either I'm going to change, or I'm going to be miserable for the rest of my life." So I determined at that point that I had to change, and just become more Godly, and not expect so much for myself, not be so selfish and expect everything to revolve around me.

Almost two decades later, marriage and life look much better for Christy, but like the husbands with the **bachelor mindset** mentioned earlier, she hit a "choice point" where she chose to shift from "me first" to "we first" thinking.

The Importance of Being "Equally Yoked"

Some of our participants did *not* weather the "very hard" early years spoken of by Terrence, Fidel, and Christy in their marital narratives—at least not during their first marriages. About 15 of the couples we interviewed included at least one partner who had been married previously, allowing us the opportunity to explore why their later marital attempts were apparently more successful than their first. A central conclusion was: *The couples whose marriages endured tended to share a unified marital and family vision—a vision that included shared religious beliefs*. For example, Ty, an African-American Christian husband, said:

> The Bible talks about, being unequally yoked. . . . It says that if you believe one thing, and the other person does not share your belief, that's just always going to be [a] problem.

Corynne, a once-divorced but happily remarried Latter-day Saint mother from Massachusetts, reflected:

> [I have] experienced two marriages, you know, one that didn't work and one that's working. I just think the commitment is deeper because we have a stronger basic foundation, which is [our common] faith. We have

> a [shared belief in Heavenly] Father. And [then there is the] common goal we have together, to be together forever . . . to keep that promise we made to each other: To be committed to each other and to be together forever. Forever.

> Life has taught us that love does not consist in gazing at each other but in looking outward together in the same direction.
> —Antoine de Saint-Exupery, from Goddard & Marshall (2010), *The Marriage Garden*, p. 161

Like Corynne and Ty, other participants compared and contrasted the personal or observed experience of being unequally versus **equally yoked**. In some marriages, one or both partners experienced a deepening of spiritual belief, a conversion, and/or a religious re-commitment after several years of marriage. These marriages offered an interesting perspective because they included the experiences of being "unequally yoked" *and* "equally yoked" within the same marriage. Shelly, a Christian mother of two from Delaware, said of her husband:

> [For the first few years of our marriage], he was living a life that I didn't agree with and that was a conflict between us. He would have to make me mad enough for me to let him go out [drinking] with his boys. . . . There was always a conflict between us. He had his life and I had mine. Not an adulterous life or anything like that, but [we were] not *together*. We were married, but not *together*. He was still "single." Once we got into our spirituality and our religion we understood that God meant for man to have this thing (marriage)—and [now this belief] influences everything we do.

A Puerto Rican Pentecostal father named Emilio and his wife experienced similar storms for a while, and they even separated at one point. He explained to us how their beliefs and a new-found "spiritual life" helped them save their marriage:

> We got separated, but we came back. But when we came back, we were missing something. We had everything: our health, our two children, our home, our jobs. We had everything a person could really ask

> for. But we both came to the core. We said, "There's something missing in our marriage. There's something missing. It's not there." And we both agreed that we needed a spiritual life. So we came to . . . the Lord. [We] gave our hearts to Him, and ever since then everything has fallen together. [Before that] it wasn't like that "one flesh" that the Bible talked about . . . that "one flesh." We weren't one flesh before we came to the ways of the Lord. She was her flesh, I was my flesh. And I mean, we would argue. I go my way; she goes her way. But when we came to the ways of the Lord, we don't argue, we communicate now. And we talk things out.

For Emilio and his wife, true marital unity did not reportedly come until they "gave our hearts to Him, and ever since then everything has fallen together." Again, we see a variation on the recurring theme regarding the importance of shared beliefs and family vision.

We now turn briefly to the topic of conflict resolution. Eddie, married for 20 years, still confessed to an occasional "battle" with his wife but also found strength in their shared belief in a sacred vow taken "before the Lord." Eddie explained:

> [My wife and me], we're individuals. We battle, you know, and a lot of times, she don't like the differences in me, and a lot of times, I don't like the differences in her. But because we both believe that marriage is a sacred vow, it's a vow we took before the Lord, we're gonna honor that vow, and . . . go through with it.
>
> (Marks et al., 2008)

Continuing on the themes of "battle[s]" and "differences" that Eddie references in marriage, we turn briefly to some work with our colleague Nate Lambert. Based on a portion of the *American Families of Faith* interviews, we have found that shared religious beliefs (and practices) helped couples: (a) avoid conflict, (b) resolve conflict, and (c) work toward relational reconciliation (Lambert & Dollahite, 2006). In connection with the preventive approach of avoiding conflict, a Baptist mother named Debby stated:

> I think that the more shared perspective on life that you have, the less inherent conflicts [you have] to begin with. So I think having a shared faith is important in that sense, in both the big picture, and hopefully, the smaller picture. But I think for me, somehow, my faith affects how I view conflict.

Phrased succinctly, a shared faith may be helpful in preventing some "conflicts to begin with." Shared beliefs can also help promote efforts at resolving conflicts when they do arise (e.g., "Let not the sun go down on your wrath," Ephesians 4:26, KJV). And, finally, shared beliefs can offer a shared pattern in how to reconcile (although this pattern differs somewhat across the Abrahamic faiths).

Conclusion

As we conclude our discussion of various challenges in marriage, we note that many people harbor the false notion that a great marriage is a relatively problem-free one. However, as we have interviewed both spouses in 200 of the strongest long-term marriages we could find, our experience has confirmed that *there is no such thing as a problem-free marriage*. Conflict, especially during the first 5 to 10 years, was the rule, not the exception for many of these marriages. Many others, like Eddie and his wife—confess to "a lot" of ongoing "battles" that may never go away. Indeed, marital researcher John Gottman (Gottman & Silver, 2004) has found that more than two-thirds of conflicts in marriage (69%) are over perpetual and irresolvable issues. While no marriage will be entirely free of issues and challenges, an important distinction of the most successful marriages is that they tend to focus time on the (other) 31% of issues that *are* resolvable (e.g., how to divide household chores) instead of beating their heads against the wall over issues that no amount of talking will magically fix (e.g., a sibling's alcohol/drug addiction).

For the married couples in the *American Families of Faith* project, challenges (including profound ones) were prevalent and, in some cases, ongoing. However, "along with the challenges came a partner one could lean on and love" (Marks, 2008, p. 178). Perhaps no one captured this better than an African-American Christian father named Earl who explained:

> [In strong marriages], the troubles will help them grow close. We had a few crises [but] we just pulled together and we got through it, and it drew us closer together as a unit. As opposed to [a husband and wife] just fighting [with] each other and snapping at each other and blaming each other, "It's your fault!"—"[No,] it's your fault!"

These experiences of marriage partners uniting in the face of challenge calls to mind the words of the late psychiatrist Viktor Frankl (1984), who said:

> If architects want to strengthen a decrepit arch, they *increase* the load which is laid upon it, for thereby the parts are joined *more firmly together*. . . . What man actually needs is not a tensionless state but rather the striving and struggling for a worthwhile goal, a freely chosen task.
>
> (p. 127, emphasis added)

The marriages of our participants had numerous "load[s] . . . laid upon" them through a variety of challenges, including constant as well as unpredictable trials. However, by joining "firmly together" while under pressure, the 200 marital arches in the couples we have interviewed have endured across time and have collectively borne significant weight without collapsing. From this standpoint, it might be proposed that one key difference between weak or failed marriages and strong, enduring marriages is that in the latter, the husband and wife "join more firmly together" when the loads of life come, instead of moving away from one another.

The standard ending in many American romantic comedy films captures some variation of a glowing bride in a white dress as "The End" spills onto the screen. For the couples we interviewed, the wedding day was the beginning—the beginning of some of the most challenging work a person can commence, the work to become a generative, committed, and unselfish partner and parent. And the most important part of their wedding was not the cake, flowers, dress, or rings—it was the vows they made and remembered and worked together to live out.

> [Do not] spend . . . time confessing [y]our partner's faults to friends . . ."
> —Wally Goddard and James Marshall, in Goddard & Marshall (2010), *The Marriage Garden*, p. 75

A Review of Connections between Religion and Marriage

To this point in the book, we have mentioned several research-based connections between religion and marriage. Some of these connections indicate benefits, and some indicate detrimental outcomes or danger. A few of these connections and findings are drawn from large, national data sets, but others are drawn from small, convenience samples and are not generalizable to the

U.S. population—it will require additional research to make that leap. With this is mind, here are several important points regarding the religion and marriage linkage:

1. Same-faith marriages are significantly more stable than inter-faith marriages.
2. Religiosity has been repeatedly correlated with increased marital satisfaction, increased commitment, and fidelity.
3. In small, qualitative, interview-based studies of long-term marriages, religious beliefs were repeatedly reported to be one of the top five helpful factors in sustaining marriage.
4. Religiosity may contribute to relationship problems when the husband's mental health is poor.
5. Case study research indicates that some religious beliefs can be damaging to marriages.
6. Field work with small samples has found that some religious beliefs (e.g., tolerance of abuse) can contribute to the ongoing victimization of battered women.
7. Shared, meaningful, (holiday/holy day) religious rituals have been linked with higher levels of marital satisfaction in research with smaller samples.
8. Home-based family worship has been linked with higher marital satisfaction in research with smaller samples but can do damage when it is forced or "compulsory."
9. In the U.S., 86% of married couples report a religious affiliation—however, identifying with a denomination seems to have far less influence than shared active involvement.
10. The local faith community provides various kinds of support for many married couples who are actively involved—however, faith communities tend to be less helpful and supportive to those in non-traditional families.

As we consider the aforementioned collection of findings regarding the religion and marriage connection, an outline begins to appear. Although many details are sketchy, an important piece of the picture created by the studies reviewed in the previous chapters and summarized here is that we see that all three dimensions of religion (beliefs, practices, and community) connect with marriage in some ways that appear to be supportive and healthy. This, however, is only part of the social science story. There are also harmful and dangerous elements of the religion and marriage connection (across all three dimensions). We must constantly bear in mind both the helpful and harmful potential of religion as we continue. On this note, many studies and reviews indicate that married persons who are involved in the same faith as their spouse tend to have longer, stronger, happier, and more satisfying marriages (Chatters & Taylor, 2005; Dollahite et al., 2004). Other studies have concluded that when beliefs are unshared, divorce rates rise significantly (Lehrer, 2009; Marks et al., 2011). Over the past 15 years, several reviews[3] have discussed connections between religiosity and marital relationships. Research specifically addressing the marriage-religion connection has yielded recurring, moderate correlations between religiosity and marital quality, marital stability (e.g., lower likelihood of divorce), and marital satisfaction (e.g., happiness in the marriage). However, we are left with very few data-based explanations regarding the whys, hows, processes, and meanings behind recurring correlations.

Throughout the book, we will ask you to come along as we try to do some digging and "mining to examine the meanings, motivations, and processes beneath the recurring findings that comprise 'correlation mountain' . . . the body of studies showing connections between religion and a variety of important" individual, marital, and family variables and outcomes (Marks & Dollahite, 2011). The correlation-rich but explanation-poor state of the field elicits the question, "*Why and how* do religious beliefs seem to influence marriage?" This is the focus of the next chapter.

Chapter Summary Points

1. Religious practices, beliefs, and community all appear to influence marriage in positive ways (e.g., higher marital satisfaction, longer marriages, increased commitment, and social support) and negative ways ("toxic faith," tolerance of abuse, higher divorce rates in inter-faith marriages) depending on how the couple uses religion.
2. A majority of Americans believe in God and claim a denomination, but only about one-third attend religious services on a regular basis.
3. Inter-faith marriages are generally less stable than same-faith marriages.
4. Along with being of the same denomination, qualitative research indicates that the strongest marriages are often between two people who share the same level of commitment to their religion, or feel they are "equally yoked" or "on the same page."
5. The *American Families of Faith* project found that even among the strongest marriages the couples faced difficult challenges and conflicts, especially in their early years of marriage.

6. Many couples reported that a shared family vision, often derived from religious beliefs, was central to the success of their marriage.

Review Questions

1. What did the research from Lee and colleagues discover about forced or compulsory family worship?
2. Based on the research of Call and Heaton, what religious behavior was correlated with increased marital stability (lower divorce rates)?
3. What seems to determine whether religious beliefs are helpful or harmful in families?
4. Why do inter-faith marriages tend to be less stable than same-faith marriages?
5. What is the difference between a "same-faith" marriage and a "matched-faith" marriage, and why does this difference seem to matter?
6. What "central conclusion" did the authors come to about strong families that were able to weather storms together successfully?
7. What percentage of marital conflicts are "irresolvable" according to marital researcher John Gottman? How might this relate to religion and marriage?

Notes

1. Portions of this chapter (about 5%) are adapted or reprinted from L. D. Marks (2006), Religion and family relational health: An overview and conceptual model, *Journal of Religion and Health, 45*, 603–618.
2. This narrative is not from the *American Families of Faith* interviews but is used with written permission of the author with the promise that anonymity be maintained.
3. These reviews include, but are not limited to, Burr et al., 2012; Chatters & Taylor, 2005; Christiano, 2000; Dollahite et al., 2004; Mahoney, 2010; Mahoney et al., 2001; Marks, 2006; Marks et al., 2011.

References

Arterburn, S., & Felton, J. (2001). *Toxic faith*. Colorado Springs, CO: Waterbrook.

Bahr, H. M. (1981). Religious intermarriage and divorce in Utah and the mountain states. *Journal for the Scientific Study of Religion, 20*, 251–261.

Bahr, H. M., & Chadwick, B. A. (1985). Religion and family in Middletown, USA. *Journal of Marriage and the Family, 47*, 407–414.

Burr, W. R., Marks, L. D., & Day, R. (2012). *Sacred matters: Religion and spirituality in families*. New York: Routledge.

Call, V. A., & Heaton, T. B. (1997). Religious influence on marital stability. *Journal for the Scientific Study of Religion, 36*, 382–392.

Chatters, L., & Taylor, R. J. (2005). Religion and families. In V. Bengtson, A. Acock, K. Allen, P. Dillworth-Anderson, & D. Klein (Eds.), *Sourcebook of family theory and research* (pp. 517–522). Thousand Oaks, CA: Sage.

Curtis, K. T., & Ellison, C. G. (2002). Religious heterogamy and marital conflict. *Journal of Family Issues, 23*, 551–576.

Doherty, W. J. (2000). *Take back your marriage*. New York: Guilford.

Dollahite, D. C., & Marks, L. D. (2005). How highly religious families strive to fulfill sacred purposes. In V. Bengtson, P. Dillworth-Anderson, D. Klein, A. Acock, & K. Allen (Eds.), *Sourcebook of family theory and research* (pp. 533–541). Thousand Oaks CA: Sage.

Dollahite, D. C., & Marks, L. D. (2006). Family and community nurturing spirituality in Latter-day Saint children and youth. In K. Yust, A. N. Johnson, S. E. Sasso, & E. C. Roehlkepartain (Eds.), *Religious perspectives on spirituality in childhood and adolescence* (pp. 394–408). Lanham, MD: Rowman & Littlefield.

Dollahite, D. C., Marks, L. D., & Goodman, M. (2004). Religiosity and families: Relational and spiritual linkages in a diverse and dynamic cultural context. In M. Coleman, & L. H. Ganong (Eds.), *The handbook of contemporary families* (pp. 411–431). Thousand Oaks, CA: Sage.

Eliade, M. (1959). *The sacred and the profane: The nature of religion*. New York: Harcourt Brace Jovanovich.

Ellison, C. G., & Anderson, K. L. (2001). Religious involvement and domestic violence among U.S. couples. *Journal for the Scientific Study of Religion, 40*, 269–286.

Ellison, C. G., Bartkowski, J. P., & Anderson, K. L. (1999). Are there religious variations in domestic violence? *Journal of Family Issues, 20*, 87–113.

Fiese, B. H., & Tomcho, T. J. (2001). Finding meaning in religious practices: The relation between religious holiday rituals and marital satisfaction. *Journal of Family Psychology, 15*, 597–609.

Frankl, V. (1984). *Man's search for meaning*. New York: Washington Square Press.

Gottman, J., & Silver, N. (2004). *The seven principles for making marriage work*. New York: Three Rivers Press.

Harris Poll #11 (2003). The religious and other beliefs of Americans 2003. Retrieved March 29, 2004, from http://www.harrisinteractive.com/harris_poll.

Harris Poll #59 (2003). While most Americans believe in God. . . . Retrieved March 29, 2004, from http://www.harrisinteractive.com/harris_poll.

Hatch, T., & Marks, L. (2014). Judaism and Orthodox Judaism. In L. Ganong, M. Coleman, & J. G. Golson (Eds.), *The social history of the American family* (pp. 781–784). Thousand Oaks, CA: Sage.

Hathaway-Clark, C. (1980). Multidimensional locus of control in battered women. Paper presented at the Rocky Mountain Psychological Association, Tucson, AZ.

Heaton, T. B., & Pratt, E. L. (1990). The effects of religious homogamy on marital satisfaction and stability. *Journal of Family Issues, 11*, 191–207.

Kaslow, F., & Robinson, J. A. (1996). Long-term satisfying marriages: Perceptions of contributing factors. *American Journal of Family Therapy, 24*, 154–170.

Kaufman, D. R. (1991). *Rachel's daughters: Newly Orthodox Jewish women*. New Brunswick, NJ: Rutgers.

Koenig, H.G., King, D. E., & Carson, V. B. (2012). *Handbook of religion and health* (2nd ed.). New York: Oxford University Press.

Koenig, H. G., McCullough, M. E., & Larson, D. B. (2001). *Handbook of religion and health*. New York: Oxford University Press.

Lambert, N. M., & Dollahite, D. C. (2006). How religiosity helps couples prevent, resolve, and overcome marital conflict. *Family Relations, 55*, 439–449.

Lee, J. W., Rice, G. T., & Gillespie, V. B. (1997). Family worship patterns and their correlation with adolescent behavior and beliefs. *Journal for the Scientific Study of Religion, 36*, 372–381.

Lehrer, E. L. (2009). *Religion, economics, and demography: The effects of religion on education, work, and the family*. New York: Routledge.

Lehrer, E. L., & Chiswick, C. U. (1993). Religion as a determinant of marital stability. *Demography, 30*, 385–403.

Lu, Y., Marks, L. D., & Apavaloiae, L. (2012). Chinese immigrant families and Christian faith community: A qualitative study. *Family and Consumer Science Research Journal, 41*, 118–130.

Lu, Y., Marks, L. D., & Baumgartner, J. (2011). The compass of our life: A qualitative study of marriage and faith among Chinese immigrants. *Marriage and Family Review, 47*, 125–148.

Lu, Y., Marks, L. D., Nesteruk, O., Goodman, M., & Apavaloaie, L. (2013). Faith, conversion, and challenge: A qualitative study of Chinese immigrant Christian marriages. *Journal of Comparative Family Studies, 44*, 227–247.

Mahoney, A. (2010). Religion in families, 1999–2009: A relational spirituality framework. *Journal of Marriage and Family, 72*, 805–827.

Mahoney, A., Pargament, K. I., Tarakeshwar, N., & Swank, A. B. (2001). Religion in the home in the 1980s and 90s: A meta-analytic review and conceptual analyses of links between religion, marriage and parenting. *Journal of Family Psychology, 15*, 559–596.

Marks, L. D. (2004). Sacred practices in highly religious families: Christian, Jewish, Mormon, and Muslim perspectives. *Family Process, 43*, 217–231.

Marks, L. D. (2006). Religion and family relational health: An overview and conceptual model. *Journal of Religion and Health, 45*, 603–618.

Marks, L. D. (2008). Prayer and marital intervention: Asking for divine help . . . or professional trouble? *Journal of Social and Clinical Psychology, 27*, 678–685.

Marks, L. D., & Dollahite, D. C. (2011). Mining the meanings from psychology of religion's correlation mountain. *Journal of Psychology of Religion and Spirituality, 3*, 181–193.

Marks, L., Dollahite, D. C., & Baumgartner, J. (2010). In God we trust: Perspectives on finances, family relationships, and faith. *Family Relations, 59*, 439–452.

Marks, L. D., Dollahite, D. C., & Freeman, J. J. (2011). Faith and prayer in family life. In T. W. Draper, A. J. Hawkins, & D. C. Dollahite (Eds.), *Strengthening our families (2nd ed.)* (pp. 185–195). Provo, UT: BYU.

Marks, L. D., Hopkins, K., Chaney, C., Nesteruk, O., Monroe, P., & Sasser, D. (2008). Together, we are strong: A qualitative study of happy, enduring African-American marriages. *Family Relations, 57*, 171–184.

Pew (2012). The global religious landscape. Pew Research Center. Retrieved December 18, 2014, from http://www.pewforum.org/files/2014/01/global-religion-full.pdf.

Robinson, L. C. (1994). Religious orientation in enduring marriages: An exploratory study. *Review of Religious Research, 35*, 207–218.

Robinson, L. C., & Blanton, P. W. (1993). Marital strengths in enduring marriages. *Family Relations, 42*, 38–45.

Stark, R. (2012). *American blessings*. West Conshohocken, PA: Templeton.

Stark, R., & Finke, R. (2000). *Acts of faith: Explaining the human side of religion*. Berkeley, CA: University of California Press.

Sullivan, K. T. (2001). Understanding the relationship between religiosity and marriage: An investigation of the immediate and longitudinal effects of religiosity on newlywed couples. *Journal of Family Psychology, 15*, 610–626.

Thomas, D. L., & Cornwall, M. (1990). Religion and family in the 1980s: Discovery and development. *Journal of Marriage and the Family, 52*, 983–992.

5

The Influence of Religious Beliefs in Marriage[1]

In this chapter, we examine the connection between religious beliefs and marriage more deeply. Namely, we will explore, uncover, and convey "insider's insights" that will be valuable to many readers, particularly to college-aged emerging adults, most of whom will marry one day. Our hope is that these previews into marriage will better inform and prepare emerging adults for success.

The *American Families of Faith* project includes 200 wives and 200 husbands from marriages or remarriages with an average duration of a little over 20 years. To frame these facts differently, our sample draws on more than eight millennia of combined marital experience (400 individuals × 20 years = 8,000 years).

As discussed previously, several research studies indicate that married persons who are actively involved in the same faith community with their spouse tend to have longer, stronger, happier, and more satisfying marriages on the whole (Chatters & Taylor, 2005; Dollahite, Marks, & Goodman, 2004; Mahoney, 2010; Marks, Dollahite, & Freeman, 2011). However, most of the related studies leave us with few data-based explanations for these trends. Why does shared religious involvement seem to correlate with strong marriage? This is an issue we addressed at length in the *American Families of Faith* project, with families where the spouses are jointly involved in their faith communities. Further, whether they are Christian, Jewish, or Muslim, most of these families worship together in their homes as well. While the dimension of religious practice and the dimension of faith community both reportedly impacted the marriages of the vast majority of the participants in the *American Families of Faith* project, the dimension of spiritual beliefs was most frequently identified as directly and indirectly impacting the participants' marriages.

Several core themes linking spiritual and religious beliefs and marriage will be discussed and illustrated in this chapter, where we try to better understand the marital processes taking place behind the scenes. The core themes that we will address include: (a) the unifying influence of pro-marriage beliefs, (b) the stabilizing influence of anti-divorce beliefs, (c) religious beliefs as a source of *harm* in marriages and families, (d) the importance of shared spiritual beliefs, and (e) faith in God as a marital support.

Theme 1: The Unifying Influence of Pro-Marriage Beliefs

Shen, a Chinese convert to Christianity, reflected on how his belief in and commitment to God had influenced his marriage to his wife, Shi. He explained:

> Marriage between a couple is a commitment—both to God and to each other. It is a life-long commitment that cannot be changed. Love, mutual respect, patience, and forgiveness are important ingredients of marriage. I cannot give you specific examples of how these virtues have influenced our marriage; however, I can say that all these together have [had] great influence on our 42 years of marriage.
>
> (Lu, Marks, & Baumgartner, 2011)

Shen's view, common among AFF participants, is that marriage is a commitment not only to each other but also to God. Previous research shows that those who believe God is a third and equal partner in their marriage often regard marriage as sacred, or as a "**three-fold cord**." Further, this belief can enhance and stabilize marital commitment (Dollahite & Lambert, 2007; Lambert & Dollahite, 2006, 2008).

Matt, a Lutheran father, used the unifying "three-fold cord" metaphor to indicate his belief in marriage as an institution that should not be dissolved (Lambert & Dollahite, 2008). He stated:

> You go to Ecclesiastes and it says that a cord of three strands is not easily broken (cf. Ecclesiastes 4:12). I think that the spiritual belief I have is that God through Christ is our example of what marriage and a family should be like. . . . [W]e also take seriously where it says the two shall become one and we try to be [united].
>
> (cf. Mark 10:8; Matthew 19:5)

In one brief response, Matt indirectly references multiple Biblical passages that are meaningful to him in connection with his lasting marriage and his beliefs about marriage.

Thomas, a Presbyterian father, similarly addressed his sacred beliefs about marriage when he explained:

> I believe [marriage] is a *covenant*. It's a three-way covenant between us and God and we believe that we're one, we're one flesh, we're one in union.
>
> (Goodman et al., 2013)

Jennifer, a Latter-day Saint mother, indicated that her religious beliefs encouraged her to look beyond "until death do you part" to a hope that she and her husband will be "together forever." She said:

> Well, we believe that families are together forever and [in our faith] we go to the temple and are sealed to one another so that we will be together forever, and I think that that's Heavenly Father's plan to have us be together forever. . . . That's the common goal we have together, to be together forever, to keep that promise [and the covenants] we made to each other, to be committed to each other and to be together forever.

Like Thomas and Jennifer, several *American Families of Faith* participants explicitly discussed marriage as a "covenant" or as a deeply sacred vow. Mitch, a Methodist father, described his experience with vow making as follows:

> [When I talk about fidelity in marriage], I mean fidelity to a vow; and making a vow in front of God and the family. That's pretty serious living up to that. And that's in our vows, that promise was indeed caring for each other through all of life's surprises. . . . And speaking those vows in front of her ten brothers . . . raised fidelity on the list.

With the exception of Shen, the participants we have heard from to this point had decades of personal history and experience in their respective faiths before getting married. We next hear from someone with a different perspective. Alberto, a Mexican-American immigrant father of two (married for eight years), explained the impact his new religious beliefs had on him as a convert to a family-centered Christian faith when he was in his late 20s. He reflected:

> Family has been one of the greatest blessings that I have experienced but when I was twenty-nine years old, I never thought of having a family, I only thought of myself. When I first learned of the church, it

> became apparent to me that God requires much more of people than their own self-interest, and recognizing this has brought me much more happiness and joy in my life than any other type of success ever could have. . . . My faith definitely influences the way I see myself as a human being. For me it's very easy to see this because I know perfectly how I was ten years ago before I became a member of my church. . . . My family (my parents and my brothers and sisters) always comment to me on the changes they see in my life. When I told them ten years ago that I was going to get married according to the teachings of my [new] church, they just laughed because I didn't have a job or a girlfriend. Two years later, when I invited them all to my wedding they were all surprised. Three months after that, when I was appointed director of an office in the Mexican government, they were surprised again. Oh yes, there's been a great change in my life.

Many of the participants we interviewed shared insights regarding how their spiritual beliefs influenced their marriages, but Alberto's narrative captures a report that his conversion to a new worldview and religious beliefs at 29 years old provided the motivation to marry in the first place. Alberto's narrative reflects the promotion of marriage and family, a focus that is clear and pervasive in the Abrahamic faiths of Islam, Judaism, and Christianity (Agius & Chircop, 1998). While research indicates that faith involvement often influences marital and fertility rates (e.g., Stark & Finke, 2000), Alberto's narrative is unique in that it captures marital and family attitudes *before* and *after* faith involvement. From Alberto's perspective, a series of changes in his life were catalyzed by his new-found sacred beliefs, including the specific belief "that God requires much more of people than their own self-interest" (Marks, 2005, pp. 101–102).

The belief that God requires much more of people than their own self-interest seems consistent with prominent developmental psychologist Erik Erikson's claim that the first developmental crisis of adulthood is the profound challenge to move beyond the self to establish true intimacy and *inter*dependence (Marks, 2005). After establishing true intimacy, Erikson viewed the second challenge of adulthood as the pull to become "generative" by using our time, talents, and resources to improve the lives of others—particularly those in the generations younger than our own (Erikson & Erikson, 1997). This generative and uplifting approach to family life often relates to parenting and raising children, but this maturation and movement away from individualism, pride, and selfishness is also fundamentally important in many successful marriages. An African-American Christian father named Larry seemed to reflect this type of generative maturity as he discussed his beliefs and his approach to his three-decade marriage. He shared:

> Marriage, for me, is a commandment of God. . . . Having faith in Him gives me the base . . . to build on, and any engineer knows that the bigger and stronger your base is, the higher you can make the building. . . . So having my faith in Him and having everything I need come from Him, there's no limit to [how much] my marriage can grow. In [response to] one of the other questions, I said self-sacrifice is not a problem to me. [God] gives me [the ability] to say, "I don't need to win this argument today" or the next one, or the next one. It's all about just getting, reaching [God, and that helps my marriage].

A Sunni Muslim father named Ahmed described his spiritual beliefs regarding marriage as well. He said:

> In Islam, marriage is a sacred institution. . . . That is why relationships outside of marriage are not permitted, to keep the entire society morally sound.
>
> (Goodman et al., 2013)

Note that for Ahmed, the issue of marriage is not only personal and marital, it is societal. This is an idea we will return to later. For now, however, we return to the influence of pro-marriage beliefs in religion.

One Mormon couple from Oregon reported that their religious beliefs promoted their marriage on multiple levels. First, they both served volunteer missions in Europe as young single adults, sharing their religious beliefs. Second, their faith promoted a marriage and familial ideal that led them to seek a specific type or quality of mate and marriage after their mission years. Third, a mutual acquaintance from Europe who was aware of their similar spiritual and familial beliefs played "matchmaker." In the couple's own words, eight children and 40 years of marriage later:

Nada: *[Question: Did your religious beliefs influence the way you met and your decision to marry?]* They definitely did, and [my beliefs influenced] the idea of what I was looking for and what I hoped to achieve in a marriage and in our family [that would] result . . from that marriage.

Lance: I think that's true. [Even the way we] met . . . happened [because we both] know a lady that we had met while serving full-time missions for our church. . . . She figur[ed] that we would be a good match for each other, and as it turned out she was right.

Lance would later add, referring to the strong, religion-based, pro-marriage beliefs held by Nada even before her missionary service, *"She was married to marriage long before she was married to me."* Indeed, this phrase seems to reflect the belief-based vision of many who taught us about their marital lives and experiences.

As we move from "pro-marriage beliefs" to our next theme, we are sensitive to the perception that it may seem like verbal hair-splitting to separate pro-marriage beliefs from anti-divorce beliefs—in fact, in some of our earlier work, we combined the two. However, although the two are closely related, they are not identical. Generative faith beliefs seem to promote marriage—but, of course, without marriage in the first place divorce could not occur. One of the important questions we had as we approached the *American Families of Faith* project was: What kept these idealistic, pro-marriage couples from divorcing after the "honeymoon effect" faded and as a long road of hard work unfolded in front of them? We turn to a partial answer next.

Theme 2: The Stabilizing Influence of Anti-Divorce Beliefs

A clear theme repeated by many of the married parents we interviewed was a strong aversion to divorce. Aaron, a Jewish father, stated, "Divorce is just not in our subset of values." Matt, a Lutheran father, said of his marriage, "I think that we take seriously where it says that God hates divorce." Brent, a Jehovah's Witness father, similarly reflected:

> We mentioned before about [marriage] being a permanent bond, that Jehovah God hates divorcing . . . because that breaks the marriage bond. And Jesus also said that adultery would be something that would, could, break the marriage bond.

Saying essentially the same thing as Aaron, Matt, and Brent, a non-denominational Christian mother named Elizabeth stated:

> God hates divorce. God instructed husband and wife to get married and stay that way forever. So who am I to say, "I can get rid of him"? [Divorce], it's just not an option.

A Latino Catholic father named Miguel invoked Elizabeth's latter phrase, almost verbatim. He said, "Divorce is not an option." Elizabeth and Miguel were not alone. Again and again, across race, religion, and region, the *"Divorce is not an option"* mantra recurred.

A Conservative Jewish mother named Rachel emphatically stated:

> *No! [Divorce is] not an option.* This is it. Contract. We made a vow to each other and we'd say this to the kids: "You'll hear us fight and you'll hear us disagree, but you'll *never* hear us talk about, 'Well, let's divorce.' "
>
> (Goodman et al., 2013)

A Jewish husband (although not Rachel's) similarly explained:

> In the Jewish tradition, marriage is a major life cycle event. . . . The Jewish faith holds marriage as being a very holy endeavor, one that is not taken lightly. . . . Divorce is not looked upon casually in any way, shape or form . . . . [Marriage is] about devoting yourself to another, in the same way that you devote yourself to God, and to the notion [that] repairing the world starts with families and starts with a one-on-one relationship.

A Chinese Presbyterian husband named Beng reflected on and shared several of his sacred beliefs related to marriage with us. He said:

> I think marriage, in the first place, is . . . designed by God and set up by God. Our faith, from the Bible, it tells us it was God who created man and woman, and put them together. Jesus emphasizes that when a man and woman are put together [by God], man should not put asunder. Man shouldn't split [a marriage] up. . . . Marriage is not our idea. It is God's idea. . . . These things are defined by God, and that's my spiritual belief on marriage. I think [we must realize] that there will be difficulties in marriage . . . [but] divorce is not an option, so we'll have to work out differences. We have to learn to accept who our spouse is, and work out differences. There will be differences, so work it out.
>
> (Lu et al., 2011)

For Beng and his wife of more than three decades, their "no divorce" stance reportedly forces conflict resolution as the only option. Mayzee, a Latter-day Saint mother in a family originally from the Pacific Isles, emphasized the same two points as Beng: (1) divorce is not an option, so (2) work it out.

> I think whenever we've had a conflict or an argument or a fight . . . we don't think about divorce. That's not a term that's . . . used [in

> our marriage]. We just think: That's not an option. We're here in this together. No matter what problems arise, or how hard that problem seems at the moment, there's got to be a way that we can overcome it and work through it and get it [resolved].

A response from a Christian mother named Kristy seemed to contain a clear echo of Mayzee as she shared her beliefs regarding marriage and belief against divorce. Kristy said:

> [I believe that] marriage is forever and divorce is not an option. Conflicts will arise and they have to be resolved. . . . Conflicts are going to be there. Conflicts are going to arise, but they have to be resolved, and the fact that divorce is not an option forces that decision [of conflict resolution] to be made.

Holly and Jared, a Mormon couple, addressed the same issues as Beng, Mayzee, and Kristy. Reflecting on their sacred beliefs involving marriage, they stated:

Holly: We know that we are gonna be married forever. *Divorce is not an option. . . .* So, we know that neither one of us is going anywhere. Even if we are having a miserable day, or week, or month, if it comes to that, we are not worried that the other person is gonna take off, and we are not worried that our marriage is falling apart. And while occasionally that might [mean] that [the] two us are taking [each other] for granted, I think that gives a lot of security, knowing that the relationship that you are building and the family you are building is something that's gonna last forever.

Jared: . . . these things [my faith] are as much a part of me as my arms, so I often don't stop and think about them, . . . [but] the whole basis of our relationship is not that we are just here to have fun now, [or that] we hope things work for a while. It's that we are building an eternal unit, that Holly and I are always [going to] be together. . . . The goals that we are aimed towards . . . [are not just] five years down the road, it's eternity, eternity, eternity.

Holly's parents had divorced while she was growing up. She converted to and became involved in her faith community during her years of emerging adulthood and married within that faith. A similar pattern was reported a handful of additional times by *American Families of Faith* participants in various faiths. It seemed that in many of these cases where participants had experienced the divorce of their parents, a conversion to or deepening of their religious faith was, at least in part, an effort to rekindle their personal hope and faith that marriage *could* endure. (We will address this issue at length in chapter 10, "Religion and Diverse Family Forms.")

The following three excerpts from Chinese Christian converts, drawn from the research of Yaxin Lu and colleagues, add similar perspectives from a different vantage point—that of U.S. immigrants. Guo, a Christian mother of four originally from Hong Kong, explained that "commitment to marriage" was central to her marriage of more than 20 years. She said:

> God created marriage, and let no man separate. Commitment to marriage is God's blessing; commitment is very important. We [do] not think about divorce, no matter how big the difficulties are. We must work out and resolve the difficulties in the Lord. We would not address divorce easily. This idea cannot emerge into my mind.
>
> (Lu et al., 2011)

Guo not only identifies commitment as "very important" to her marriage; her statement also includes a refusal to even "think about divorce." This idea of refusing to entertain divorce, even in word or thought, was an idea addressed by others as well, but this ideal was reportedly put to the test in some cases. Another Chinese Christian wife recalled:

> We were full of pain and hav[ing] difficulties when [my husband] Lei lost his [job]. If I had not believed in God, I would have . . . left him. I would have left him suddenly. . . . It is wrong to have this idea. We [must] come back to God.

Wang, another Chinese convert to Christianity, similarly explained:

> In [the] Chinese tradition [I held] before [my conversion to Christianity], if the husband and the wife couldn't get along very well, they would divorce; this is very common among non-believers. After we [came to] believe in God, we realized that [although] we are not perfect [and] have many shortcomings, we will make up with each other and help the other. [We try] not to look at the speck of sawdust in other's eyes [while we] pay no attention to the plank in our own eyes. Marriage, which is established by God, is very holy. Our relationship is more stable than before. These spiritual beliefs made our marriage more stable.
>
> (Lu et al., 2011)

Some of the couples we interviewed added another explicit level of aversion to divorce. They did not even speak the word in their home and referred to it, even in their interviews with us, as "the 'D' word." Ashley, a Christian mother of seven married for 40 years, said:

> The "D" word does never come up in the house. [Marriage] is not about getting mad at somebody and throwing that word out there. When you're at the very beginning of your marriage . . . you already [need to] have that in your mind, that [the "D" word is] not an option.

Laura, a Full Gospel Christian mother of two married for about 10 years, expressed a perspective similar to Ashley's. Laura, a Washington State native, said:

> The "D" word's never an option. . . . That's not even a word in our family. That's never an option. When we got married that was something that we talked about. This is never going to be an option, both coming from divorced families [and dealing with that pain as kids]. [We're] not even going to mention the word because it's not valid in this family; it is not an option. . . . [Our] faith is the glue that holds it all together.

Note Laura's repeated and almost emphatic aversion to divorce. In just five lines, she mentions that divorce is "never an option" four separate times. Further, other than mentioning that she and her husband are both from "divorced" families, Laura never explicitly mentions "divorce." Instead, she uses four euphemistic replacements: "the 'D' word," "that," "this," and "it." This aversion was explained by Laura and her husband, Jason, who, elsewhere in their interview, related their traumatic childhood experiences of watching both sets of their parents go through volatile divorces.

Some readers might wonder if Laura and Jason's religious involvement might also be a reactionary response to having parents who were not involved with faith. On the contrary, Laura's family of origin was heavily involved in religious activities (perhaps "too involved," by her report). Similarly, Jason's father was a pastor—a pastor who managed (from Jason's point of view) to almost always place other congregational members above his own wife and children. Laura's final comment is that for her and Jason, "Faith is the glue that holds it all together." However, it seems from this couple's reports that a non-generative and hyper-involved version of religion may have done more damage than good in their parents' marriages. Both Laura and Jason acknowledge this and struggle for a healthier balance of religious faith involvement in their own married life.

Although Laura and Jason reportedly strived for a more balanced religious life than their divorced parents had modeled for them, many other participants were either religious "converts" or nominal church members who became religiously involved *after* coming from religiously indifferent families. Michelle, a Presbyterian mother from California, was one of these—and she tied her marital success closely with her faith. She contrasted her marriage to her husband with her family of origin and said:

> I look at our [marriage] relationship as very intentional. . . . I could not be married [and stay married without my faith]. I look at [it this way], it's the grace of God that we're married for 19 years. There's no way, I don't believe there's any way that we would be able to be still be married [without our shared faith]. Let's look at it this way. My sister has been married four times and divorced [all four]. My mother has been married three times now. My father has been married three times and divorced three times. Everyone in my immediate family has not been able to stay married and they're not religious. . . . [I believe that] it's only by the grace of God that we've been able to [stick].

Alexis, a Christian Scientist wife and mother married for the same duration as Michelle (19 years), explained how her faith helped her stay committed to marriage during difficult times.

> We've been married over 19 years and sometimes your spouse drives you crazy, but you love him. And sometimes you just have to see him as God sees him. Not sometimes—all the time, actually. . . . [If you can remember] the set of wonderful qualities that you married him for . . . it just helps you get over the tough spots.

One of the more dramatic histories from the AFF project involved Angie, a Muslim mother of two from Pennsylvania. Angie had seen her minister and then her parents have affairs while she was a teenager—both situations resulted in divorces. Like Michelle (mentioned earlier), Angie's parents' (and her minister's) infidelity weighed heavily on her, and she looked for a different way. That way, for her, ultimately involved a conversion to Islam. She was, for a time, what one minister has called a "**religious refugee**" (cf. Bengtson, Putney, & Harris, 2013, p. 60). Looking back, Angie explained:

> My husband knows my worst fear before we got married was that I would divorce. That he would leave or I would leave, an affair, whatever. . . . But now, I have no fear that my husband will have an affair. I know him. I know his religion. . . . I've seen a lot of men that when things get tough, they take off. . . . I can sit here and look you in the eye [and tell you that my husband will not cheat and will not leave].

Later in the interview, Angie's husband, Omar, shared the following narrative that seemed to capture and illustrate why Angie displays such confidence in his fidelity. He reported:

> At work, our offices look out on to the parking lot. Every morning, all the engineers gather into this one guy's cubicle at 7:45 [as the women start to arrive] and say, "Ah, look what *she's* wearing. She looks good!" Typical, it's a normal thing between guys. But by saying these things you are degrading that woman, you are gossiping. Knowing that these things will be written [in my heavenly book] prevents me from [participating] and from that your entire behavior is changed. [Instead], you are sitting in your office doing your work, which is what you are supposed to be doing.
>
> (Marks, 2005, p. 101)

Omar had previously offered a detailed explanation of his spiritual belief that our deeds and misdeeds will be written in a personal book of life that will one day be opened before the world—and that this belief keeps him in constant check (Marks, 2005). This religious belief is an example of how deeply held convictions have both individual *and* marital consequences.

Omar's work narrative is relevant to our discussion in that it captures and reflects an ideal encompassed by most of the Abrahamic faiths; namely, that it is wrong for a man to even *look* inappropriately at a woman. For many of those in the *American Families of Faith* project, the line for divorce is reportedly drawn on the side of caution and prevention, but living out this ideal is not easy. Brett, a Presbyterian father, said:

> Everyone has hard times in a marriage, and certainly, there are times when it would be easy to walk out the door. But I think that having made a commitment that's a promise, that makes you stop and think, "Well, yeah, I could just walk out the door"—but "No, there's something bigger here than me just getting fed up and walking out the door."

An African-American Baptist father and armed forces veteran named Stewart had seen his wife, Annie Mae, face this very decision (to stay or to "just walk out the door") during their more than 30 years of marriage. He recalled, as she listened quietly:

> I was in [the wars in] Korea and Vietnam and I experienced some things that I don't even want to remember. I lost friends. . . . When I returned from Vietnam, I was messed up. [I was messed up] a little bit physically and a lot mentally. I was suffering from post-traumatic stress and I was approaching a state of becoming an alcoholic. And my wife and I talked about this and prayed over this and worked with this and she was right there by my side. She didn't turn her back on me and she very easily could have.

Stewart went on to explain that even several decades later,

> The post-traumatic stress thing is something that I still deal with. It's something that I'll probably live with the rest of my life. But she understands and helps me. . . . She is a very strong person. My wife ha[s] overcome things that the average woman would probably just keel over and say, "It's over." She's very strong and I guess her most significant strength is God. Her belief in God is . . . her main strength.

Annie Mae, Stewart's wife, seemed uninterested in discussing her marital heroics. She immediately turned the interview discussion toward the topic of Stewart's caregiving for her following her aneurism a couple of years before the interview and reported:

> Well, I feel that *he's* very strong in many, many ways. Because all the obstacles that we had in our lives, the medical [obstacles], *he* had to be the one to take over and to help. . . . He had to speak for me when I couldn't talk . . . he had to do everything for me. . . . He's a very, very strong man.

At the conclusion of their interview, Stewart was asked what advice he would give to young couples about marriage. He responded:

> Throw out all of the theory. Get rid of a large percentage of the advice [you will be given] and concentrate on each other. . . . Say to one

> another, "We are going to build this life for you and me" and let everything else other than God be secondary.

On the heels of Stewart's counsel, we shift gears. Although the frequently held perspective of anti-divorce beliefs among the AFF participants has been covered at length, these beliefs were not held by all. Some participants were more open to the idea of divorce. Brett (the same father who discussed not walking out the door under most circumstances) would later emphasize:

> [But] I'm certainly not a hard core person that says, "We can never get divorced." I understand that there are situations . . . [where] that may be the best option.

Brett's statement brings us to an important point in the chapter and to a discussion of a perspective that counters much of what we have discussed to this point. The participants we have heard from have largely discussed how their religious beliefs have strengthened and supported their marriages. However, religious beliefs can also challenge or damage family relationships as well. It is to this reality that we now turn in Theme 3.

Theme 3: Religious Beliefs as a Source of Harm in Marriages and Families

The findings of scores of empirical studies, including several from the *American Families of Faith* project, seem to indicate that there are "healthy-souled" expressions of religion that are linked with positive outcomes for individuals, marriages, and families. However, as mentioned in chapter 2, it is apparent that there are "sick-souled" expressions of religion and religious beliefs that harm individuals and families—as William James, Rodney Stark, and others have empirically and historically documented. Researcher-clinicians Arterburn and Felton (2001) refer to the harmful and sick-souled ways of being religious and/or misapplication of beliefs as "toxic faith."

Harm 1: Excessively Rigid Anti-Divorce Beliefs

In the preceding section, we introduced the strong "anti-divorce beliefs" of many AFF participants. It may be pointed out, however, that these same beliefs that helped keep several AFF couples together (and reportedly kept them from quitting on their marriage and one another during difficult times) might be harmful and damaging under different circumstances. What about marital situations involving domestic violence or abuse? What about marriages where one partner is faithful and keeps his/her covenants, while the other engages in infidelity? These, and other scenarios, constitute (even for many persons with strong anti-divorce beliefs) reasonable exceptions to the rule of "divorce is not an option."

During our 15-year process of conducting interviews with diverse families around the United States, we visited and attended (as guests) many different services at churches, synagogues, and **mosques** in various cities and towns. During one church visit on the East Coast, Loren attended a service with a friend named Pearl. As they pulled into the parking lot, Pearl abruptly braked, hustled from the car, and broke up a physical fight between the legal wife and current girlfriend of a male church member who had brought his girlfriend to a "family day" at the church. The violence would likely have been far more severe without Pearl's early intervention. Pearl later explained to Loren that the congregation did not believe in divorce, but that as a result of this belief (and a stigma on those who did choose to divorce) there were several couples who "probably should have divorced" who did not—including the couple involved in the love triangle just mentioned. This couple was not interviewed for our project, but their situation presents a counterexample that we should consider for balance. There are almost certainly contexts where anti-divorce beliefs can be damaging instead of preventive. In a book entitled *Sacred Matters: Religion and Spirituality in Families* (2012), Wes Burr and colleagues explained:

> It is variation in what people *do* as a result of their ideals and beliefs about the sacred that determines whether the sacred is helpful or harmful in families, and it is not the mere presence of religion [or religious belief] . . . that makes the difference.
>
> (p. 17)

From this perspective, a religious belief that is lived out and honored with kindness, consideration, and wisdom will likely help marriages and families. By contrast, the same belief may be held, but violated or hypocritically or self-righteously misapplied in actions toward others. Hence, it is not only what one believes but what one *does* with those beliefs that matters most. Anti-divorce beliefs that are applied by a couple to promote their positive marriage in one circumstance might be misapplied by the same couple if they engage in harsh and ill-informed judgment of a couple who is divorcing in another circumstance. From Burr's perspective, we must attend carefully not only to professed *beliefs* but to how those beliefs are *applied* and lived out. Having briefly discussed challenges and complexities associated with anti-divorce beliefs, we now turn to another religious belief that was identified as potentially harmful by several *American Families of Faith* mothers and fathers.

> Reason and religion teach us that [women] too are primary existences, that it is for us to move in the orbit of our duty around the holy center of perfection, the companions not the satellites of men.
>
> —Emma Hart Willard, 1787–1870

Harm 2: "Male Headship"

One question our AFF participants were asked was: "Are there any religious beliefs that, if misunderstood or misapplied, could harm families?" A recurring response to this question from Christian women and men familiar with the New Testament was a concern over the following teaching of the Apostle Paul, expressed in his letter to the Colossians—"Wives, submit yourselves unto your own husbands, as it is fit in the Lord" (Col. 3:18, KJV)—and again in his letter to the Ephesians:

> Wives, submit yourselves unto your own husbands, as unto the Lord. For the husband is the head of the wife, even as Christ is the head of the church: and he is the saviour of the body. Therefore as the church is subject unto Christ, so let the wives be to their own husbands in every thing.
>
> (Eph. 5:22–24, KJV)

Some participants quoted portions of these verses verbatim and had clearly studied, and in many cases wrestled with, them before. Other participants referred to these verses by the concept of "male headship." Interpretations and responses to these verses varied. Among the wives, a couple of women reportedly embraced this teaching. One mother explained that she had advised her (now adult, married) daughter not to compete with her husband and warned that if both the wife and the husband "want to be the head of the family, there will be conflict." Even so, the same mother conceded that "as a wife, it's not easy to accept" (Lu et al., 2013). Other mothers and fathers seemed to accept a modified form of the teaching as a personal belief but emphasized the related and often overlooked verses from Ephesians 5 that read:

> Husbands, love your wives, even as Christ also loved the church, and gave himself for it. . . . So ought men to love their wives as their own bodies. He that loveth his wife loveth himself.
>
> (Eph. 5:25, 28, KJV)

One wife we interviewed challenged this belief:

> [A danger is the belief that] "the head of the wife is the husband." This is misapplied if a husband suppresses his wife with this, just for his own benefit and authority. . . . They have both responsibility and obligation. We should not choose a special sentence to defend ourselves. . . . Why should I submit to him [my husband] if he is wrong?
>
> (Lu et al., 2011)

One husband, originally from Hong Kong, said:

> [The Bible states], "The husband is the head of a family, a wife should submit to her husband." It's harmful to marriage if this is misunderstood and we misapply this Bible teaching. Our pastor also taught us that it was male chauvinism if the husband requires the wife to obey him in everything no matter what it is; it is [a] misunderstanding of the Bible verse. The rest of the passage states that "the husband should love his wife with the love of Christ."
>
> (Lu et al., 2011)

In our collaborative work with diverse scholars and with diverse populations, many Christian wives and a significant minority of the husbands wrestled with if and how to implement the doctrine of "**male headship**" (Burr, Marks, & Day, 2012; Lu et al., 2013). While the specific term "male headship" was specific to Protestant Christians, a profound concern over sexism, male chauvinism, or, as one father put it, "unrighteous dominion" was evident among some Jewish, Mormon, and Muslim wives and husbands as well. Having discussed two expressions of religious belief that reportedly can be damaging to marriages (i.e., anti-divorce beliefs and "male headship"), we now turn to another challenge that emerged in some *American Families of Faith* folks—harm to family relationships as a result of divergent religious beliefs.

Harm 3: Family Conflict and Tension Due to Divergent Religious Beliefs

A common faith and unified set of religious beliefs reportedly provided a shared family vision for many of the marriages and families in our *American Families of Faith* project. Religious faith, however, can be a source of anguish when a family member leaves the family faith, "falls away," or marries outside a family's cherished faith. Let us revisit a narrative from a Jewish father named Seth, presented earlier in the book, this time in slightly expanded form.

> (Two of my brothers) married persons out of the faith and I don't think they'll have much religion of any sort now. I don't think they'll have much Christianity or much Judaism. I see the family dynamics, the relationship between my parents and them. . . . I mean, my parents love them very much but it *hurt* my parents.

The pain was not limited to Seth's parents, but also reportedly spilled over to his passionately Jewish grandfather. Seth's own pain is apparent as well. Less apparent, however, is the probable pain of Seth's brothers and their non-Jewish wives at a being considered "outsiders" by the rest of the family.

We see that Seth's reflections on family life within Judaism are not idiosyncratic. They seem to resonate with those of Erik, a 24-year-old observant Jewish male in Bengtson and colleagues (2013) longitudinal study who explained:

> I see that I'm Jewish, and I see that my parents are Jewish, [and] my grandparents are Jewish. . . . This is just the way I am supposed to do it.
>
> (p. 54)

Miriam Bornstein, a Modern Orthodox Jew from Bengtson's study, stated that if her children married outside of Judaism:

> What would be lost would be the feeling of being Jewish, following the laws of Judaism, the traditions of being Jewish, celebrating the holidays and the Jewish festivals. Being Jewish is not simply a religion, being Jewish is a way of life.
>
> (p. 57)

Our AFF participant Seth explained his extended family's current situation, in connection with his brothers' decisions to marry outside of Judaism—a situation that reflects some of the realities that Miriam Bornstein (from Bengtson's study) mentioned. Seth said:

> Being Jewish within a family of Jews was really important and marrying Jewish was real important to me. I wanted to be married to someone who had as much in common with me as possible. . . . There's a certain framework for life and marriage in Judaism. . . . I look at the dynamics of a happy family, and it's just all part of it.

The "certain framework for life and marriage in Judaism" that mattered profoundly to Seth and his wife, Sarah; to his parents; and to his late grandparents is *not* an integral part of life for his two brothers who married outside the Jewish faith. These marital decisions caused evident pain and tension for family members on both sides of the divide. Further, the predicament seems to fall under the heading of what marriage researcher John Gottman (Gottman & Silver, 2004) would refer to as a perpetual problem—one that is long-term and difficult or even impossible to fully resolve. For Seth's extended family, a "shared family vision" has become a literal "di-vision" of faith. Something that was once shared and seen similarly came to be seen and practiced differently (Marks, 2002). Indeed, beliefs that unite can also divide.

Another example of religious beliefs as a source of di-vision (two different visions) is the case of a Korean immigrant couple who switched religions during their emerging adulthood. Oui and Kim both converted to Christianity as young adults in their native Korea, but none of their family members have joined them in their new-found faith. The husband, Oui, soberly explained:

> We have a deep problem with religion with our families. So actually, that's the reason religion is not good sometimes. We can't have our relatives praying for us. That's a terrible feeling. . . . It has been a challenge [to not have the same faith as our parents].

While Kim and Oui had found a sense of joy and meaning in their new faith, their faith had become a virtual line of demarcation between generations. As with Seth, the Jewish father whose brothers had married outside the faith, religion had become a source of "di-vision" for Oui and Kim instead of a shared family vision (Marks, 2002, 2004).

In summary, rifts related to religious beliefs can occur within a marriage, between siblings, and across generations. These rifts can arise through inter-faith marriage, "falling away," conversion to a different faith, or even significantly decreasing or increasing religious involvement or orthodoxy in the same faith.

As we conclude this section on "Family Conflict and Tension Due to Divergent Religious Beliefs," we gain an additional perspective of the complexities involved at the intersection of family relationships and religious beliefs. In the next theme, we address the strength that many reported when they enjoyed shared religious beliefs in their marriages.

Theme 4: The Importance of Shared Religious Beliefs in Marriage

The couples in the *American Families of Faith* study repeatedly emphasized the importance of shared religious and spiritual beliefs. A Jewish father of two said of his marriage, "Our values are always very, very close, which is why we're so close. [Having shared values] has positively affected our marriage." Li, a Chinese father married for more than 20 years, likewise reported:

> Our core values of our belief are very consistent. The aim of our marriage, the fundamentals of our marriage, and [our] core belief[s] are the same. [Our shared faith] is the central part of our life . . . our service and our work.
>
> (Lu et al., 2013, p. 236)

Shana, a Latina LDS mother of five, added some more depth to the concept of a shared faith or spiritual connection at the center of her marriage—a marriage that had seen some very rough patches. She explained:

> Because we believe in the same things, it makes [life] different. We feel that spiritual connection is [something that's] real and true. It's different than just a physical connection. . . . Those feelings pull you together, not only as husband and wife but as members [of the same faith]. I guess it's just a spiritual thing.

Shana considered divorce at one point in her marriage, primarily due to her husband's substance abuse problems through several years of their early married life. Shana's husband, James, became involved in and eventually joined Shana's church and attributes that involvement as a key factor in his "getting clean." Shana's emphasis on "connection" and being pulled together with her husband by their faith illustrates the same reported benefit identified by Seth and Li—that sharing sacred beliefs has benefitted their marriages.

A more cultural aspect of shared religious beliefs and their importance was captured by a Jewish father of two from our AFF project who recalled:

> I knew very early on that I wanted to marry Jewish. I never questioned that, I always knew. I always knew that it was the right path to take. I always believed, and still do, that the cultural upbringing of being Jewish is so deep that being married to someone who is not Jewish, they just wouldn't get it. They wouldn't laugh at the same jokes. They wouldn't enjoy the same foods I enjoy on the same levels, you know? . . . . I thought, who would want to go through life not being able to share that and understand that?

A Jewish mother named Miriam in Bengtson and colleagues' (2013) study similarly explained that to her, "I identify family as being Jewish—to me, being Jewish is very connected with being family-oriented" (p. 57). We are reminded by these two Jewish parents (from different studies) that religious beliefs often serve as a family framework and the foundation for culture and subculture. "Indeed, for those who are deeply connected to their faith, the influence of religion may literally carry into jokes, foods, holidays, rituals, and—in a word—*life*" (Marks, 2005, p. 104).

Several couples mentioned that having shared spiritual beliefs helped them avoid many (but certainly not all) points of conflict. However, when conflict did arise within the marriage (or from challenges from outside the marriage) many expressed their gratitude for the strength of shared faith—and, in some cases, for the "formal" steps of conflict resolution promoted by their religion. A Latino Catholic father named Enrique stated:

> In Catholicism, divorce is not an option. It happens, but it shouldn't be an option [under most circumstances]. The thing is that in Catholicism, what you do is you work through your problems, whatever contradiction that you have, you try to work through that spiritually. The sanctity of marriage is very important to Catholics. . . . In the Catholic Church, divorce is a thing that you don't want to do. It happens, but every step to reconciliation should be made before divorce is the final answer.

An Arab-American Muslim wife named Tagreed similarly explained that in Islamic belief and practice:

> If you have [marital] differences that you cannot solve together, [Islam] gives guidelines on how to involve others into the mediating position in order to help you resolve the issues.

A Latino family from the East Coast, Javier and Julia Morales, provided another example of turning to faith during challenges. Following a year that included tragedies in both their business and at the family level, Javier reflected:

> Definitely our [shared Catholic] faith is a strength. This past year our faith has been a big strength to our relationship too. What we've been through this past year would put a strain on any marriage, but we have [been reminded] that our family is the most important thing to us and that we're in this together. Our faith is all involved with that.

Elsewhere in their interview Javier and Julia offered some additional thoughts on their shared faith, particularly during difficult times:

Javier: [Our faith] has been our safe haven. It works better than a second bottle of wine. (Laughing). . . . [There's] no headache the next day. . . . [Faith is] a hunger, and it's also what satisfies that hunger.

Julia: There's a hymn we sing at church that says, "As a deer longs for running streams, so I long for you." Faith is that longing and knowing that it's God [that you need]. Some people don't have that, but I've grown up with that and have the understanding as an adult that . . . I [need] God in some fashion and that it's a natural, instinctive thing. As you grow and learn more about yourself and your spirituality broadens and you understand certain things in relationship to God, you learn that you need to *feed* that faith.

Javier: As you go through life and its steps, you seek fulfillment and we would say, . . . "When we finish med school it'll be great. When I finish residency, it'll be great. When I get my own [medical] practice, it'll be great." But you get to each step (and it's cool) but there's still that longing. . . . That's why we need our faith. That's why faith is important to us, because ten years ago we were trying to "make it" [on the world's terms] but that's not what satisfies the longing. . . . [Only] faith satisfies that hunger and that longing that seems insatiable.

The "longing" and "hunger" in the soul that Julia and Javier both reference is at the heart of the work of one of the great students of world religions,

Huston Smith, who spent his life delving into the whys and hows of religious belief and practice. Late in his lengthy career, in his book *Why Religion Matters* (2003), he explained:

> There is within us—even the . . . most lighthearted among us—a fundamental dis-ease. It acts like an unquenchable fire that renders the vast majority of us incapable in this life of ever coming to full peace. This desire lies in the marrow of our bones and the deep regions of our souls. All great literature, poetry, art, philosophy, psychology, and religion tries to name and analyze this longing.
>
> (p. 28)

Omar, an Arab-American Muslim father of two, expressed a concept similar to Julia and Javier's idea regarding the hunger for God by relating the following Arabic story about Allah.

> A Bedouin, who believed in God, was asked by a man who did not believe, "Why do you believe in God? What can you tell me? How did you get to this realization?" The Bedouin said, "When I leave my camel in the desert, it goes back to where it came from. That tells me there is a God."

Omar's personal interpretation of the story was two-fold. First, those who truly want to see God will see Him in everything, including a camel's homecoming. Second, just as the camel in a strange land intuitively knows the way home, a person of faith is drawn—though in a strange world—toward his heavenly home. Shared beliefs like these reportedly unite Omar with his wife, Angie.

Some of the couples we interviewed reported their explicit belief that without shared religious beliefs fusing their marriage, "it wouldn't work." A Jewish couple, Saul and Ruth, were one of these. Saul said:

> I believe [marriage is] a partnership, and I believe that it is deeply rooted in where I come from, and where Ruth comes from. And frankly . . . I . . . never even dated anyone who wasn't Jewish. That was my choice. I knew that if I didn't marry somebody that shared the same belief system, fundamentally, that it wouldn't work.

One specific shared religious belief that many participants referenced was the conviction that God had a vested interest in their marriage. In many cases, this belief ran so deep that they viewed God as a third partner in the marriage. For example, a number of couples directly or indirectly invoked the idea of the divine marital triangle with one spouse at each of the sides of the base and God at the peak. For example, Angelica, a Christian mother, explained:

> Marriage is kind of like a triangle, with God at the top. . . . The closer you get to Him the closer you get to each other. And so I really like that example. [Likewise], I think that once you start to drift away from God, you start to drift away from each other.

An African-American, non-denominational Christian husband similarly explained that from his perspective:

> Marriage is God's design and you can't truly experience marriage without having God be a part of it. When God is part of your marriage, that's when you can experience the true fulfillment of what a marriage is. The two come together and they may be different in many, many ways, but when they come together and love each other and respect each other and do marriage the way God has designed it . . . it's very fulfilling. Even though you may not agree upon everything, by allowing God to show you how to be a husband or wife you can live a very fulfilled life.

Sam, an LDS father and husband, also talked about the connection between God and his marriage. He explained:

> I believe in order to be with God someday in heaven I need to have my wife by my side. I don't walk ahead of my wife and she doesn't walk ahead of me; we walk side by side. So without her I don't feel like I could reach my highest potential that [our] Heavenly Father has set out for me.

Mei, a Chinese Christian wife and mother of two, similarly reflected:

> This is very good that we have the same religious beliefs. We will become closer and closer, and [we] meet on the spot where God is the common center of our life.
>
> (Lu et al., 2011)

Again, repeated reports across religion and race seem to indicate that both wives and husbands view their shared beliefs as a unifying force that allows them to "meet on the spot where God is the common center of our life." Such reports may offer a partial explanation of significantly lower divorce rates among same-faith marriages, as discussed in the previous chapter (see also, Lehrer, 2009; Lehrer & Chiswick, 1993). We turn next to another source of strong marriage that our participants identified, a shared faith in God as a marital support.

Theme 5: Faith in God as a Marital Support

The most pervasive and salient spiritual belief reported by the couples in connection with marriage was that their shared faith in God provided them with marital support. Indeed, a sizable minority of the couples explicitly stated that they did not believe their marriages would even still be intact were it not for their faith in, and support from, the Divine. Consider the following narratives from participants. When asked, "Has your relationship with God influenced your marriage?" a Presbyterian wife named Shelly responded:

> It has kept me in it. [*Laughter from both her and her husband Greg*]. There are many times when it's been very rough going, I'm sure for Greg as well as myself, and there are lots of times when we would have some conversations, and . . . [my relationship with God] just helped keep me married.

Cristen, a Christian wife, likewise commented (with her husband agreeing):

> I don't think . . . we'd be together anymore if we didn't have God in the middle. You know, we've often said that, when we've hit struggles and stuff. If we didn't have God, I don't think we would have been able to get through our struggles intact.

Jessica, a non-denominational Christian mother of four, similarly said of her 25-year marriage to Joseph:

> We have disagreements, we have things we don't see the same sometimes, and [our faith is] a source of help. We can pray about things together and the Lord can help us work things out. Sometimes one person has to give in and accept the other person's point of view, it helps to be able to pray about things. God [is] the best counselor you could ever have. I don't know how marriages can work without God. I'm sure that

> there are people who are so compatible that they can still get along, but [faith] has been really helpful [for us].

Abdul, an Arab-American Muslim father, although from a different world religion and cultural background than Shelly, Cristen, and Jessica, had views that seemed to harmonize with theirs in some ways. Of his marriage to his wife, Zahra, he said:

> As a human, we get into fights, we get into disagreements on things. But, knowing that God is watching you, you cannot hurt your partner, or do something bad to her, or He that is greater than you can hurt you at the same time. He can do something to you. So that's what kept me calm. Allah . . . my relationship [with Him] prevents me from doing such things. . . . Allah has helped me overcome it. . . . If I [did]n't have this relation[ship] [with] Allah, [our marriage] would [have] failed a long time ago.

It is interesting to note that for Shelly, Cristen, Jessica, and Abdul, the element of their faith that reportedly sustains them most during the "very rough going," the "struggles," the "disagreements," and the "fights" is not merely an abstract belief, but a sense of *relationship* and close connection with their God.

John, a Christian husband in an interracial family, reported: "We probably have more conflicts than the normal couples because we are interracial. Lots of issues come up because of different expectations and different cultures." The research of Deborah Tannen (1991) indicates that many differences may be rooted in gender (as well as in race and culture)—but the salient point is that differences exist. John's Chinese Christian wife, Cindy, added:

> The Bible teaches us we should be kind to each other. If you are a Christian, you care about people, [and] of course [you are supposed to] care about your spouse. I have already mentioned we should practice understanding and forgiveness. John sometimes gets angry easily. . . . He los[es] his control, so I [will just] be quiet, calm down, and pray. Later on when he regains his composure, he would apologize. If I were . . . non-Christian, I would have said "bye" to him already.

A connection between making it through difficult times in life and marriage and a deep faith in (and a sense of relationship with) God was also emphasized by Rashaad, an African-American Methodist from Delaware, who said of his marriage:

> We both feel that a marriage is a bonding thing. As God says, "Whatever I join together let no man put asunder." I believe that my faith made me love my wife a lot more. We are very different. If it weren't for faith, I probably would have run a long time ago. [I'd have said], "You don't want to do what I want to do. We just don't see eye to eye. I'm gone." But when you believe in God . . . yes, the boat still gets to rockin' but the Bible says, "In me you can weather the storm."

Chelsea, a Methodist like Rashaad but from Louisiana, said:

> You don't just throw in the towel when times get tough. You work it out. *You work it out*. And, a lot of that deals . . . not just [with] communication, but I think having a relationship with God and a prayer life really helps that. [You need] that connection, that bond [with God].

We have now heard variations on the concept of the importance of having a relationship with God from several diverse participants—participants from different races, genders, religions, and regions of the nation. We pause here for a brief but scenic detour that will allow us to more closely examine this important concept of "a relationship with [a] God" who is perceived to be involved in the details of personal, marital, and family life. In doing so, we will consider some parallel research.

Psychologist Katie Cherry of Louisiana State University has spent more than a decade studying the long-term coping efforts of 125 diverse individuals and their families in the aftermath of Hurricane Katrina, one of the worst natural disasters in U.S. history. In her recent edited volume, Professor Cherry and her colleagues reach the following conclusion in their chapter addressing "Faith and Coping":

> As we consider what our participants conveyed and taught us about the influence of their spiritual beliefs and religious practices, their shared experiences and insights, and their coping with both the immediate and long-term aftermath of two catastrophic hurricanes [Katrina and Rita]. . . *Perhaps the most profitable and profound finding is that the participants who reportedly received the deepest measure of support from their spiritual beliefs and religious practices were those who tended to speak of God in the closest and most personal terms*. These men and women conceptualized and discussed God in ways that captured and reflected not only a belief but a *being*, not only religion but a *relationship*, not only faith but a *friend*.
>
> (Marks et al., 2015, p. 385, emphasis added)

For some of the participants in Cherry's study, "God" was not a distant abstraction or force but a personal, relational being who was reportedly involved in their individual and family lives—and not peripherally involved, but at the very center of their lives.

Moving back to the *American Families of Faith* project and the topic of marriage, Kelsey, a Lutheran wife, addressed the perceived involvement of God in her marriage in the following way:

> I can't even comprehend a marriage that doesn't have God at the *center*. To me . . . it would seem so difficult to me. I can't imagine what would hold it together. . . . I guess [if you had no faith] I can understand how divorce could [happen] because there would not be anything solid [to hold on to].

Yang, a Chinese-American immigrant wife and an adult convert to Christianity, explained that, in her view, her religious conversion (along with her husband's) stabilized and strengthened their marriage (Lu, Marks, & Apavaloiae, 2012). She said of their experience:

> Believing in God (was) the most important transition of our marriage; [our faith] became the base of our marriage. We didn't understand the meaning of marriage before . . . (but) the more we know God, the more we understand the meaning of marriage. As I grow up in spirit, I submit myself before God. This is a very important part to make the marriage stable. Considering many broken marriages, they don't deal with their own problems, but [attribute] the conflicts to the other side, [to the other person]. Blaming the other is a sin. On the contrary, we should confess our own sins before God . . . [this] is very important for building a stable marriage. [When we are humble and acknowledge our own sins], then the marriage is on the proper way.
>
> (Lu et al., 2012)

Yang's portrayal of God as both a close confidant and the one to whom she can "submit" and "confess [her] own sins" conveys—like the previous reports, reflections, and testimonies—a sense of relational closeness. Yang, like several of the flourishing Hurricane Katrina survivors studied by Katie Cherry, seems to be one who discussed "God in ways that captured and reflected not only a belief but a *being*, not only religion but a *relationship*, not only faith but a *friend*."

In sum, for *American Families of Faith* participants in strong, enduring marriages, their shared religious beliefs reportedly impacted marriage through several channels:

1. Pro-marriage beliefs encouraged marriage.
2. Anti-divorce beliefs discouraged divorce.
3. Shared religious beliefs helped provide similar worldviews and "visions" of family life.
4. A belief in God as a marital support was repeatedly mentioned as a strength and support without which many of these couples' marriages would, by their reports, have failed.

Further, these reports often focused not only on a belief in God but on a close and relational connection with God. As we discussed in the middle of the chapter, however, there are also multiple ways in which "religious beliefs [can be] a source of harm in marriages and families," including: (a) excessively rigid anti-divorce beliefs, (b) misapplied "male headship," and (c) family conflict and tension due to divergent religious beliefs. As we consider all the issues presented in this chapter, we gain a greater appreciation for the validity of the subtitle of sociologists Robert Putnam and David Campbell's (2010) book-length study: *How Religion Divides and Unites Us*.

Conclusion

A team of marriage and family therapists who jointly authored a volume entitled *Beliefs: The Heart of Healing in Families* conceptualized beliefs as fundamental to understanding ourselves and others (Wright, Watson, & Bell, 1996). For many individuals and families, religious beliefs are central to other beliefs they hold. Family professionals, educators, clinicians, and clergy who are sensitive to beliefs (including religious beliefs) held by their clients will gain a more comprehensive understanding of the individual and/or family they are serving. This idea is valid whether an individual is atheistic, devout in a faith, or somewhere in between (Marks, 2006). For example, an individual or family's spiritual beliefs regarding divorce, sexuality, death, and family relationships are all of pragmatic significance and warrant the helper's awareness, sensitivity, and consideration. As Julia, a Catholic mother in our study, emphasized:

> I think it is important to address faith [as a counselor], especially with someone who has brought it up. . . . To at least ask questions regarding

> how important faith is [to the individual or couple] and then to treat them sensitively. I think from my own experience, if I was going to a counselor, faith is so much a part of who I am that I couldn't separate faith and family, and when a counselor is treating a person, they should be treating the whole person and [be aware] of the issues they're dealing with.
>
> (Marks, 2005, p. 107)

It is important to note that it is not necessary for a family professional to share the client's beliefs, only that s/he be aware and sensitive with respect to the individual or family's beliefs (Marks, 2005).

While it is true that religion is not an important factor in many American marriages, religion is "the single most important influence in [life]" for "a substantial minority" of Americans (Miller & Thoresen, 2003, p. 25). Subsequently, for that substantial minority, including families like those from *American Families of Faith*, scholarly and clinical awareness of and sensitivity to the marriage and religion connection remains vitally important (Marks, 2004).

The prior chapter (chapter 4) discussed several research studies that connected shared religious involvement with marital stability and satisfaction. In the present chapter, drawing heavily from interviews with the diverse wives and husbands in the *American Families of Faith* project, we have learned some central reasons how and why shared religious beliefs present several supports to marriage. In the next two chapters, we will direct our attention toward the connection between parent-child relationships and religion.

Chapter Summary Points

1. For many families, a religiously based, pro-marriage belief impacts marriages through greater commitment to marriage and through a sense of greater accountability before God to be a good spouse.
2. For many families, a religiously based, anti-divorce belief helps prevents divorce and can stabilize marriages.
3. Religious beliefs can also be harmful in families. For example, a strong aversion to divorce can be damaging in situations where divorce may be warranted; religious beliefs may be applied and interpreted in ways that are sexist or abusive; and conflict or tension in marriage or across generations can arise due to differing beliefs.
4. Family professionals who are sensitive to and respectful of the religious beliefs of those they serve are likely to be more effective (whether the professional shares the same beliefs or not).

Review Questions

1. How many years of combined marital experience does the *American Families of Faith* sample draw on?
2. What does the research say about the consequences of having a marriage in which both spouses are actively involved in the same faith community?
3. List at least two specific religious beliefs that reportedly can have a positive impact on marriage.
4. List at least two specific religious beliefs that can reportedly be harmful to families.
5. This chapter refers to both the positive and negative impacts of anti-divorce beliefs. What do you think makes the difference between the positive or negative influence?

Note

1. In this chapter we draw excerpts from previously published work (including Goodman et al., 2013; Lu et al., 2011, 2012, 2013; Marks, 2005; Marks et al., 2008; Marks et al., 2012), as well as from previously unpublished *American Families of Faith* data.

References

Agius, E., & Chircop, L. (1998). *Caring for future generations: Jewish, Christian, and Islamic perspectives*. Westport, CT: Praeger.

Arterburn, S., & Felton, J. (2001). *Toxic faith*. Colorado Springs, CO: Waterbrook.

Bengtson, V. L., Putney, N. M., & Harris, J. (2013). *Families of faith*. New York: Oxford.

Burr, W. R., Marks, L. D., & Day, R. (2012). *Sacred matters: Religion and spirituality in families*. New York: Routledge.

Chatters, L., & Taylor, R. J. (2005). Religion and families. In V. Bengtson, A. Acock, K. Allen, P. Dillworth-Anderson, & D. Klein (Eds.), *Sourcebook of family theory and research* (pp. 517–522). Thousand Oaks, CA: Sage.

Dollahite, D. C., & Lambert, N. M. (2007). Forsaking all others: How religious involvement promotes marital fidelity in Christian, Jewish, and Muslim couples. *Review of Religious Research, 48*, 290–307.

Dollahite, D. C., Marks, L. D., & Goodman, M. (2004). Religiosity and families: Relational and spiritual linkages in a diverse and dynamic cultural context. In M. Coleman, & L. H. Ganong (Eds.), *The handbook of contemporary families* (pp. 411–431). Thousand Oaks, CA: Sage.

Erikson, E. H., & Erikson, J. M. (1997). *The life cycle completed*. New York, NY: Norton.

Goodman, M., Dollahite, D., Marks, L., & Layton, E. (2013). Religious faith and transformational processes in marriage. *Family Relations, 62*, 808–823.

Gottman, J., & Silver, N. (2004). *The seven principles for making marriage work*. New York: Three Rivers Press.

Lambert, N. M., & Dollahite, D. C. (2006). How religiosity helps couples prevent, resolve, and overcome marital conflict. *Family Relations, 55*, 439–449.

Lambert, N. M., & Dollahite, D. C. (2008). The threefold cord. *Journal of Family Issues, 29*, 592–614.

Lehrer, E. L. (2009). *Religion, economics, and demography: The effects of religion on education, work, and the family*. New York: Routledge.

Lehrer, E. L., & Chiswick, C. U. (1993). Religion as a determinant of marital stability. *Demography, 30*, 385–403.

Lu, Y., Marks, L. D., & Apavaloiae, L. (2012). Chinese immigrant families and Christian faith community: A qualitative study. *Family and Consumer Science Research Journal, 41*, 118–130.

Lu, Y., Marks, L. D., & Baumgartner, J. (2011). The compass of our life: A qualitative study of marriage and faith among Chinese immigrants. *Marriage and Family Review, 47*, 125–148.

Lu, Y., Marks, L. D., Nesteruk, O., Goodman, M., & Apavaloaie, L. (2013). Faith, conversion, and challenge: A qualitative study of Chinese immigrant Christian marriages. *Journal of Comparative Family Studies, 44*, 227–247.

Mahoney, A. (2010). Religion in families, 1999–2009: A relational spirituality framework. *Journal of Marriage and Family, 72*, 805–827.

Marks, L. D. (2002). Illuminating the Interface between Families and Faith. Unpublished dissertation. University of Delaware.

Marks, L. D. (2004). Sacred practices in highly religious families: Christian, Jewish, Mormon, and Muslim perspectives. *Family Process, 43*, 217–231.

Marks, L. D. (2005). How does religion influence marriage? Christian, Jewish, Mormon, and Muslim perspectives. *Marriage and Family Review, 38*, 85–111.

Marks, L. D. (2006). Religion and family relational health: An overview and conceptual model. *Journal of Religion and Health, 45*, 603–618.

Marks, L. D., Dollahite, D. C., & Freeman, J. J. (2011). Faith and prayer in family life. In T. W. Draper, A. J. Hawkins, & D. C. Dollahite (Eds.), *Strengthening our families (2nd ed.)* (pp. 185–195). Provo, UT: BYU.

Marks, L. D., Hopkins, K., Chaney, C., Nesteruk, O., Monroe, P., & Sasser, D. (2008). Together, we are strong: A qualitative study of happy, enduring African-American marriages. *Family Relations, 57*, 171–184.

Marks, L. D., Hopkins, K., Nesteruk, O., Chaney, C., & Baumgartner, J. (2012). A qualitative exploration of why faith matters in African-American marriages and families. *Journal of Comparative Family Studies, 43*, 695–714.

Marks, L., Lu, Y., Cherry, K., & Hatch, T. (2015). Faith and coping: Spiritual beliefs and religious practices after Hurricanes Katrina and Rita. In K. Cherry (Ed.), *Traumatic stress and long-term recovery: Coping with disasters and other negative life events* (pp. 369–388). New York: Springer.

Miller, W. R., & Thoresen, C. E. (2003). Spirituality, religion, and health: An emerging research field. *American Psychologist, 58*, 24–35.

Putnam, R. D., & Campbell, D. E. (2010). *American grace: How religion divides and unites us*. New York: Simon & Schuster.

Smith, H. (2003). *Why religion matters*. San Francisco, CA: Harper San Francisco.

Stark, R., & Finke, R. (2000). *Acts of faith: Explaining the human side of religion.* Berkeley: University of California Press.

Tannen, D. (1991). *You just don't understand: Women and men in conversation.* New York: Ballantine.

Wright, L. M., Watson, W. L., & Bell, J. M. (1996). *Beliefs: The heart of healing in families and illness.* New York: Basic.

Parenting in Faith—What Research Has Found[1] 6

In chapter 3, we introduced a conceptual model that illustrates many of the connections between various family relationships and the three dimensions of religion (religious practices, spiritual beliefs, and faith community). In chapter 4, we took a closer look at the connections between the marriage relationship and the three dimensions of religion—with an in-depth examination of spiritual beliefs in chapter 5. In the present chapter, we turn our focus and attention to parent-child relationships. More specifically, we examine how the three dimensions of religion influence (1) the mother-child relationship and (2) the father-child relationship (see Figure 6.1). We begin by looking at the connection between religious practices and the mother-child bond.

> A little girl gets out her crayons and begins drawing a picture on a paper. Her mother asks, "What are you drawing a picture of, sweetheart?"
> "I am drawing a picture of God," the young girl responds.
> "But we don't really know what God looks like, do we?" the mother gently suggests.
> "Well, in a few minutes, when I'm finished with my picture, you'll know," responds the daughter.

Religious Practices and the Mother-Child Relationship: Arrow 1B

Research that addresses religious practices in connection with the mother-child (M-C) bond includes Boyatzis and Janicki's (2003) study based on surveys

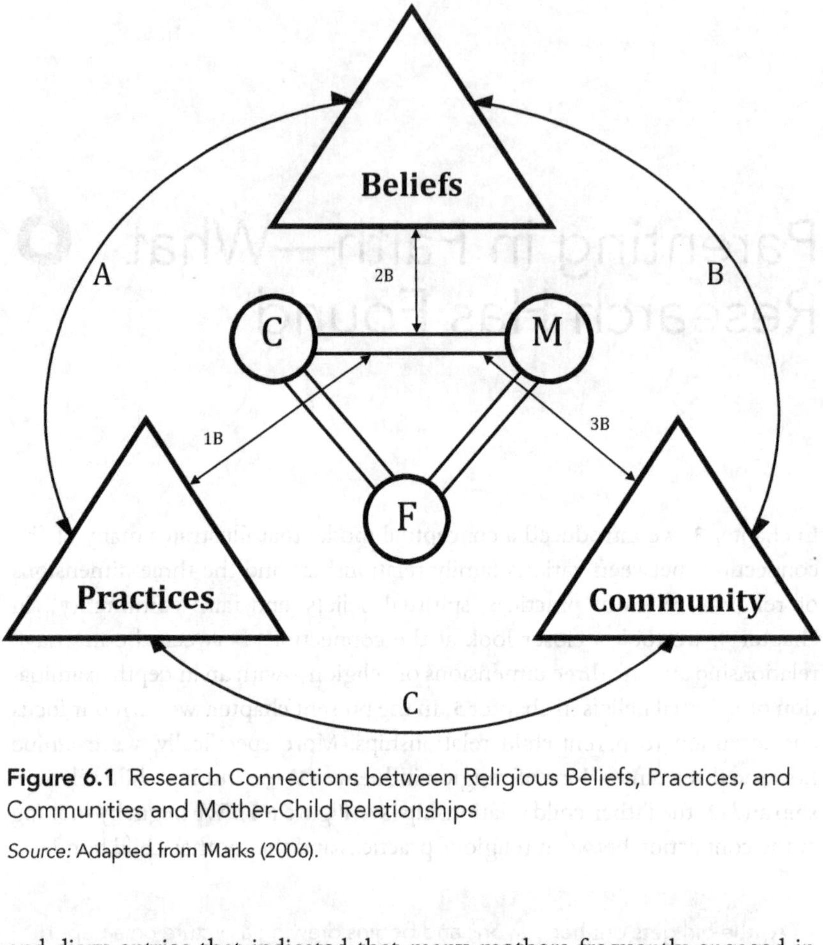

Figure 6.1 Research Connections between Religious Beliefs, Practices, and Communities and Mother-Child Relationships

Source: Adapted from Marks (2006).

and diary entries that indicated that many mothers frequently engaged in bidirectional communication with their children regarding matters of faith, a practice that has been reported to be beneficial and influential later, even decades later, in children's lives (Wuthnow, 1999).

Other mother-child linkages include Pearce and Axinn's (1998) finding that "various dimensions of family religious life [including religious practices] have enduring effects on mothers' and children's perceptions of the quality of the mother-child relationship" (p. 810). Other studies have also noted that parallels exist between children's conceptualizations of what God is like (God images) and parent-child interactions and relationships (Bengtson, Putney, & Harris, 2013; Vergote, 1980).

Research has also indicated that kind, loving behavior by parents facilitates the ability of a child to conceive of and believe in a loving God, while hostile parental practices tend to dispel a child's faith in a benevolent supreme being (Dollahite, 1998; Vergote, 1980). Fathers' parenting practices were the primary focus of early research on children's God images, but mothers began to be studied as well, and one research study has indicated that in some respects "parenting by mothers *more than by fathers* predicts youths' images of God" (Hertel & Donahue, 1995, p. 196, emphasis in original). Such findings indicate the importance of including *both* parents in research on the religion-family connection if we are to best understand religion's influence in children's lives.

Recent, cutting-edge findings from longitudinal work across 35 years have indicated something that is likely more important than mother-father comparisons. In their landmark book-length study, *Families of Faith: How Religion Is Passed Down Across Generations*, Vern Bengtson and colleagues (2013) reported that there was "no significant difference between mother-child and father-child religious similarity" (p. 76). Neither mothers nor fathers had significantly more influence on their children's later religious affiliations than the other. However, what did matter (with respect to whether adult children followed in their parents' footsteps of faith or not) was *how close and warm their parent-child relationships were.* For all six religious categories studied,[2] and for both mothers and fathers, those who reported "close" relationships with their parent(s) remained affiliated with their parents' faith at measurably higher levels than those whose parent-child relationships were "not close" (p. 78). For Protestants, the mother-child differences in shared religious affiliation with respect to "close" versus "not close" mother-child relationships were measurable but modest. However, for Catholic, Mormon, and Jewish families, the connection between close mother-child relationships and ongoing affiliation with the mother's faith ranged from strong (a 10% increase for Catholic adult children with "close" mother-child relationships) to very strong (a 22% increase for Mormons and a 30% increase for Jews). Again, it appears that closeness of relationship, not gender, is more foundational in determining whether a child holds to his or her parents' faith. Even so, gender still matters.

In a review of several empirical studies, Koenig, McCullough, and Larson (2001) emphasized in their *Handbook of Religion and Health*:

> Women are more likely to attend religious services, pray privately, say religion is important in their lives and depend on religion as a coping [support]. Thus, it is possible that religious . . . practices are more deeply ingrained into the social and psychological lives of women and therefore confer greater health benefits.
>
> (p. 329)

Some studies, however, seem to indicate that although men are generally less religious and less religiously involved than women, for men who *are* involved in religion, there also appear to be personal, relational, and familial benefits, as well as costs and challenges (Burr, Marks, & Day, 2012; Mahoney, 2010; Marks, Dollahite, & Freeman, 2011; Snarey & Dollahite, 2001).

Qualitative work involving Christian, Jewish, and Muslim families has revealed that these faiths include practices that reportedly promote a sense of closeness with each other and with God. As previously addressed, studies drawn from the *American Families of Faith* project have found that influential practices include saying grace for Protestant Christians, offering **novenas** for Catholic Christians, **Family Home Evening** for Latter-day Saints, the *Shabbat* meal and accompanying ritual for Jewish families, and the Ramadan fast for Muslims. In most cases (and across several studies), these rituals and practices were reportedly meaningful for both mothers *and* fathers (Dollahite & Marks, 2005; Marks, 2004; Dollahite & Marks, 2005; Marks & Dollahite, 2012).

> No man is poor who has had a Godly mother.
>
> —Abraham Lincoln
>
> God could not be everywhere, so He made mothers.
>
> —Jewish proverb
>
> All that I am or ever hope to be, I owe to my angel mother.
>
> —Abraham Lincoln

Religious Beliefs and the Mother-Child Relationship: Arrow 2B

Research that has connected religious beliefs and the mother-child relationship has included the work of Bao and colleagues (1999), who found that mothers in more positive mother-child relationships were more likely to transmit their religious beliefs to their adolescent children, consistent with the later findings of Bengtson and colleagues (2013). Another study found that when mothers and their children have religious agreement or "concordance," this seems to "protect against depression" in the children (Miller et al., 1997, p. 1416).

Several studies in the 1970s and 1980s examined the strength of the connection between parent and child beliefs. Many of these parent-child "transmission" studies indicated that mothers were influential in religious socialization (Acock & Bengtson, 1978; Clark, Worthington, & Danser, 1988; Hoge, Petrillo, & Smith, 1982; Kieren & Munro, 1987). However, the emphasis of these studies was typically on transmission, not on the meaning and influence of religious beliefs in the mothers' lives or on the impact these beliefs had on mothers' parenting practices. Two examples of scholarship that *does* delve into deeper connections between religious belief and motherhood include: (1) Kaufman's (1991) *Rachel's Daughters*, which qualitatively examined Orthodox Jewish women, and (2) Stacey and Gerard's (1990) study of Evangelical Christian women. Unfortunately, such studies are rare.[3] A comparatively rich set of research is found, however, on the connection between religious *community* and the mother-child relationship. It is to that connection that we turn next.

Religious Community and the Mother-Child Relationship: Arrow 3B

First, we note that a mother's level of involvement with religion seems to influence not only how she parents her children, but whether she will choose to have children at all. As we have summarized elsewhere:

> Women who are involved in a faith community (as measured by reported attendance) are significantly more likely to have children. Pearce's (2002) work emphasizes a mutual relationship in the religiosity [and] childbearing connection—namely, that the importance of religion in a woman's life appears to shape childbearing attitudes and behaviors, and that family situation (such as the presence of children) also seems to influence religiosity.
>
> (Marks et al., 2011, pp. 187–188)

This finding that more religious women are more likely to have children has been confirmed and extended in more recent research by Abma and Martinez (2006), who found that among more than 4,000 women, ages 35 to 44, the choice to be voluntarily childless was linked with lower levels of religious involvement at every survey point for nearly 25 years (Marks et al., 2011; see also Stark, 2012).

Research indicates that in the United States, women attend religious services far more frequently than men, generally speaking (Koenig, King, &

Carson, 2012), and that religious communities have long been important, even vital, resources for many American women (Ozorak, 1996). In a finding that linked church attendance with social support, Ellison and George (1994) noted that:

> Frequent attenders at religious services have larger nonkin networks than do infrequent church attenders or unchurched persons . . . [and] frequent churchgoers benefit from a wider array of supportive transactions than do their less religious counterparts, including instrumental support (i.e., money, goods, and services) and socioemotional support. (p. 57)

The larger, stronger, and more supportive social networks generally enjoyed among those who frequently attend worship services at their church, synagogue, temple, or mosque is one of several factors that likely contributes to significantly better health and years of additional longevity enjoyed by the highly religious, as documented in several empirical studies (Hummer et al., 1999; Koenig et al., 2012; Koenig et al., 2001; Marks et al., 2005).

Returning to the mother-child connection specifically, in summary, women who are actively involved in faith communities tend to have larger and more supportive social networks; they generally have better social, emotional, and psychological health; and they have significantly better physical health and longevity, but this is not the whole story.

> If you bungle raising your children, I don't think whatever else you do well matters very much.
>
> —Jacqueline Kennedy Onassis, *Women's Wit and Wisdom*
>
> At the end of your life you will never regret not having passed one more test, winning one more verdict or not closing one more deal. You will regret time not spent with a husband, a child, a friend or a parent.
>
> —Barbara Bush, *Women's Wit and Wisdom*

Potential Harmful Aspects of Maternal Religious Community Involvement

There are, however, potentially negative aspects of the religion-mother connection. In this section we briefly explore some of these. Burr and colleagues

(2012) reported the following narrative from "a recently married man in his middle twenties" to demonstrate harm that can be done by a mother who lives out her religion in relationally damaging ways.

> Our family was so religious when I was growing up that we went to church every week. My mother was clearly the leader in this, and she was intense in the ways she brought God and religion into our home. She did it in a very demanding way that was often critical and cynical; and when one of the kids did something they shouldn't, she'd talk about how God was displeased and we ought to feel guilty. She put more guilt on us than you can believe, and it was painful the way she treated us. Unfortunately, the words that best describe the way she treated us are brutal and abusive. I was the oldest and was an obedient child, so I didn't get yelled at as much as the others, and it was sad the way she treated my sister and brother who weren't as inclined to do what she wanted. Now that I'm away from the home and able to make my own choices, I don't want to have anything to do with her God and with her religion. There was little love and a lot of anger in our home, and my little sister hates my mother so much that whenever she can she stays with someone else on weekends when our mother is around the house. My brother is now away from home . . . and his resentment toward my mother and feelings of always being pressured and never loved has been getting in his way.
>
> (Burr et al. 2012, p. 25)

This young man's discussion of his mother bringing "God and religion into our home . . . in a very demanding way that was often critical and cynical" seems to reflect a central finding from the research of Lee, Rice, and Gillespie (1997), who found that heavy-handed, compulsory family worship may be more detrimental for children than no family worship at all. This is the apparent situation of the prior family as described by the young man. Indeed, although social and instrumental support from the faith community is a valuable resource for many mothers and families, the young man's narrative from Burr's research demonstrates that the religion-mother-child connection can be a negative as well.

Marital Status and Maternal Support in Religious Communities

Additional research has also indicated that a woman's marital status seems to influence whether (or at least how much) she is supported by the faith community. Sorenson, Grindstaff, and Turner's (1995) study of depression in unmarried adolescent mothers found that young single mothers who were *not* religiously involved reported lower levels of depression, while the combination of religious involvement and non-marital motherhood *was* stressful for religiously involved young women. Additionally, Sorenson and colleagues found that "even greater distress [was] experienced by young women who lived in an unmarried relationship while at the same time taking part in religious activities" (p. 80). In contrast, religiosity was not related to depression among religiously involved, *married* teen mothers. In sum, the relationship between religious involvement and depression seems to vary considerably across personal, marital, and family situations.

A second example of the importance of a mother's marital status to her and her faith community may be drawn from the work of Taylor and Chatters (1988), who found that divorced and separated women tended to receive less social support from their faith communities than did widows. Findings like these contextualize Dollahite, Marks, and Goodman's (2004) conclusion that a "key challenge for [many] American churches in the 21st century will be to find a balance between supporting the standard of marriage-based families that are idealized [by most churches] . . . while addressing the pluralistic family realities that confront them" (p. 414). Phrased a little differently, faith community leaders and faith communities themselves are increasingly presented with the challenge of pursuing certain spiritual and structural ideals that are harder and harder to find in the real world. This challenge relates not only to mothers, but also to fathers. We now turn to the connection between father-child relationships and religious practices.

Religious Practices and the Father-Child Relationship: Arrow 1C

In the preceding section addressing the mother-child relationship, we referenced Bengtson and colleagues' (2013) report regarding both mothers and fathers. You will recall that adult children who reported "close" relationships with their parent(s) remained affiliated with their parents' faith at higher levels than those whose parent-child relationships were "not close" (p. 78). Bengtson and colleagues additionally reported that in four of the six religious affiliations studied, "What is really interesting is that, for religious transmission, having a close bond with one's *father* matters even more than a close relationship with the mother" (p. 76, emphasis in original).

Exceptions to this tendency included Jewish mothers (who scored as significantly more influential than did Jewish fathers) and Mormon mothers, who scored only 2% higher than Mormon fathers. However, for the other four affiliations, the differences favored fathers, and profoundly so for both Evangelical and Mainline Protestant denominations. The data led the study's authors to conclude: "Clearly, the quality of the child's relationship with his or her father is important for the internalization of the parent's religious tradition, beliefs, and practices" (p. 76).

Although Bengtson and colleagues' study sample (more than 3,000 persons over four generations) and methods were outstanding, more research on the religion-fathering connection is needed, particularly in connection with religious practices. A few in-depth qualitative studies indicate that some religious practices, including prayer, reportedly strengthen the father-child (F-C) bond for many fathers who face pronounced challenges, including having a child or children with special needs (Dollahite, 2003; Dollahite, Marks, & Olson, 1998, 2002; Marks & Dollahite, 2001). In other qualitative work with 64 diverse fathers, Palkovitz and Palm (1998) found that fatherhood often prompts men to reassess their religious faith and that many "become more involved and increase [their] participation in religious practices" after becoming fathers (p. 36). Indeed, children sometimes pull their parents back into religious involvement.

For some fathers (and to a lesser extent mothers because more women tend to be more involved in religion before becoming parents than men), this influence of parenthood promoting increased religious involvement is pronounced enough that we call it the "and a little child shall lead them" phenomenon. This idea is not new, but dates to the writings of the Jewish prophet Isaiah (see Isaiah 11:6) that are embraced by all of the Abrahamic faiths. This idea also surfaces in literature, including the following reference from Mary Ann Evans (better known by her penname, George Eliot) in the classic novel *Silas Marner*, where the title character is led by degrees from a broken faith and empty life to a life of unselfishness, meaning, and renewed faith by a presumed orphan named Eppie, who literally toddles into Silas Marner's home and life. Eliot writes:

> In old days there were angels who came and took men by the hand and led them away from the city of destruction. We see no white-winged angels now. But yet men are led away from threatening destruction; a hand is put into theirs, which leads them forth gently towards a calm and bright land, so that they look no more backward; and the hand may be a little child's.
>
> (Eliot, 1861/2007, p. 134)

Like Eliot's *Silas Marner* and the work of developmental psychologists Rob Palkovitz and Glen Palm (1998), the *American Families of Faith* project includes some families (and/or fathers) who attributed their return to religious engagement during adulthood to the "pull" of a child or children born to them. Although the related stories were not necessarily as dramatic as those of *Silas Marner*, examples did include some Jewish couples who were minimally or marginally involved in Judaism during early adulthood but, after marriage and the arrival of a child or two, felt an increasing desire to "raise their children in the Jewish way" and enrolled their child(ren) in Jewish and/or Hebrew day school and were themselves pulled into increasingly full participation in Jewish faith community life (Hatch & Marks, 2014). Similar reports were occasionally offered by participants from other faiths (Christian, Muslim, LDS) where parents reported that they felt the need to "get back" for the sake of their children.

In a few cases within the *American Families of Faith* project, this experience of being "pulled" back into involvement by one's children was reportedly experienced with family life itself. Jacoby, an African-American Baptist father, discussed how (about 10 years into his marriage) he had literally separated himself from both his family and his faith community. He recalled that his children helped him drop his pride and reunite with his wife following a formal separation. Jacoby reflected:

> My children influence [me and] my marriage every day. One Christmas, [my wife and I] were separated, I was living somewhere else at the time. . . . [But] I came over, dropped my pride a little bit. . . . [Even though I was living somewhere else at the time], my daughters still got me something for Christmas. I felt really awkward; good, but awkward. Well, it made me want to come back. [They] had that kind of influence. When I realized what I was messing up here, in terms of the marriage, [I thought], "Maybe everything I have and need is right here." I knew that I had to get back here.

A reflection from an African-American Christian father named Earl captures a frequently expressed feeling among *American Families of Faith* fathers that children "deepened the commitment" in the fathers' marriages. Earl said:

> I think that having [children] just deepened the commitment that we had made to each other through getting married. It was a responsibility that I feel that we both took very seriously. . . . My kids influenced my

> marriage in so many ways. I just couldn't see nobody else raising them. I thank God for my kids and I thank God for my family. They've been my strength [and] they've been my joy. They've been my happiness. [My kids and wife] have been my life.

However, the prior happy and helpful reports regarding children and marriage only capture part of the complexity involved. Many fathers, like Larry, could recall times when their children added strain to their marriage. Larry illustrated:

> Sometimes [kids] play both sides of the parents. They know you, [just] like you know them. They know you and they push your buttons and play off the parents. . . . I think kids can impact marriage and they can impact them positively or negatively, just depending on what they got going on in their own lives. . . . Sometimes [a kid] brings out the dysfunction or any holes in the relationship between the parents. . . . The other side of that coin, [there's] been things that they've done that made us gleeful and happy and [make us feel] like we did a good job [as parents]. [Those times] made it feel closer [in our marriage], so it goes both ways: (kids stress you and they bless you).

This final point that "kids stress you and they bless you" seems to capture the reported influence of children on their fathers' marriages and their faith life as a complex and mixed bag (Marks et al., 2010).

Previous work by Dollahite and Thatcher (2006) and Palkovitz and colleagues (2003) has emphasized a *transactional* relationship between parents and children. In transactional relationships, *both* parties are influenced by the other. Social scientists have long been aware that parents influence their children in several ways, including faith (Bengtson et al., 2013). However, the research of Palkovitz and others has shown that the influence of having a child sometimes stimulates increased religious practice, attendance, and involvement in parents—indicating a reciprocal influence between (1) parents and child and (2) family and religion (as represented in Figure 6.2).

These findings and concepts elicit questions regarding the less frequently examined influences of family on religion and children on parents (Dollahite et al., 2004; Palkovitz, 2002). Our hope is that these important but historically overlooked issues will receive additional attention. We now turn from the behavioral dimension of religious practices to the more cognitive dimension of religious beliefs (see Figure 6.3).

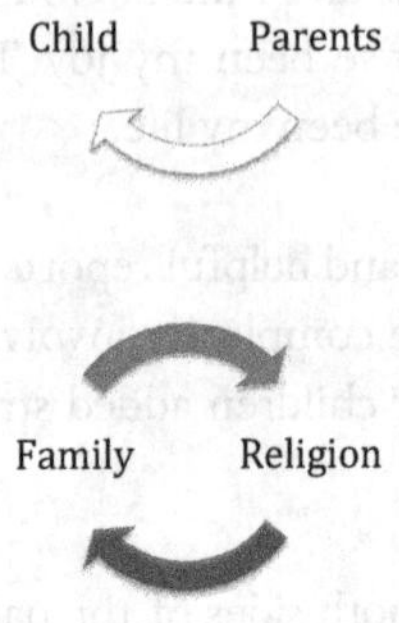

Figure 6.2 Transactional Relationships in Religion and Families

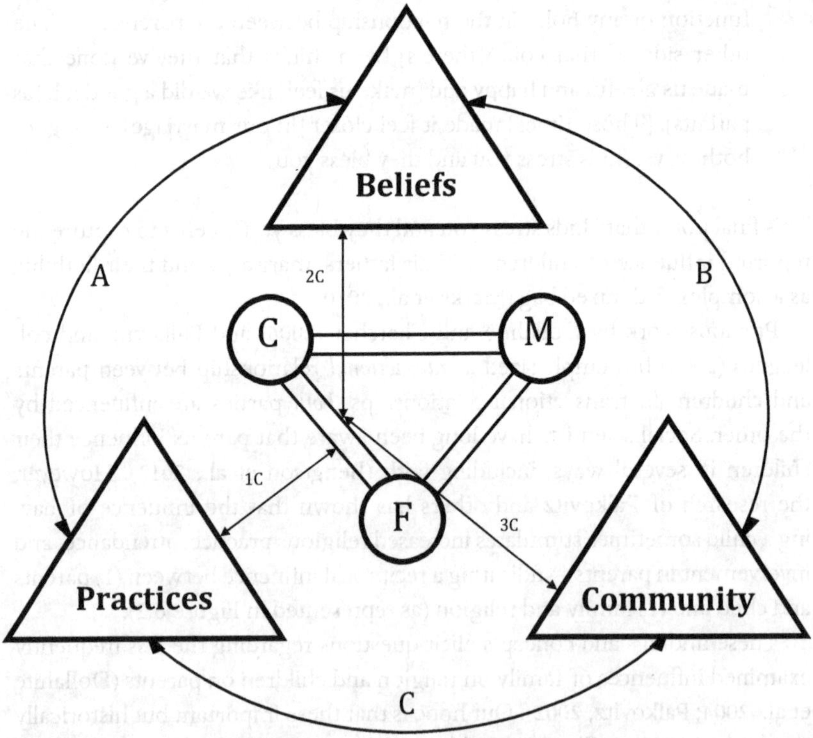

Figure 6.3 Research Connections Between Religious Beliefs, Practices, and Communities and Father-Child Relationships

Source: Adapted from Marks (2006).

Religious Beliefs and the Father-Child Relationship: Arrow 2C

Arrow 2C, the connection between the dimension of religious beliefs and the father-child (F-C) relationship, was addressed in early studies that correlated some religious beliefs with lower father absence rates—and with higher levels of paternal devotion (Fichter, 1962). Other work has linked religious beliefs with higher levels of generativity and commitment to children (Christiansen & Palkovitz, 1998) and increased father-child involvement (Bartowski & Xu, 2000; Wilcox, 1999, 2002). A related study by King (2003) examined religiousness in connection with eight aspects of father involvement among both married and divorced fathers and concluded that "certain aspects of father involvement are more frequent among the more religious, including better quality relationships . . . and stronger feelings of obligation for contact with children" (p. 392). Our own findings have typically been consistent with those of King and others, but we have also had participants talk about warm and devoted *non*-religious fathers, as reflected in the following interview excerpt from Ray, a father of a child with severe developmental disabilities, who recalled:

> My father was not a religious man but one of the things that I remember [from my childhood] is when we were working on the yard [at our] cabin in Minnesota. We children would get tired and leave and go play, but my father would always stay until the job was done. It would always impress me that I would be playing with my friends, and then I would still see my dad working on the same job, until the job was done. It always impressed me and has carried throughout my life that that's what men do. They accomplish the job. . . . I think the feeling that I have is, "Yeah, [having a child with severe disabilities] is tough, it is a disappointment. This is not fair." But I think that this is what you are dealt and this is what you play with. You don't just sit and whine and moan about it. You just get up and go to work and do the things that you need to do and deal with it. As far as spiritual things, I see from my father through his example that this is my job (to be a good father). I am to finish the job, so no matter what it takes or how long it is, you just stick to it and go to work, until the job is done. It is the father's responsibility—you are responsible, you are the support.

While much of our interview data in the *American Families of Faith* project mesh well with the concept that religious beliefs seem to generally promote better and warmer father-child relationships, there are also occasional references to religious men who were harsh, cruel, or distant fathers—or kind, positive fathers, like Ray's, who were not religious.

Although several studies and our own findings primarily link religious belief to responsible fathering, there may be a darker side to this connection as well. It has been posited that religious parents, especially conservative Protestant fathers, may be more authoritarian (low warmth, high control) than others since this is what some religious leaders advocate. A survey of the literature indicates mixed results regarding the linkage between conservative religiosity and parenting beliefs, especially fathers' beliefs (Ellison, Bartkowski, & Segal, 1996a, 1996b). Laythe et al. (2002) reported that Christian orthodoxy *is* correlated with fathers holding authoritarian attitudes toward their children.

By way of comparison, King (2003) reported that religious fathers are "*more* likely to . . . [agree that husbands should share] housework and child care equally with their wives" (p. 390, emphasis added). Other studies by Gunnoe, Hetherington, and Reiss (1999) and Wilcox (1998) have linked religiosity predominantly with high warmth parenting, while aspects of colder, authoritarian fathering were negatively correlated with religiosity. In another study, Wilcox (1999) found that Evangelical Christian fathers were more "traditional" (e.g., in expectations of obedience by children) but were also relatively highly involved fathers and were found to be "more expressive than most fathers" (p. 236). So, on the whole, many fathers seem to be striving to live out religious beliefs that promote kindness, warmth, and support in their fathering efforts in ways consistent with the idealized, gentle, and highly involved "new father" (Wilcox, 2004).

To summarize, research on the religious beliefs–fathering linkage has produced a mixed profile that combines elements of authoritarian and authoritative parental typologies. More specifically, some data indicate that religiously conservative fathers tend to be cold, hard, and authoritarian in some of their attitudes and expectations of obedience from their children—but other research also seems to indicate that many religious fathers are warm and supportive in the love they reportedly demonstrate and express to their children. One touching example from our early work was a religiously devoted father named Tom Boyer (actual named used by request) as he attended to his five-year-old daughter, Megan (actual name used by request), during her final stages of terminal leukemia. Tom shared:

> I was always there for her. Megan got my time. She had leukemia and I was going to make sure that I spent time with her when I wasn't at

work. Maybe the hospital is the part we like to forget but can't. When her pain got to the point that she couldn't go to the bathroom, I was the one that did her bedpans for her. She would only let me do it; I was the one that did that. It wasn't a thing for Mom, and she didn't want anybody else in the room. She kicked everybody out of the room; nurses, Mom (Mom had to be outside the door), and I would get the bedpan as best as I could under her bottom without hurting her. Moving the sheets hurt her. It was not a good thing. But she let me do that for her, and I was able to take care of her needs, and it helped me that I was the only one she'd let do it. You wouldn't expect bedpan shuffling to be a wonderful memory, but it was. She trusted me to do my best job not to hurt her, and that was special to me that she let me do that.

> I know only scientifically determined truth, but I am going to believe what I wish to believe, what I cannot help but believe—I expect to meet this dear child in another world.
>
> —Louis Pasteur (at the bedside of his dying daughter)
>
> To her the name of father was another name for love.
>
> —Fanny Fern [Sara Payson Willis]

Over the years, Tom and Megan's story has served as an inspiring example to us and our students of living out a sacred charge of the Abrahamic religions to "turn the heart of the fathers to the children" (Malachi 4:6, KJV). Our focus now turns from the cognitive dimension of religious beliefs to the social dimension of the religious community.

Religious Community and the Father-Child Relationship: Arrow 3C

At the turn of the 21st century, the connection between religious community and the father-child (F-C) relationship began receiving heightened attention from an array of researchers, family professionals, and policy makers. Two central themes in some of this work include the following: (1) father involvement in the United States is declining in several respects, as evidenced by high divorce and non-marital birth rates, and (2) religious communities are in a unique position to make efforts to reverse these trends (Eberly, 1999; Horn, 2001; Wilcox, 2004).

An African-American father named Ty from our *American Families of Faith* project was asked if his religious involvement influenced his fathering. He responded:

> [Oh] yeah, it reinforces that I have a greater role and responsibility than I ever thought. There is a higher standard, there is a much higher standard I've learned about and what that standard means is . . . that I must give my life for my family. And there's no limit to what I should give to my family. . . . I should be willing to give [my all] to my family. And I've been challenged by that, I've been tested by that . . . [but] through the strength of my Creator I've been able to keep my family together.

For Ty and others we interviewed, their religious involvement has "challeng[ing]" and "test[ing]" functions that reportedly call on them to be committed, responsible fathers. Research has indicated that active church attendance correlates with lower rates of unwed teen paternity (Hendricks, Robinson-Brown, & Gray, 1984) and with warm, affectionate parenting (Bartowski & Xu, 2000). The late Steven Nock (1998) emphasized that a man is known and respected in his religious community for filling his responsibilities, including his responsibilities to his child(ren).

Sociologist William Marsiglio and colleagues (2000) addressed the religious community as a social support in fathering and emphasized that fathers "contribute to their children's development through their connections with other individuals and organizations" and mentioned faith communities as one of the contexts where "social capital is created" (p. 1176). Specifically, the social connections that religious communities facilitate are helpful in creating opportunities, including employment and networking opportunities, not only for fathers but for all family members.

Continuing on the social network theme, a qualitative study by Dollahite et al. (1998) found that "help from the church" was a primary resource that highly involved fathers of children with special needs relied on as they tried to meet both the everyday and extraordinary needs of their children (p. 77). In a follow-up study that explored this "help from the church" finding in more depth, fathers gave specific narrative accounts of how their religious communities had offered social, emotional, spiritual, financial, and temporal support (including transportation and housing) in times of need.

When they work well, the multi-faceted help systems provided by many religious communities do seem to offer social, emotional, spiritual, and temporal support. Additionally, religious communities offer opportunities to serve others that can foster a sense of meaning and connection (Cherry, 2009, 2015; Dollahite & Marks, 2005; Marks, 2004). In contemporary and largely individualistic U.S. society, this benefit can be overlooked. Patricia, an LDS mother of six (now adult) children, mentioned service as not just an activity but as a teaching tool for her children that both she and her husband, William, have used. She explained:

> I see [giving] service as being a big part of the impact [of faith] on the kids. Dad gathers them up on Sunday morning when there's three feet of snow and they all march down the street to shovel out the neighbors that are too old to shovel themselves out. They think, "We're shoveling snow on [the Sabbath], but you know what? It's the right thing to do because we are helping somebody else."

Patricia later added:

> [There is a] comfort of knowing that we are doing what we are supposed to be doing, serving unselfishly. And because we are keeping that commandment, we can ask the Lord, in turn to bless us . . . knowing that we are doing our part.

Patricia's husband, William, identified several purposes, meanings, and products of active involvement and service in their religious community. Fittingly, Loren interviewed them both at their East Coast church between service commitments they had there. William commented on the children-oriented nature of much of their service and involvement:

> There's an old adage, "It takes a village to raise a child." Our congregation is the [village] that we have chosen to focus our energies on and I think our kids felt comfortable in that community and have drawn a lot of strength from it. It's a diverse community . . . and there's strength in that diversity. . . . We [Patricia and I] have both taken time to go on scout camps and girls' camps and spent time with the children in their youth activities. A lot of things that [our] church provides as part of their standard program are faith-initiated and it's only because persons of faith are involved that there is enough energy around to make them happen, and I think that [those programs] have had a big impact [on the children involved].

> Help thy brother's boat across, and lo! thine own has reached the shore.
>
> —old Hindu proverb
>
> You can't imagine how difficult [moral training] is. As soon as you've overcome one thing, others crop up, and you have to start all over again. Without the support of religion . . . no father would be able to bring up his children by his own efforts.
>
> —Leo Tolstoy, *Anna Karenina*

In addition to his involvement with children and youth, William had spent hundreds of hours in voluntary counseling with adult members of his congregation over the previous five years. In connection with the time and energy this commitment required, he mentioned two "blessings" he believed he received. William reflected:

> I think when we work with people, it helps us to keep our own struggles in a better perspective and they don't become a burden, [we view our struggles as] just a part of life. We see so many other people, and we're just glad we're not in their shoes.
>
> I personally believe that people are at their happiest when they're serving others, no matter who they are. Everybody I've talked to—I've done this at work at lunch time sometimes, [and when] I've interviewed people for jobs—I've asked people, "What's been the most rewarding thing you've ever done?" Very seldom do they [say], "It was the day I completed my degree. . . ." It nearly always focuses on doing things for people. Really, that's what service in the church . . . is based on. Doing things for other people, [going] outside yourself.

Patricia and William remind us that religious communities, at their best, provide the opportunity to discard our personal "It's all about ME" t-shirts and instead focus on "doing things for other people, [going] outside" ourselves. The example offered by Patricia and William reminds us that faith communities can help turn the hearts of mothers and fathers toward children in loving and generative ways and that the hearts of the children can indeed turn away from self-absorption and toward their parents and others as they serve and love. These objectives are central to optimal development, according to social science perspectives (see Erikson & Erikson, 1997) and several world religions (see Malachi 4:5–6).

However, as with mothers, there can be negative aspects of the father–religious community connection. Our own research indicated that while the aforementioned supports from faith communities can be helpful for fathers and their families, conversely, when the fathers' religious communities *failed* them, "it was both disappointing and hurtful in ways that seemed to elicit deeper frustration and pain than failures by secular agencies and institutions" (Marks & Dollahite, 2001, p. 636). To capture the full range of fathers' experience, it must be acknowledged that faith communities do influence some fathers, but this influence can be positive, negative, or both (Burr et al., 2012; Palkovitz & Palm, 1998).

Conclusion

In this chapter, we have discussed findings from previous research as well as narratives that capture largely positive but sometimes negative connections between religion and parenting. Our AFF data and previous data on the topic all seem to support the notion that lived parental example is of foundational importance in the religion-family connection. Indeed, a core principle from our research, our teaching, and our experience is the **principle of lived invitation**: "Our behavior is permission to others to behave similarly, but it is more than that—it is an *invitation* to do so." Perhaps this holds especially true in the context of parent-child relationships.

Chapter Summary Points

1. Religious practices—including conversations about faith—often have positive influences on mother-child relationships and faith development.
2. Women tend to attend services, pray, and rate religion as more important in their lives than men do.
3. Beliefs are most likely to be transmitted between mothers and children (and fathers and children) when there is a strong and nurturing relationship between the parent and child. Further, harmony of religious beliefs is an apparent protection against depression.
4. Women who attend worship services regularly are more likely to have children.

5. While religious community involvement is often correlated with positive outcomes, non-traditional family forms (including divorced, separated, and unmarried mothers) tend to receive less support and receive fewer benefits.
6. Children often increase the level of religious involvement of their parents.

Review Questions

1. Based on Bengtson and colleagues' research, what factor is the best predictor of whether a child will remain actively involved in his or her parent's faith?
2. What do the authors cite as a reason for why women may enjoy greater health benefits than men?
3. "Women who are involved in a faith community . . . are significantly more likely to have children." What reason do the authors cite to explain this phenomenon?
4. Does a woman's marital status affect the support received from a faith community? If so, how?
5. From the standpoint of religious involvement, how is a parent-child relationship transactional?

Notes

1. Portions of this chapter are adapted with permission from L. D. Marks (2006), Religion and family relational health: An overview and conceptual model, *Journal of Religion and Health, 45*, 603–618.
2. The six religious categories used by Bengtson and colleagues (2013) were Evangelical Protestant, Mainline Protestant, Catholic, Jewish, Mormon (Latter-day Saint/LDS), and None (meaning no religious affiliation) (p. 78).
3. While we do not take the time here to provide a thorough summary of the findings of these two studies, we highly recommend them.

References

Abma, J. C., & Martinez, G. M. (2006). Childlessness among older women in the United States: Trends and profiles. *Journal of Marriage and the Family, 68*, 1045–1056.

Acock, A., & Bengtson, V. (1978). On the relative influence of mothers and fathers: A covariance analysis of political and religious socialization. *Journal of Marriage and the Family, 40*, 519–531.

Bao, W., Whitbeck, L. B., Hoyt, D. R., & Conger, R. D. (1999). Perceived parental acceptance as a moderator of religious transmission among adolescent boys and girls. *Journal of Marriage and the Family, 61*, 362–372.

Bartowski, J. P., & Xu, X. (2000). Distant patriarchs or expressive dads? The discourse and practice of fathering in conservative protestant families. *The Sociological Quarterly, 41*, 465–485.

Bengtson, V. L., Putney, N. M., & Harris, J. (2013). *Families of faith*. New York: Oxford.

Boyatzis, C. J., & Janicki, D. L. (2003). Parent-child communication about religion: Survey and diary data on unilateral transmission and bi-directional reciprocity styles. *Review of Religious Research, 44*, 252–270.

Burr, W. R., Marks, L. D., & Day, R. (2012). *Sacred matters: Religion and spirituality in families*. New York: Routledge.

Cherry, K. (Ed.) (2009). *Lifespan perspectives on natural disasters*. New York: Springer.

Cherry, K. (Ed.) (2015). *Traumatic stress and long-term recovery: Coping with disasters and other negative life events*. New York: Springer.

Christiansen, S. L., & Palkovitz, R. (1998). Exploring Erikson's psychosocial theory of development: Generativity and its relationship to paternal identity, intimacy, and involvement in childcare. *The Journal of Men's Studies, 7*, 133–156.

Clark, C. A., Worthington, E. L., & Danser, D. B. (1988). The transmission of religious beliefs and practices from parents to firstborn early adolescent sons. *Journal of Marriage and the Family, 50*, 463–472.

Dollahite, D. C. (1998). Fathering, faith, and spirituality. *The Journal of Men's Studies, 7*, 3–16.

Dollahite, D. C. (2003). Fathering for eternity: Generative spirituality in Latter-day Saint fathers of children with special needs. *Review of Religious Research, 44*, 339–351.

Dollahite, D. C., & Marks, L. D. (2005). How highly religious families strive to fulfill sacred purposes. In V. Bengtson, A. Acock, K. Allen, P. Dillworth-Anderson, & D. Klein (Eds.), *Sourcebook of family theory and research* (pp. 533–541). Thousand Oaks, CA: Sage.

Dollahite, D. C., Marks, L. D., & Goodman, M. (2004). Religiosity and families: Relational and spiritual linkages in a diverse and dynamic cultural context. In M. J. Coleman, & L. H. Ganong (Eds.), *The handbook of contemporary families* (pp. 411–431). Thousand Oaks, CA: Sage.

Dollahite, D. C., Marks, L. D., & Olson, M. M. (1998). Faithful fathering in trying times: Religious beliefs and practices of Latter-day Saint fathers of children with special needs. *The Journal of Men's Studies, 7*, 71–94.

Dollahite, D. C., Marks, L. D., & Olson, M. M. (2002). Fathering, faith, and family therapy: Generative narrative therapy with religious fathers. *Journal of Family Psychotherapy, 13*, 263–294.

Dollahite, D. C., & Thatcher, J. Y. (2008). Talking about religion: How religious youth and parents discuss their faith. *Journal of Adolescent Research, 23*, 611–641.

Eberly, D. E. (Ed.) (1999). *The faith factor in fatherhood* (pp. 219–240). New York: Lexington.

Eliot, G. (1861/2007). *Silas Marner*. New York: Signet Classics/Penguin.

Ellison, C. G., Bartkowski, J. P., & Segal, M. L. (1996a). Conservative Protestantism and the parental use of corporal punishment. *Social Forces, 74*, 1003–1028.

Ellison, C. G., Bartkowski, J. P., & Segal, M. L. (1996b). Do conservative Protestant parents spank more often? Further evidence from the National Survey of Families and Households. *Social Science Quarterly, 77*, 663–673.

Ellison, C. G., & George, L. K. (1994). Religious involvement, social ties, and social support in a southeastern community. *Journal for the Scientific Study of Religion, 33*, 46–61.

Erikson, E. H., & Erikson, J. M. (1997). *The life cycle completed*. New York, NY: Norton.

Fichter, J. H. (1962). Religion and socialization among children. *Review of Religious Research, 4*, 24–33.

Gunnoe, M. L., Hetherington, E. M., & Reiss, D. (1999). Parental religiosity, parenting style, and adolescent social responsibility. *Journal of Early Adolescence, 19*, 199–225.

Hatch, T., & Marks, L. (2014). Judaism and Orthodox Judaism. In L. Ganong, M. Coleman, & J. G. Golson (Eds.), *The social history of the American family* (pp. 781–784). Thousand Oaks, CA: Sage.

Hendricks, L. E., Robinson-Brown, D. P., & Gray, L. E. (1984). Religiosity and unmarried black adolescent fatherhood. *Adolescence, 19*, 417–424.

Hertel, B. R., & Donahue, M. J. (1995). Parental influences on god images among children: Testing Durkheim's metaphoric parallelism. *The Journal for the Scientific Study of Religion, 34*, 186–199.

Hoge, D. R., Petrillo, G. H., & Smith, E. I. (1982). Transmission of religious and social values from parents to teenage children. *Journal of Marriage and the Family, 44*, 569–580.

Horn, W. F. (2001). Turning the hearts of the fathers: Promoting fatherhood through faith. In J. Fagan, & A. J. Hawkins (Eds.), *Clinical and educational interventions with fathers* (pp. 191–214). New York: Haworth.

Hummer, R., Rogers, R., Nam, C., & Ellison, C. G. (1999). Religious involvement and U.S. adult mortality. *Demography, 36*, 273–285.

Kaufman, D. R. (1991). *Rachel's daughters*. New Brunswick, NJ: Rutgers University.

Kieren, D. K., & Munro, B. (1987). Following the leaders: Parents' influence on adolescent religious activity. *Journal for the Scientific Study of Religion, 26*, 249–255.

King, V. (2003). The influence of religion on father's relationships with their children. *Journal of Marriage and the Family, 65*, 382–395.

Koenig, H. G., King, D. E., & Carson, V. B. (2012). *Handbook of religion and health (2nd ed.)*. New York: Oxford University Press.

Koenig, H. G., McCullough, M. E., & Larson, D. B. (Eds.) (2001). *Handbook of religion and health*. New York: Oxford.

Laythe, B., Finkle, D. G., Bringle, R. G., & Kirkpartick, L. A. (2002). Religious fundamentalism as a predictor of prejudice: A two-component model. *Journal for the Scientific Study of Religion, 41*, 623–635.

Lee, J. W., Rice, G. T., & Gillespie, V. B. (1997). Family worship patterns and their correlation with adolescent behavior and beliefs. *Journal for the Scientific Study of Religion, 36*, 372–381.

Mahoney, A. (2010). Religion in families, 1999–2009: A relational spirituality framework. *Journal of Marriage and Family, 72*, 805–827.

Marks, L. D. (2004). Sacred practices in highly religious families: Christian, Jewish, Mormon, and Muslim perspectives. *Family Process, 43*, 217–231.

Marks, L. D. (2006). Religion and family relational health: An overview and conceptual model. *Journal of Religion and Health, 45*, 603–618.

Marks, L. D., & Dollahite, D. C. (2001). Religion, relationships, and responsible fathering in Latter-day Saint families of children with special needs. *Journal of Social and Personal Relationships, 18*, 625–650.

Marks, L. D., & Dollahite, D. C. (2012). Don't forget home: The importance of sacred ritual in families. In J. Hoffman (Ed.), *Understanding religious rituals* (pp. 186–203). New York: Routledge.

Marks, L. D., Dollahite, D. C., & Freeman, J. J. (2011). Faith and prayer in family life. In A. J. Hawkins, D. C. Dollahite, & T. W. Draper (Eds.), *Successful marriages and family life* (pp. 185–195). Provo, UT: BYU Studies.

Marks, L. D., Hopkins, K., Chaney, C., Nesteruk, O., & Sasser, D. (2010). My kids and wife have been my life: Married African American fathers staying the course. In R. Coles, & C. Green (Eds.), *The myth of the missing black father* (pp. 19–46). New York: Columbia University.

Marks, L. D., Nesteruk, O., Swanson, M., Garrison, M. E. B., & Davis, T. (2005). Religion and health among African Americans: A qualitative examination. *Research on Aging, 27*, 447–474.

Marsiglio, W., Amato, P., Day, R. D., & Lamb, M. E. (2000). Scholarship on fatherhood in the 1990s and beyond. *Journal of Marriage and the Family, 62*, 1173–1191.

Miller, L., Warner, V., Wickramaratne, P., & Weissman, M. (1997). Religiosity and depression: Ten-year follow-up of depressed mothers and offspring. *Journal of the American Academy of Child and Adolescent Psychiatry, 52*, 41–49.

Nock, S. J. (1998). *Marriage in men's lives*. New York: Oxford University Press.

Ozorak, E. W. (1996). The power but not the glory: How women empower themselves through religion. *Journal for the Scientific Study of Religion, 35*, 17–29.

Palkovitz, R. (2002). *Involved fathering and men's adult development*. Hillsdale, NJ: Erlbaum.

Palkovitz, R., Marks, L. D., Appleby, D. W., & Holmes, E. K. (2003). Parenting and adult development: Contexts, processes and products of intergenerational relationships. In L. Kucynski (Ed.), *The handbook of dynamics in parent-child relationships* (pp. 307–323). Thousand Oaks, CA: Sage.

Palkovitz, R., & Palm, G. (1998). Fatherhood and faith in formation: The developmental effects of fathering on religiosity, morals, and values. *The Journal of Men's Studies, 7*, 33–52.

Pearce, L. (2002). The influence of early life course religious exposure on young adults' dispositions toward childbearing. *Journal for the Scientific Study of Religion, 41*, 325–340.

Pearce, L. D., & Axinn, W. G. (1998). The impact of family religious life on the quality of mother-child relations. *American Sociological Review, 63*, 810–828.

Snarey, J. R., & Dollahite, D. C. (2001). Varieties of religion-family linkages. *Journal of Family Psychology, 15*, 646–651.

Sorenson, A. M., Grindstaff, C. F., & Turner, R. J. (1995). Religious involvement among unmarried adolescent mothers: A source of emotional support? *Sociology of Religion, 56*, 71–81.

Stacey, J., & Gerard, S. E. (1990). We are not doormats: The influence of feminism on contemporary Evangelicalism in the United States. In F. Ginsburg, & A. Tsing (Eds.), *Negotiating gender in American culture* (pp. 98–117). Boston: Beacon.

Stark, R. (2012). *America's blessings: How religion benefits everyone, including atheists*. Conshohocken, PA: Templeton Press.

Taylor, R. J., & Chatters, L. M. (1988). Church members as a source of informal social support. *Review of Religious Research, 30*, 193–202.

Vergote, A. (1980). Religion after the critique of psychoanalysis. *The Annual Review of the Social Sciences of Religion, 4*, 1–29.

Wilcox, W. B. (1998). Conservative Protestant childrearing: Authoritarian or authoritative? *American Sociological Review, 63*, 796–809.

Wilcox, W. B. (1999). Emerging attitudes about gender roles and fatherhood. In D. E. Eberly (Ed.), *The faith factor in fatherhood* (pp. 219–240). New York: Lexington.

Wilcox, W. B. (2002). Religion, convention, and parental involvement. *Journal of Marriage and Family, 64*, 780–792.

Wilcox, W. B. (2004). *Soft patriarchs, new men: How Christianity shapes fathers and husbands.* Chicago: University of Chicago Press.

Wuthnow, R. (1999). *Growing up religious: Christians and Jews and their journeys of faith.* Boston: Beacon.

Parenting and *American Families of Faith*[1] 7

In this book, we have discussed the power of religious faith to unite families—and to divide them (see Burr, Marks, & Day, 2012). In this chapter we move to an in-depth examination of what we have learned about parenting in faith from our *American Families of Faith* project. First, let's set the stage a bit.

Commentaries and insights on the parent-child connection are not uncommon in the scriptures of the Abrahamic faiths. A proverb from King Solomon (king of Israel) reads, "Train up a child in the way he should go: and when he is old, he will not depart from it" (Proverbs 22:6, KJV). As we will see in this chapter, social science does offer some moderate support for this idea, but the findings indicate only tendencies, not immutable laws. Indeed, Solomon's own later life provided an exception to his proverb as he violated and "departed" from the core Israelite belief in the "one true God" (1 Kings 11:4, KJV). The effort of parents to share their religious faith with their children—and children's subsequent decisions to embrace or reject the faith of their parents—is not a new story, but it is one that remains relevant today, millennia after Solomon and his father, David.

Our colleague, respected sociologist Vern Bengtson, wrote in his book-length study *Families and Faith: How Religion Is Passed Down Across Generations*[2] (2013) that his own experience with his mother, with respect to religious faith, had been a trying and divisive one. He reflected that "it seemed I was to become the weak link in [the] chain that had connected generations through faith." Over the course of his life, Bengtson shifted from being a "fundamentalist Evangelical to a moderate Presbyterian to a skeptical nonbeliever."

These personal religious changes reportedly created intense and profound distress for his mother. Bengtson explained:

> Religious differences in families can create profound distress. As I moved away from the Christian fundamentalism that characterized my childhood, my widowed mother became more and more distraught. . . . She wrote to me saying that I was "breaking her heart." In another letter she said this: "Vern, if I have to choose between you and my Jesus, I will choose Jesus." I couldn't understand. Why such a choice? What had I done? "You have turned your back on Jesus," she said.
>
> (pp. viii–ix)

Bengtson continued his discussion of his experience with his mother by revealing:

> For the remaining twenty-six years of her life, my mother and I lived in a sort of uneasy truce. We had to avoid talking about religion—which was difficult, considering her faith and her church were the very focus of her life. To my everlasting regret, my mother died with sorrow and anger, believing that because of my "hardness of heart" she would never be able to see her only child and grandchildren in heaven. Each of us loved the other so much, but we were formal and uneasy together because of the religious gulf between us.
>
> (p. ix)

The jacket of Bengtson's book *Families and Faith* claims that "few things are more likely to cause heartache to devout parents than seeing their child leave the faith"—a phenomenon Bengtson himself experienced from the child's perspective. Unlike Solomon, however, late in his life, after his mother's passing, Bengtson seemed to fulfill the proverb, "Train up a child in the way he should go: and when he is old, he will not depart from it" (Proverbs 22:6, KJV). Bengtson revealed to his readers that "something unexpected happened" as he neared the culmination of his research project on families and faith:

> On Easter Sunday three years ago, I wandered into a church service. Suddenly I was overwhelmed by the music and beauty, and bowled over by recollections and revelations—utterly "surprised by joy," as C.S. Lewis described his own later-life religious experience. I came back.

> So these days I'm in church every Sunday, singing away in the choir. Every Thursday I'm there at a noon Bible study. . . . [I'm now on] the church governing body, so I'm spending even more time there. In looking back over how things have turned out for me religiously, I think my father and grandfather would be pleased. I hope my mom would too.
>
> (p. xi)

By way of comparison, the Christian apostle John expressed, "I have no greater joy than to hear that my children walk in truth" (3 John 1:4, KJV). Two brief examples of this latter concept from our *American Families of Faith* participants (with young children) include, first, an African-American Christian father named Rashaad who referenced the pride and emotion he felt for his daughter following her simple participation in a worship service. He said:

> What really got me was that . . . last week, [a] lady said to one of my daughters, "Would you like to close up with a prayer?" And she said yes and she did it and I was proud of her. It wasn't something long-winded, it was something short and simple, but that's all that matters. . . . A little tear came to my eye, and then she came running over after and said, "Daddy, I love you." And I said, "I love you too." Now she could have said, "I don't want to pray," but she didn't. I want you to know that [wasn't] a wasted trip.

A Jewish mother recalled a similar recent experience with one of her two daughters at synagogue. She shared the following:

> My daughter participated in a Sabbath service and was up there singing. There's a pride that you feel that's just incredible and that makes me feel even closer to my husband and also to my Mom and my in-laws too when they are there. Because you just know how everyone feels . . . we are all standing there together. I mean it's something that you all share that's very special. Having [my daughters] learning things that I learned certainly makes me feel closer to them.

In these examples, we see the meaning and sense of pride and closeness that can accompany a parent seeing his or her child share that sacred religious and family vision. Religion, when combined with family relationships, seems capable of producing both sorrow and joy, while it both "divides and unites us" (Putnam & Campbell, 2010).

How and Why Does Religion Help and Harm Parent-Child Relationships?

We will now take a closer and deeper look at *how* and *why* religion can harm or help parent-child relationships. Emerging research also indicates that relationships can influence religious faith, but we will examine that phenomenon more closely in chapter 11.

One of the leading scholars of world religions, Huston Smith, focused his life's research efforts primarily on what we refer to as the religious dimensions of beliefs and practices. Because he was not a family studies scholar, family relationships were not a central (or even a secondary) focus in most of his work. Yet, in an influential book he wrote in his 80s entitled *Why Religion Matters*, Huston Smith (2003) offered a rare peek behind the scenes into his personal and family experience. In the following narrative, we become privy to the driving force in his life's efforts to share and promote the best of what a variety of world religions offer. Behind it all, for Huston Smith, was a powerful parental example of lived faith. He explained:

> I was born into a loving family whose parents committed their lives to the highest calling they could conceive—that of being missionaries to China. Sacrifices were to be expected, and (in the disease-ridden China of that time) they arrived on schedule; their firstborn died in their arms on his second Christmas Eve. . . . The most important thing I inherited from my parents was faith.
>
> (p. xiii)

Smith witnessed in his parents a deep and authentic faith that was "inherited," lived, and further developed in his own life. The recently culminated and published study by Vern Bengtson, Putney, and Harris (2013) found a similar pattern across more than three decades among those who were raised in devotedly religious homes. Bengtson and colleagues' findings corroborated similar patterns detected by sociologist Christian Smith and his colleagues in the first of a series of book-length studies on religion in the lives of youth across time. In *Soul Searching: The Religious and Spiritual Lives of American Teenagers*, Smith and Denton (2005) concluded:

> Contrary to misguided stereotypes and frequent parental misperceptions, we believe that the evidence clearly shows that *the single most important social influence on the religious and spiritual lives of adolescents is their parents.*
>
> (p. 261, emphasis added)

Additional findings from the National Study of Youth and Religion (NYSR) show that the greatest evidence of religiosity influencing youth's lives for the better can be seen when comparing the lives of the most religious youth, "The Devoted" (8% of American youth), with the lives of the average American youth (Smith & Denton, 2005). "The Devoted" youth claimed that their religion was "very or extremely important in [their] everyday life" and reported that they felt "very or extremely close to God"; they attend religious services, pray, read scripture, and participate in religious youth groups more than other American teens (p. 220). In the area of family relationships, this group of extremely religious youth reported having the highest quality of parent-child relationships in every area studied, including levels of honesty, acceptance and understanding, getting along, and feeling loved by and close to their parents (cf. Dollahite & Thatcher, 2007). In an earlier study, also based on data from across several years, Scott Myers (1996) similarly found that "parents' religiosity is *the primary influence* on the religiosity of their adult offspring" (p. 864, emphasis added).

To restate, the shared conclusion of three of the most rigorous longitudinal studies on religion and "transmission" of parents' beliefs and practices to their children to date is that when a teen's parents are actively involved in religious faith, it is significantly more likely that the teen will be actively involved in a life of religious faith as an emerging adult (Smith & Snell, 2009) and middle-aged adult (Bengtson et al., 2013).

Conversely, those who did not see or witness a modeling of parental involvement in faith in their childhood and youth were significantly less likely to have ties to religion as adults—and these patterns seem to endure to a measurable degree across generations. Even so, a 2008 Pew Forum on Religion and Family Life found that 44% of Americans reported that they had changed or dropped the religious affiliation of their childhood—while a bare majority had retained the affiliation of their formative years. Parent-child **religious transmission** is an empirical probability, but it is far from a law. Further, we know relatively little about *how* and *why* it happens (or fails to happen) (see Bengtson et al., 2013, p. 12).

The central and recurring findings of scholars including Bengtson and colleagues, Scott Myers, and Christian Smith and colleagues are reflected in our *American Families of Faith* project as well. A majority of the parents we interviewed, although not all, indicated that their own parents were authentically and actively involved in faith during the participant's formative years. Next, we strive to add color to these ideas, and perhaps a little more about the missing hows and whys, by sharing some of our participants' own narratives.

Parenting and Congruence in the Faith Walk

Our participants repeatedly discussed the meaning, influence, and power of religious practices including family prayer, the study of sacred texts, family rituals (e.g., the Ramadan fast for Muslim families, the *Shabbat*/Sabbath meal and rituals for Jewish families, and Family Home Evenings for LDS/Mormon families) (Dollahite & Marks, 2005, 2009; Marks, 2004; Marks & Dollahite, 2012). As important as these practices and rituals were, however, a recurring report by mothers and fathers (across races and religions) was that *the* most important religious practice was parents "practicing what they preach."

> What you do speaks so loudly that I cannot hear what you say.
>
> —Ralph Waldo Emerson

The importance of "practicing what you preach" was most apparent in the context of *parental example*. In fact, some parents emphasized "practicing" so heavily that "preaching" was downplayed as almost unnecessary (Marks, 2004). Angie, a Muslim mother of two, explained in her interview:

> In terms of religion, it doesn't matter how much the father talks to the children [about religion], the children will learn from what the father *does*. . . . If my children see my husband go to the Mosque every night for prayer [which he does], he is setting an example. I don't have to "teach" it. They are seeing it.

Angie's narrative as a Muslim mother is almost interchangeable with that of Marisol, a young Catholic mother from Bengtson and colleagues' (2013) study. Marisol says:

> We . . . have to show our kids that this is the way we want them to be, and in order to do that, we have to go to church and we have to practice it.

> *Religion is at its best when it relies on the strength of . . . example. It is at its worst when it seeks to impose truth by force.*
>
> —Rabbi Jonathan Sacks (2015), *Not In God's Name*, p. 234, emphasis in original

Moving back to our own AFF participants, a Korean Christian father of two named Oui shared a reflection on living an exemplary religious life as a father that harmonized closely with Angie's and Marisol's comments. He expressed his perception that:

> A person who *really* believes in Christ often has parents who have a good faith in God. . . . If we can help my son be like Jesus Christ or close to Jesus Christ, what else can we worry about for our child? I can't really "teach" . . . we have to *show* him by what we do during our life. If we do very well for God and other people, then he will know what he has to do.

Notice the focus by both Angie and Oui, mother and father, Muslim and Christian, on the same point: the importance of a lived parental example. Angie modestly emphasizes (consistent with Islam) that her husband "is setting an example" and that their children "are seeing it" (Marks, 2004). Speaking of his young son, the Korean Christian father Oui posited that "we have to *show* him by what we do . . . then he will know what he has to do." Evidence of the validity of the "practicing over preaching" approach in parenting promoted by Angie and Oui was also offered by Joseph, a Christian father of four, who reflected back to his own childhood. He recalled:

> I could see from my parents' behavior over time that faith was something that matters. This is something that is real, this is something you invest in. My parents were very formative in providing a foundation for my faith.

Notice that Joseph referred, first and foremost, to his parents' *behavior*. Teaching and instruction may have been influential as well, but these were not mentioned. Joseph again referred to the power of **behavior-belief congruence** in connection with his own parenting when he explained:

> Kids just want to know the truth and you have . . . to represent that in a way that's meaningful and in a way that's real. . . . Your kids live with you, they see you. They see if this is a Sunday morning thing or a 24/7 thing. When Dad slams his thumb in the car door, what does he do? When something goes wrong, does he freak out or does he have faith?

Joseph's reference to his children seeing through his example "if this is [just] a Sunday morning thing" is illustrative of a concept we refer to as

temporal compartmentalizing. If parents seem to compartmentalize and confine "faith" to a certain time, space, or setting, the meaning and influence of faith will likely be diluted. Some of the participants' shared experiences seemed to indicate that the compartmentalizing approach to religion was harmful due to the contradictory messages sent to children (Marks, 2004). Returning to Joseph's efforts to be congruent and "real," how was Joseph doing in his efforts to make his faith a "24–7 thing"? Jessica, Joseph's wife, gave the following account:

> In our family . . . [Joseph is] an excellent role model. The kids need to be able to look up to him and see the God in his life . . . [so] that they'll want to pattern their lives after him. It's always great for kids to be able to look up to their Dad and see someone that they respect. . . . I've seen him changing over the years. He loves the Lord and wants to do what pleases Him . . . modeling what he sees as being valuable for the kids to see. He has an important role in being like Jesus to the kids. A lot of our understanding of who God is comes through fathers, because God is presented as a father in the Bible. If a kid grows up having a father who is loving and kind and supportive and strong, I think it is easier for them to understand God and who He is. . . . The kids see in their father aspects of God, a perfect God.

Jessica's synopsis of Joseph's concerted efforts to be a congruent, faithful father and the influence this has on their children climaxes with her conditional statement, "If a kid grows up having a father who is loving and kind and supportive and strong, I think it is easier for them to understand God." Jessica's insight here was not solely grounded in 20 years of parenting experience; her insight was also based on 12 years of volunteer work with a faith-based youth group that had exposed her to a diverse array of youth and an accompanying variety of family situations.

Interestingly, Jessica's report mirrors similar statements drawn from clinical experience (Dollahite, 1998) and previous research on "God images" by Hertel and Donahue (1995) and Antoine Vergote (1980) that indicate that children with warm parents are more likely to conceptualize and believe in a warm God, while those with more punitive parents have conceptualizations of a colder God and are, understandably, less likely to have a faith at all. As a Catholic Bishop, Kenneth J. Povish, has written, "If children have no experience of a present, caring, loving, providing father at home, they are not apt to understand what [is] meant [when they hear] about a present, caring, loving, providing Father in heaven" (Povish, 2003, p. 14).

> It is difficult for a child to find a father in God, unless the child first finds something of God in his father.
>
> —Robert Ingersoll

Talking the Talk: Encouraging Youth-Oriented Religious Conversations[3]

In the previous section we demonstrated that "walking the walk" (as parental example of a religious life) is extremely important to how children respond to parental efforts at religious socialization. However, the research also indicates that "talking the talk" (parent-child religious conversations) can also play an extremely important role in how children come to feel about the faith of their parents. Research by Dollahite and Thatcher (2008) found that among 20 different kinds of home- and family-based religious activities (e.g., family prayer, singing hymns, watching religious videos, reading sacred texts, sacred family celebrations, family religious meals) the *most* important and the second most frequent activity was parent-child religious conversations.

In connection with this same topic of conversations, Smith and Denton (2005) asked adolescents how often they and their families talked together about God, scriptures, prayer, or other religious or spiritual issues. About one-third (34%) said a few times a week or more, 28% reported a few times a month or weekly, and 38% said a few times a year or never. In a study on religious conversations, Flor and Knapp (2001) found that the more frequently parents and younger adolescents had bidirectional discussions on issues of faith, the more likely the adolescents were to place importance on religion and to exhibit religious behavior.

When religious parents and their adolescent children talk about religious matters, or about other issues with religious implications, the potential exists for strong positive or negative emotion in both parent and child, for the parent-child relationship to be strengthened or weakened, and for the child's interest in future religious discussions with the parent to be enhanced or diminished. In our *American Families of Faith* project we found that there were two main kinds of parent-adolescent religious conversation: parent centered or youth centered. We discuss both of these next.

Parent-Centered Conversations

Four main characteristics of **parent-centered conversations** were: (a) parents talk too much, (b) parents' talk is unsolicited or unwanted, (c) parents give demands without explanation, and (d) conversation is too restrictive for the adolescents.

Parents Talk Too Much

Some parents acknowledged that they had the tendency to talk to their children about religion more than the children preferred. Heidi, a 35-year-old Latter-day Saint mother of four, reported, "We talk to them an awful lot more than they want us to."

Adolescents reported some frustration with religious conversation when their parents talked too much. Chad, a 12-year-old Episcopalian youth, explained how his parents sometimes made him talk with them longer than he would like:

> Sometimes I ask a question and then I think that they go too far because they start talking too much. . . . And then I say that I don't want to discuss it anymore and I try to walk away and then they have me come back in and I'm, like, really mad.

Parents' Religious Talk Is Unsolicited or Unwanted

Some parents and adolescents indicated that, at times, the parents spoke to the children about religion when it was unsolicited or unwanted by the child. Hailey, a 14-year-old, was irritated that her father always spoke of religious principles: "He always, for every situation, even something [like] a math problem, he can relate a scriptural principle. . . . And it can get really annoying."

Parents Give Demands without Explanation

Charlotte, a 56-year-old Presbyterian, recounted a conversation in which she made her 14-year-old son, Shane, go to church:

Charlotte: But you've [Shane] made a comment a lot about, "How come we have to go to church? None of my other friends do. Why are we the only ones?" Which we're not.

Interviewer: And how do you respond to that when Shane asks that question? What do you say?

Charlotte: What do I say? "Because that's what we do. We're going to church and you'll be better off for it. So get out of bed and get in the car."

Conversation Is Too Restrictive

Some families reported that when religious conversation was too restrictive for the adolescent children, it was a negative experience. Rachel, a 38-year-old Hasidic Jewish mother of seven, learned that, "If [they] have to sit rigidly—the children of all ages, and . . . you have this long lecture, it can actually be a very negative influence. . . . The kids will feel restricted."

Having overviewed our research findings on parent-centered conversations and four of their limiting features, we now turn to **youth-centered conversations.**

Youth-Centered Conversations

Youth-centered conversations manifested the following characteristics: (a) adolescent talks more and parents listen, (b) adolescent seeks and receives understanding from parents, (c) religion is related to adolescent's life, (d) conversation is open, and (e) parent-adolescent relationship is nurtured.

Adolescent Talks More and Parents Listen

Kira, a Lutheran mother, responded why she thought it best to use fewer words: "I've learned that less words are better because sometimes if you just plant the seed, their mind will work on it." Brent, a Jehovah's Witness father, suggested that by letting his adolescent children express themselves, he could better understand them: "And also [I try] understanding what their thinking patterns are, and what they're going through. And allowing them to communicate that."

Adolescent Seeks and Receives Understanding from Parents

Mandy, a 15-year-old Christian and Missionary Alliance youth, commented about her parents' readiness to answer her questions: "They're always willing to talk to me about any questions I had. And they explained what they believed to me." Kelsey, a 13-year-old Orthodox Christian, commented, "Sometimes my parents don't know the answer so then it's kind of a discussion because they don't have the answer to give me." Another way that parents tried to help their children understand their religious views was by reasoning on the child's level. Yuusif, an East Indian Muslim father, said that one element of religious conversations is "explaining to them [my children] in a way they can understand . . . and reason[ing] with them."

Religion Is Related to Adolescent's Life

Parents and adolescents recognized the importance of having religious conversations that link faith beliefs with the adolescent's life. Scott, a 14-year-old Catholic, spoke of his parents: "I just feel like they always try to bring religion into our lives and (try) to make us better." Shawn, a Baptist father, said the following when speaking of family devotions: "There's always the challenge of, 'Okay, let's really make this relevant,' or helping them see the usefulness."

Conversation Is Open

There were many families who spoke about how they valued openness in their religious conversations, which allowed everyone to speak their minds. Alecia, a 20-year-old Latter-day Saint, gave an adolescent perspective when she said she enjoyed casual conversation where she could talk:

> If it's a one-on-one conversation, it's usually pretty interesting. It's interactive. I enjoy talking about religion. . . . Most of the time when we're just talking as friends more than anything like on a casual basis, it's usually pretty cool. . . . I'll say something to [my mom] about religion and she'll be like, "Yeah, that's awesome. I have a story that goes with whatever you were talking about." And I'm like, "Oh that's really cool." And we can talk about it casually and not have to worry.

Aisha, a 46-year-old African-American Muslim mother of 11, said:

> We talk a lot. We have very in-depth conversations because you can see they're very verbal. They have their opinions. And we've always told them that you can always say what you need to say, but just say it with

> the right tone. You know, so they're allowed to express themselves, even if they disagree with us. We don't have a problem with that, it's just how you say it.

Parent-Child Relationship Is Nurtured

Yuusif, an Arab-American Muslim father, spoke of the need to be "constantly alert with them and close to them in understanding what they're going through." Amy, a 45-year-old Baptist mother of two, expressed her efforts to compliment her children and to be a good friend to them. She explained:

> Trying to encourage them and to just let them know how much I respect and admire them and appreciate them as people and who they are and how proud I am of them [is important]. . . . I still play with my kids; and I'm very affectionate and I hug them. And even though I'm their mother, I'm also their friend.

Jack, an 18-year-old Baptist, told how his friends' parents neglected the parent-child relationship while still trying to transmit beliefs:

> I've seen some of my friends . . . where parents are slamming Bible verses in their face, and really not loving them, not helping them grow. It's more like a forceful thing, at unnecessary times, when it really would have been helpful just for them to sit down and talk with their kid.

Both parents and youth reported that youth-centered conversations fostered adolescent interest and engagement in the conversations. Parents—including the more "traditional" ones—also seemed to enjoy and value more youth-centered conversations since it was apparent to them that their children were more likely to feel better about their parents and their faith during and after these kinds of conversations. In summary, the core finding of this in-depth qualitative study was: *When parent-adolescent religious conversations are youth centered, the emotional experience is more positive for parents and adolescents than when they are parent centered.* This research suggests that parents who desire to see their adolescent children more willingly, happily, and frequently engage with them on matters of faith would be well-advised to adopt a conversational style that focuses on the needs, interests, questions, and perceived time constraints their kids bring to the conversational table.

When Parents Are Not What They Should Be

In this section we share some examples of less-than-ideal parenting in a context of religion. Based on their findings from a 35-year longitudinal study with more than 3,000 participants, sociologist Vern Bengtson and colleagues offered this conclusion:

> Throughout [our] book[-length study] we can see how a distant or non-affirming parent-child relationship—particularly with a father—is often mentioned in our interview as a catalyst for conversion to another faith or dropping out of religion altogether.
>
> (Bengtson et al., 2013, pp. 78–79)

Previously in this chapter, we shared research and data that demonstrated the profound influence of an exemplary parent who "walks the walk" and "talks (and listens to) the talk." We now pause for a very different perspective. We present a unique counter-narrative shared with us by a student and friend, a 22-year-old African-American woman.[4]

"Daddy, Where Are You?"

I was born . . . to two people who were never supposed to be together. I was never supposed to be born, and I say this because my dad was married [to another woman] at the time that he got my mom pregnant. My mom says [she didn't know he was married], he was there every day with her so she really couldn't imagine that he [was] married and had so much time to spend with her. Due to the circumstances, I was the last thing that he wanted, for sure. I am living, breathing proof of his infidelity. [It] is really crappy to come into the world under such circumstances, but needless to say, I'm here. . . . [Even worse] is the fact that I didn't find this out until my senior year of high school.

The story [I was told] was that my dad was an attorney . . . but hold on, the lie gets better. At the time of my birth, he "felt" it; he felt the moment I came into the world. This was the story that I grew up believing. I remember having him call me from time to time. From hearing his voice, I always imagined that he'd look like Michael Jackson because his voice was really soft. I didn't have a face to match that voice until about 7 years old when I met him for the first time. He started coming around and buying me lots and lots of things, then he'd disappear again and I wouldn't hear from him. It [has] stayed like that, even now. One [rare] day we were together and he asked me what I wanted to be when I grew up. I said, "A lawyer, just like you," and he looked at me crazy. Now I know why, he was never a lawyer, [he was] a finance manager at a car dealership.

There would be times when he'd promise me things and never deliver, or he'd tell me he was going to come see me and I'd sit for hours and hours and he wouldn't show or call. Some people say you can't miss what you never had, but I had it, then I lost him, then I had him, then I lost him, then I had him, then lost him again. It was a never-ending cycle. That really hurt me, but what hurt me the most was the fact that he has other children: two with his wife, and another [one] with another woman, and the relationship [he has with them] is so close and everything that I always wanted. They have memories they can talk about, they have the closeness. Whenever I was alone with my dad I felt awkward most times, as if I was with a stranger. It hurt me to see how he was with [his other children], knowing that I didn't have that. For the longest [time], I battled myself, "What is wrong with me?" "Why am I not enough?" These are things that I battle still.

There was a time where I really thought I had him. My senior year of high school, everything [about the real story] came out. I was having a really rough time living with my mom. She built a brand new house . . . [but] I was never treated the same as my other siblings. I felt like I didn't have family other than my grandparents. I finally broke [down and poured my heart out] to my dad, thinking that he could finally be the hero that I needed him to be and save me. I told him everything that had been going on, how my step dad . . . hit me, everything. It angered him, but not once did he say that I could come live with him. I was heartbroken by the man that was supposed to dust off my knees and help heal [my] broken heart.

From then [on], I was just done with it and with him. Since then I have tried to reach out, but a relationship only exists when I reach out. I'm constantly seeing pictures of [him] and his family and things they're doing together, and I'm here with almost no family. It still hurts, but I push forward. Get this, [now] my dad is a *Pastor.*

How have I responded? I thank God every single day for blessing me in all the ways that he has and opening all the doors that he has, and continues to open for me. My grandparents are the most amazing thing that could've happened to me, because without them [stepping in and] raising me up in the way in which they did, I wouldn't have made it. I'm so happy I have the opportunity to [improve and to] be better and do better. I . . . [promise] on everything that means anything to me that I *will* be an AMAZING mom and marry an AMAZING . . . guy so that my children will never have to feel anything that I've felt. This is *so* important to me . . .

I want other young people to know . . . I have incredibly strong faith in God because although there are things in my life that are awry, I can look around me and see things that are so beautiful. Whether it be my grandparents who love me unconditionally, my professors that believe in me, or just where my life is headed and all of the things that I am blessed to have; it all reassures me that there is a God. This God has never once let me down and has remained the constant in my life when all else has wavered. There are people that have been through what I have or even worse, and some aren't fortunate to make it through, but I have. God took my life in his hands and he's molding it and making me into who He wants me to be and I couldn't be happier to oblige, for I know with God at the forefront, I will always be protected. [My constant prayer is]: "My life is not my own, to You I belong, I give myself to You."

—author's name withheld

We are grateful for the willingness of this remarkable young woman to share her story, first with us, and now with you. We appreciate her invitation to each of us to step onto her personal sacred ground, and we are grateful for her friendship and example. Her life experience illustrates that there are often complex connections between faith and family life that are not easily or fully explained without in-depth information shared by those who have lived their faith out over several years. Her experience also demonstrates in living color that, for some people, struggles and challenges in one area—faith or family life—are addressed by strengths in the other area.

Several research studies indicate that, for most young adults, "parents have been the primary influence on their religious development" and that their relationships with their parents (whether positive or negative) tend to be "linked to their first conceptions of God" (Bengtson et al., 2013, p. 71; see also Smith & Denton, 2005). These studies, and others, verify a measure of truth in Robert Ingersoll's statement that "it is difficult for a child to find a father in God, unless the child first finds something of God in his father." Even so, our friend's recollections in "Daddy, Where Are You?" show that there are notable exceptions that warrant our attention. Some participants in our *American Families of Faith* project mentioned hypocritical or even faith-damaging patterns of behavior in their parents. Our aim in the project was not to go digging in the dirt to ask for specifics about parental failures, but we were eager to learn about the paths of highly religiously involved individuals who had built strong marriages and families without having the advantage of positive parental models during their formative years. In the next section we get a brief view of a few such persons. Like the author of "Daddy, Where Are You?" these individuals may have lacked ideal models in their own parents, but they found influential and powerfully positive models in other persons, including grandparents and parents of peer-aged friends.

The Congruent Example and Faith Walk of Non-Parents

While parents are often a powerful force in their children's faith development, in some instances the congruent example of a *non*-parent can be salient enough to encourage and promote faith. A Jewish father named Seth repeatedly mentioned his grandfather as a powerful influence in his own faith life, although Seth's parents were reportedly less faith oriented. Seth recalled:

> I have seen people who, from the outward appearance, seem to center on their religion. They say the right things but then you look at their lives and you say, "These are not spiritual people, they're not living everyday what they're saying." They may read the Bible three times a day but in their relationships with their kids and their family you don't see God-like behavior.

Seth mentioned that his own parents fit his description of "hypocritical" and that they seemed to be focused on appearances instead of on relationships. Seth, however, had an alternative example that convinced him that religion and faith could be authentic. In the face of the hypocrisies that he observed in his parents and some of their synagogue members, Seth emphasized with conviction:

> But then I look at someone like my grandfather, he never changed. . . . Some people go to synagogue and act holy and then go home and revert to their own lives. But . . . my grandfather never put on a front for anyone, he didn't *act* spiritual in synagogue, he *was* spiritual.

Seth spoke of his grandfather's behavior-belief congruence and conviction with profound admiration. Seth said that he had not reached his grandfather's level in his faith development but explained with emotion that his grandfather's example remained impressed upon his mind and heart long after his grandfather's passing (Marks, 2004).

Shana, a Latina Christian mother of five, received no faith training from her parents, who had an array of significant problems, but she was deeply influenced by her neighbors' example during her childhood.

> My neighbors from the age of six all the way up until I was ten, they were born-again Christians. Even though that's not the [denomination] I'm in now, it's a little bit similar to it. Anyway, I felt different when I walked in their home. They were really humble people, they always wanted to help people. They prayed as a family together. They read the Bible together, they were never out of place with anything. It was different from anything I'd ever seen. [There was] peace, as soon as I'd walk into their home I'd just feel at ease.

Shana indicated that she now prays with her children like her neighbors did more than 30 years ago. She commented on the benefits she perceives from this family practice.

> [Family prayer] feels right. It feels good. It feels like this is what every family should be doing. I'm grateful to . . . be able to do that. If my family that I grew up with ever would have done that . . . it would have been a fond memory that I would have held, but we never did. [Our family now] should pray more, but when we kneel together and hold hands as a family, it brings a spirit of love into [our home] and makes the children feel right and lets them know that this is what is right and that this is what they need to do with their families and I'm sure they'll remember it.

It is likely that Shana's children *will* remember this ritual and the relational and emotional connections associated with it. Based on a review of the religious transmission literature, children with two parents who actively worship together are most likely to remain involved in faith themselves (Bengtson et al., 2013; Smith & Denton, 2005). However, as seen in Seth's and Shana's narratives, a congruent role model does not have to be a parent to have a significant faith-related influence on a person's life.

Conclusion

In chapter 6, we reviewed many statistically based research articles by a variety of social scientists to create an outline of what we know about how religion seems to influence parent-child relationships. In the present chapter, we have presented a more in-depth and personal view of the hows, whys, and processes at work behind this connection. Instead of focusing primarily on quantitative research findings, we focused on stories behind the research. We heard several details regarding sociologist Vern Bengtson's personal return to faith, and we heard about the profound sacrifices made by the missionary parents of religious scholar Huston Smith. We were presented with a detailed life narrative from a 22-year-old woman who has witnessed and personally experienced piercing parental hypocrisy with respect to faith and fidelity—but who also has developed a profound and personal relationship with her Creator. We have heard from *American Families of Faith* participants who enjoyed the benefits of loving and faithful parents and from some who did not.

We learned that the most powerful religious practice in which parents can engage is not necessarily prayer, or Bible study, or church attendance. Across faith, race, gender, geographic region, or context, the most powerful and influential religious practice appears to be walking a congruent faith walk—or, phrased differently, "practicing what you preach." Indeed, we see Wes Burr et al.'s (2012) assertion confirmed and corroborated—the assertion that what matters most is not merely what is believed, but how those beliefs are *lived out* in family life. Even so, in-depth qualitative research from our project indicates that "talking the talk" is also influential and vital, especially when the conversations are youth centered.

In our classes on family, we ask students to frequently write, reflect, and process their experiences in order to promote growth and self-awareness. One student's extraordinarily positive written reflections on her family across three years of classes together led me (Loren) to contact her parents, who were Catholic, to offer my thanks to them for their example to me as a fellow parent—and to thank them for sharing their daughter with me. With permission, we offer the following excerpt from this mother's return letter, which seems to embody some of the best of what we have been trying to convey to you as an emerging adult and potential parent. Speaking of her husband of nearly 30 years and their four daughters, this mother summarized:

> I never knew how much I would love being a mother. Someone once told me that whatever you didn't like about your childhood you would have the opportunity to change with your own children. It has been so true. I kept the parts that I loved about my childhood and did things with my children that I wish I would have had when I was a child. . . . God had a plan.

We have not encountered any perfect marriages or families during our 15-year journey to study and explore strong families of faith. We have met many, however, like the family just mentioned, that are doing well enough to inspire us and offer hope that it *can* be done. As researchers and parents, we are profoundly and personally grateful to these families. Indeed, in spite of the pain and challenges discussed by the 200 families of faith that we interviewed, many of them (like the mother just mentioned) seemed to believe that with respect to the children they brought into the world and nurtured—"God had a plan."

Chapter Summary Points

1. Research from several sources indicates that parents are a primary factor in their children's religious and spiritual lives and that this influence remains into adulthood.
2. Although it is probable that a child will stay in his or her parent's religious denomination, almost half do not remain affiliated with their parents' faith. A strong predictor is whether a close relationship existed between the parents and child.
3. Research and conceptual work both indicate that the charge to "practice what you preach" is an important and powerful call for religious parents to remember and live. In addition, it is important for religious parents to learn how to talk about religious matters with their children—especially teenaged and young adult children—in ways that promote strong families and strong faith.
4. Research on "God images" shows that children's perceptions of God are moderated by perceptions of parents, including fathers and mothers.
5. While some children do not have parents who live what they profess to believe, research indicates that non-parents can be a profound and positive influence in some cases.

Review Questions

1. What are the differences between the stories of King Solomon and Vern Bengtson?
2. According to the text, what appears to be the single most important social influence on the religious and spiritual lives of adolescents?
3. What percentage of American teens are considered as "The Devoted"? What has research found regarding the quality of their relationships with their parents compared to other American teenagers?
4. What percentage of Americans report they have changed or dropped the religious affiliation of their childhood?

5. Explain behavior-belief congruence, and give an example of how this might apply in a real-life situation.
6. Read the story "Daddy, Where Are You?" What most stood out to you from this young woman's experience?

Notes

1. Portions of this chapter are adapted or drawn from D. C. Dollahite & J. Y. Thatcher (2008), Talking about religion: How religious youth and parents discuss their faith, *Journal of Adolescent Research, 23*, 611–641.
2. In our estimation, this is one of the finest and most rigorous studies on religion and family to date. The study's featured strengths include its (rare) longitudinal design and its inclusion of three (or even four) generations.
3. This section draws on and is adapted from the results section of Dollahite & Thatcher (2008). For more on the topic of youth-centered religious conversations, see Dollahite & Thatcher (2007, 2008), Flor & Knapp (2001), and Smith & Denton (2005).
4. This narrative is not from the *American Families of Faith* interviews, but is used with written permission of the author with the promise that anonymity be maintained.

References

Alghafli, Z., Hatch, T., & Marks, L. (2014c). Sharia law. In L. Ganong, M. Coleman, & J. G. Golson (Eds.), *The social history of the American family* (pp. 1175–1177). Thousand Oaks, CA: Sage.

Bengtson, V. L., Putney, N. M., & Harris, J. (2013). *Families of faith*. New York: Oxford.

Burr, W. R., Marks, L. D., & Day, R. (2012). *Sacred matters: Religion and spirituality in families*. New York: Routledge.

Dollahite, D. C. (1998). Fathering, faith, and spirituality. *The Journal of Men's Studies, 7*, 3–16.

Dollahite, D. C., & Marks, L. D. (2005). How highly religious families strive to fulfill sacred purposes. In V. Bengtson, A. Acock, K. Allen, P. Dillworth-Anderson, & D. Klein (Eds.), *Sourcebook of family theory and research* (pp. 533–541). Thousand Oaks, CA: Sage.

Dollahite, D. C., & Marks, L. D. (2009). A conceptual model of family and religious processes in a diverse, national sample of highly religious families. *Review of Religious Research, 50*, 373–391.

Dollahite, D. C., & Thatcher, J. Y. (2007). How family religious involvement benefits adults, youth, and children and strengthens families. In L. D. Wardle, & C. S. Williams (Eds.), *Family law: Balancing interests and pursuing priorities* (pp. 427–436). Buffalo, NY: W. S. Hein & Company.

Dollahite, D. C., & Thatcher, J. Y. (2008). Talking about religion: How religious youth and parents discuss their faith. *Journal of Adolescent Research, 23*, 611–641.

Flor, D. L., & Knapp, N. F. (2001). Transmission and transaction: Predicting adolescents' internalization of parental religious values. *Journal of Family Psychology, 15*, 627–645.

Hertel, B. R., & Donahue, M. J. (1995). Parental influences on god images among children: Testing Durkheim's metaphoric parallelism. *The Journal for the Scientific Study of Religion, 34*, 186–199.

Marks, L. D. (2004). Sacred practices in highly religious families: Christian, Jewish, Mormon, and Muslim perspectives. *Family Process, 43*, 217–231.

Marks, L. D., & Dollahite, D. C. (2012). Don't forget home: The importance of sacred ritual in families. In J. Hoffman (Ed.), *Understanding religious rituals* (pp. 186–203). New York: Routledge.

Myers, S. M. (1996). An interactive model of religiosity inheritance: The importance of family context. *American Sociological Review, 61*, 858–866.

Povish, K. J. (2003). *The peace I leave with you*. Lansing, MI: Xulon Press.

Putnam, R. D., & Campbell, D. E. (2010). *American grace: How religion divides and unites us*. New York: Simon & Schuster.

Smith, C., & Denton, M. L. (2005). *Soul searching: The religious and spiritual lives of American teenagers*. New York: Oxford.

Smith, C., & Snell, P. (2009). *Souls in transition: The religious and spiritual lives of emerging adults*. New York: Oxford.

Smith, H. (2003). *Why religion matters*. San Francisco, CA: Harper San Francisco.

Vergote, A. (1980). Religion after the critique of psychoanalysis. *The Annual Review of the Social Sciences of Religion, 4*, 1–29.

Muslim Families in the United States

8

In 2004, we drew attention to the fact that almost all of the social science research on religion and families examined Christian families—and only Christian families (Dollahite, Marks, & Goodman, 2004). Specifically, we noted a "conspicuous" absence of research on both Muslim and Jewish families (p. 422). We have made a pronounced effort to include both Muslim families and Jewish families in the *American Families of Faith* project, and virtually all of our work includes both along with Christian families from various denominations. Some of our recent work has focused solely on Muslim families or Jewish families (e.g., Alghafli, Hatch, & March, 2014a, 2014b, 2014c; Hatch & Marks, 2014a, 2014b, 2014c; Marks, Hatch, & Dollahite, unpublished manuscript). In the next two chapters, with *American Families of Faith* project members Trevan Hatch[1] (who holds a graduate degree in Jewish Studies) and Zahra Alghafli (a practicing Muslim from Saudi Arabia who has researched and published several recent works on Muslim families), we take a closer look at Muslim (chapter 8) and Jewish families (chapter 9).

When students, friends, or family ask us what we research, and we include Muslim and Jewish families in the response, they often say something like, "Wow, that's so interesting!" Similarly, when we are in the presence of a group of scholars, it is not uncommon for many in the group to want to discuss our research on Muslim and Jewish families—and what we are finding and publishing.

What makes Muslims (and Islam) and Jews (and Judaism) of such interest to so many people? What can we learn about how religion influences family life from these two religions? Further, what can we learn from Muslims and Jews about what it is like to be a religious minority family in the United States?

In the next two chapters, we will highlight multiple aspects of Islam and Judaism that may answer some of these questions. Specifically, we will briefly examine, for both Muslim and Jewish families, two of the three dimensions of religion (as defined in chapter 2): *religious practices* and *religious community*.[2]

Before continuing, we will briefly address the question: Why, of all the religions in the world, do we choose to focus only on Muslim and Jewish families? First, most of the research we have cited throughout this book is based on samples of Christian families in the United States. Therefore, much of what you have learned in the previous chapters of this book (with the exception of our AFF data) has been drawn from studies of Christians. Thus we feel a need to devote chapters to the two other "Abrahamic faiths" that constitute the great majority of American families of faith.

But why focus only on the Abrahamic faiths and not on other religions? Regarding what are often called the "Eastern religions" (Buddhism, Hinduism, Jainism, Sikhism, etc.), very little empirical research has been conducted on the religious experience of these families. In addition, the Eastern religious traditions are less familiar to most Western students, and, therefore, much more space would be required in this book to adequately address these traditions. Judaism and Islam, on the other hand, are typically more familiar to many Western readers, perhaps because these religions are featured in the media more often and also share some roots with Christianity (Agius & Chircop, 1998). In fact, Judaism and Islam, along with Christianity, are often grouped and labeled together as "Abrahamic religions" because they trace their heritage back to the ancient patriarch Abraham. As readers attempting to learn more about how religion impacts families, it is vital for us to explore Jewish and Muslim populations because they are important and influential religious minorities in the United States.

The rich context of religious minority families offers the chance to highlight issues like identity formation in youth and emerging adults, the importance of social support from their religious community, and the unique challenges religious minorities face as they strive to live their religion. In this chapter we feature Islam and the 25 Muslim families from the *American Families of Faith* project.

What Is Islam? Who Is a Muslim?

The words "Muslim" and "Islam" come from the same root (*slm*), meaning "peace" or "submission." Islam is the name of the religion, and a Muslim (literally meaning "one who submits") is an adherent of that religion.

Islam is the religion of over one billion people worldwide, roughly 20% of the world's population. Islam was founded by the Prophet **Muhammad** in the seventh century CE. Muhammad was born in Mecca, the home of the Káaba sanctuary of over 350 idols. Beginning at age 40, Muhammad reported that he had received several revelations from the heavenly messenger Gabriel that were later transcribed and combined in one volume known as the **Qu'ran (Koran)**.

The death of Muhammad fractured the Muslim community. One segment maintained that Muhammad's son-in-law, Ali bin Abi Taleb, should lead the **Umma** ("Muslim community"). Ali's followers were known as *Shi'at Ali*, or the "Party of Ali," more commonly referred to today as Shi'ites or **Shia Muslims**. The other major segment argued that the Umma should choose the next leader, as Muhammad did not specifically identify his successor before his death. This group selected Abu Bakr, Muhammad's father-in-law, as the next leader, and are commonly known as **Sunni Muslims** or Sunnis (meaning a clear path or right way of practice). Today, roughly 80%–85% of Muslims worldwide follow Sunni Islam. Within 300 years of Muhammad's death, Islam had spread from Arabia to China and India in the East to Spain and Portugal in the West and from Morocco to southern Africa.

Muslims in the United States and Muslim U.S. Demographics

Historians are unsure about the location of the first mosque in the United States (Howell, 2007) let alone when the first Muslims immigrated to the United States. It is likely that African Muslims, brought to America during the slave trade, represented the first sizable group of Muslims in America. Some have estimated that up to 15% of African slaves brought to the U.S. were Muslim (Diouf, 2013). The most recent study on American Muslims (Pew, 2016) estimated that 3.3 million Muslims live in the United States—about 1% of the total population. Some have projected this figure to double within three decades. Only about 10% of the U.S. Muslim population are legal immigrants, and roughly 20% of adult Muslims in the United States are converts (Pew, 2016). According to one source, 75% of converts to Islam in the United States in the five years following September 11, 2001, were women (Haddad, Smith, & Moore, 2006). Another study of Muslims in 39 countries revealed that a majority of self-identified Muslims are deeply devoted to the beliefs and practices of Islam (Pew, 2013). Of course, as among all faiths, there is a range of degree of religious adherence among Muslims.

We now turn attention to various aspects of Muslim family life that illustrate ways religion impacts Muslim individuals and families in the United States. Specifically we will review: (1) some of the challenges that Muslims face as a religious minority in the United States; (2) the impact of the religious community and social support for Muslim families; and (3) a few important aspects of religious observance in the home.

Challenges of Being a Religious Minority: Muslim Perspectives

In the years since 9/11 and the subsequent War on Terror, Islam and the Muslim population have been front and center in Western media. The three issues involving Muslims and/or the Middle East that seem to garner the most attention in the media are terrorist groups, the Arab-Israeli conflict, and the treatment of women. All three issues are highly charged with emotion and are often represented in sensationalized ways. In other words, most of what Americans hear in the media about Islam is negative and may or may not be representative of Islam or the majority of Muslims. Those in the popular media rarely discuss Islamic theology or Islamic religious practices in the home as practiced by most Muslim families. The focus tends to be on violent and extremist groups that are not representative of the majority. As a result of both 9/11 and subsequent media coverage, hate crimes against Muslims reportedly increased by 1600% (from pre-9/11 levels) in both Canada and the United States (Canadian Islamic Congress, 2002; Cheng, Ickes, & Kenworthy, 2013).

The Muslim Practice of *Hijab*

Two of the most commonly discussed topics on Islam in the media are violence and the treatment of women. Concerning the latter, the female head covering, called **hijab**, receives significant media (and scholarly) attention. Typically ignored is that Muslim men are also enjoined to cover their heads during worship and the fact that the practice of covering the head or hair for women and/or men when in public or at worship is practiced by millions of people in other faiths as well (e.g., Orthodox Judaism, Orthodox Christianity, Sikhism).

In connection with *hijab*, it is a common practice in Islam for Muslim women to cover their hair in public or in the presence of men who are not part of their family—although individual and cultural adherence and expression vary widely. In Islam, the principle of *hijab* is a system of modest dress implemented, ideally, to protect humanity against illicit sexual interaction between men and women who are not married. *Hijab* means "curtain" and usually refers to the head covering, although the extension of *hijab* might include a full body covering and a veil (*niqab*) that completely covers the face. The broader principle of *hijab* is widely applied in Islam as a head covering, even though none of the seven references to *hijab* in the Qur'an concern head coverings or women's dress, but rather a general separation of the sexes (White & Mir, 2007). Due to the ambiguous nature of the scriptural passages regarding female dress, some Muslim feminist commentators have suggested that *hijab* and other similar traditions must be reinterpreted for modern times.

Given both media-related and academic attention to the principle and/or practice of *hijab*, and the highly visible expression of the practice, it is not surprising, then, that several participants in the *American Families of Faith* project discussed *hijab*—and many did so at length and in depth. While most Muslim AFF participants (female and male) spoke positively about *hijab*, a few implied challenges were identified. Many participants went beyond the physical manifestations of *hijab*, like veiling and covering, to discuss what they saw as the underlying and foundational principles, including modesty and appropriate barriers and distance between the sexes. The following excerpts are illustrative. As Tamara, a Shia wife and mother, explained:

> In my opinion, *hijab* is not just about clothes. . . . It is a whole institution of separation [between men and women] that was made by the creator of everything. . . . God has set certain standards. According to my religious belief . . . one of the things is modesty at a level where you have to totally ignore the other gender. . . . That is a sacrifice, especially when you are a teenager.

Jane, a Sunni wife and mother who was also an adult convert to Islam, similarly reported:

> I cover my head. Why do I cover my head? Because in our religion, I do not want men to flirt with me. Let's face it, if I were standing next to a woman in a bikini, men would lust over her and not over me. I don't want men to lust over me, whether I'm married or not. One of the ways to prevent that is to cover up . . . I don't call this a sacrifice. Think about all the women who spend hours and hours doing their hair, I

> don't have [to do] that . . . I used to have to get up at the crack of dawn to style. [Now] I can get up and wash it, dry it, braid it, and go. I don't have that pressure or the pressure of wearing fad clothes. I don't think it's a sacrifice in any way. I think I gained beyond my wildest dreams . . . I feel that in Islam, *I have more rights than I did before.*

Ali, a Shia husband and father, referenced past discussions he and his wife had regarding *hijab* and said:

> Something we [as a couple] have grown to agree about [is] there has to be a gender separation in the sense that she would not communicate . . . much across gender and [that] she would [dress] conservatively. That keeps the woman away from a strange man and by covering half of her face or more. What this does is block identity, because if you have many people who dress that [modest] way, the woman is not going to be talked about. So if they dress that way there is a barrier and I think that is what *hijab* is in Islam.

Notice the language used in these quotes regarding the justification of *hijab*: gender "separation," "blocking identity" of women, placing "barriers" between genders, "modesty at a level where you have to totally ignore the other gender." This type of language was mentioned in a positive context with affirming undertones by practicing Muslims, both men and women. The laws concerning the separation of sexes implemented in Islam to guard against illicit sexual practices were portrayed and viewed as noble among the Muslims we interviewed.

Many non-Muslim Americans, however, may perceive the justifications and practices associated with *hijab* as sexist, primitive, and a stumbling block for women rather than a stepping stone to a higher functioning society. This is where the challenge arises for Muslims in many Western countries. It may not be the *hijab* in and of itself that is the challenge, but rather (1) the perception of *hijab* that perpetuates the media narrative that Muslim women are mistreated and that they have minimal or no individualized identity because they must cover up to avoid inciting sexual thoughts in men; and (2) the separation of the sexes in American society is extremely difficult in a practical sense, as mentioned by one Muslim: "As a Muslim, we don't shake hands with the opposite sex, so that sometimes creates problems. When you meet someone for the first time . . . that sometimes creates a problem."

Another Muslim husband, Mohammad, explained that his wife, Alya, an American convert to Islam, experiences frequent persecution because of *hijab*:

> Some of the people who are ignorant in American society view [her] as almost like a traitor to her own country [the U.S.]. You know, people get really irritated with her. They just see her and they just start shouting out kind of hate speech because they see that she is a white lady wearing a scarf. It is something I do not have to endure because when I go out, nobody knows that I am a Muslim. Nobody cares, but when they see her, it hurts big time for me that she has to go through this sometimes.

Speaking generally, whether a given individual, Muslim or non-Muslim, female or male, is supportive of *hijab* or opposed to the practice, the *American Families of Faith* interview data reveal an important issue relating to *hijab*. Namely, the practice is negotiated and discussed by marital partners and has relational implications—both positive and painful. It seems that *hijab* carries with it both identity and ostracism. We now move from the personal (and relational) issue of *hijab* to a discussion of the Muslim religious community.

Muslim Religious Community

Social support from the local religious community can be important for an array of families, but it may be particularly vital for the social well-being of religious minorities, both as individuals and as families. We will not revisit previously reviewed research again here; however, the following quotes from AFF participants provide us more to think about. Further, because most available data are drawn from white, Christian samples, we have the relatively novel opportunity to learn more about how the faith community serves Muslim (and diverse but predominantly non-white) families. Ahsan, a Middle Eastern immigrant and Muslim husband, discussed the personal and familial importance of his mosque:

> Not being from here, I don't have any immediate family around us, and most of us [at my mosque] are like that. So all these, as you would call it, your congregation, is sort of like your extended family. So, yes, it does affect your family, in that you have your children to bring too, and they would intermingle with other children that ARE like them.

A Middle Eastern wife and mother, Asheka, similarly said of her mosque:

> [My religious congregation] is important because when I take my son to the congregation and he sees other people who have the same religious beliefs, it [helps] him to grow in an Islamic religious community.

> So, especially for the kids it's really important to go to the religious congregation and especially it's more important in this society because we can only meet other people of my religion when I go in the religious congregation. . . . It's also (especially) important for me and other women because they don't go outside so much, but when they go to the congregation they can learn from other people and they can have some socialization and [this] helps build their mind . . .

Another Muslim wife and mother, a white U.S.-born convert to Islam, explained:

Alya: [Our religious] community is good for the kids. [It helps them] to be able to see other kids who are Muslims. They do not have a lot of interactions at school. They do not see a lot of Muslims at school. So, it is good when our oldest daughter can see other girls with *hijab* on and she feels more normal. She sees other people like her.

Mohammad, husband of Alya, reflected:

> Whe[re] I grew up, there were a lot of Muslims. Lots of what I learned was through that interaction. So, thank God, it happens in this community that at least we can get some of it. Without the community, I think we would be lost completely because it is very hard because [Alya] comes from a culture that had no Islam in it. I came from a culture that split half-and-half; [there was half of the] culture that had Islam in it. So really, the community helps. Without the community we really would be struggling. [Actually], I think we are struggling now, without the community we would be drowning. That is one thing we look at—you know, maybe one day down the road we [will] move somewhere where the [Muslim] community is bigger. I mean, there might be an Islamic school that [is] well enough [established] for the children to go to. That is something we look at and talk about.

In the preceding interview data excerpts, we have heard mothers and fathers repeatedly reference the religiously specific social support that Muslim faith communities offer to their children, and this theme recurred often in the data. However, some participants also talked about personal, qualitative, and social benefits that they received as adults. Omar, a Sunni Muslim originally from Jordan and a father of two, said:

> When you go to pray at the mosque, [for men] it is obligatory to go to the mosque. Everyone is equal at the mosque, you can stand wherever you want. The poor person is standing next to the rich man . . . the sick

> is standing next to the healthy, the white is standing next to the black. There is an equality. From a societal standpoint, that brings the society together. No one is better than another, except by his good deeds. . . . Everyone stands in line. Before prayer, the prayer leader tells you to close the gaps (so your shoulders are touching your neighbor) . . . and then we pray together. . . . This brings a society together.

Omar's wife, Angie, one of a few white, U.S.-born, adult converts to Islam in the AFF sample, went on to explain:

> We dress humbly [in the mosque] so that we don't make poor people feel bad. That way you don't know whether you are standing next to a doctor or a poor man. You can't tell. Where I used to go to church, you wore your very best (and I was guilty of this) and then [when someone is dressed poorly] you think, "Oh, what are they doing here?"

In this section on Muslim faith community we first documented the child-centered benefits reported by parents. We then moved to personal and social influences of the mosque on the perceptions, attitudes, and thinking of the parents themselves—as the latter few excerpts illustrate. In the next section, we move from the mosque to the home as we examine family-based religious observance in Islam.

Muslim Religious Observance in the Home

We have written elsewhere, in connection with family and home-based religious rituals and observances:

> The small body of research that examines religious, family-level ritual has yielded some interesting findings—namely, that shared religious activities may contribute to intimacy and commitment in marriage and that family religious activities "also represent a potentially unique pathway to facilitate family cohesion" (Mahoney et al., 2001, p. 590). . . . [Even though we know relatively little about the whys and hows of family-level religious rituals] family ritual (especially religious family ritual) seems a promising phenomenon for social researchers to examine.
>
> (Marks & Dollahite, 2012, pp. 187, 186)

Our interviews with Muslim families have delivered some valuable insights on the phenomenon of religious family (and individual-level) rituals. Based on *American Families of Faith* data, two of the most salient rituals or religious observances in the Muslim home are: (1) daily prayer (**salat**) and (2) fasting during the holy month of **Ramadan**.

Prayer (salat)

We turn first to prayer or *salat*. Omar, an Arab-American Muslim father, explained, "Prayer in Arabic is called *salat*. . . . [*Salat*] means connection, it is your time to connect with God" (Marks & Dollahite, 2012, p. 198). Another Muslim husband, Tal, said:

> There [have] been times when [I] was mad and I had to go and pray to calm down. When you pray, you have to center yourself and you have to submit to Allah and you can't be angry and submit—it just does not work. So yes, prayer can help, definitely. You will become more rational [and] reasonable.

From Tal's reflection, we see that even apparently individual-level rituals like personal prayer can have family-level and relational implications. Another Muslim husband explained the influence of family prayer:

> When you pray you have to center yourself and . . . submit to Allah. You can't be angry and submit. It just does not work. . . . Especially after prayer . . . the whole house [will settle] down. There is no TV, there is no internet, there is nothing, and there is pureness of communications there and it comes straight from the heart. You know, you just can't get that any other way . . . especially [the] close[ness] with the children.

Ashekah, a Muslim mother and wife, also took time to discuss and explain the familial nature of prayer in her home.

> [Prayer] is something we do as a family. You are worshiping as a family and it gives everybody time to stop and *interact with each other* afterwards. And you know, you're teaching your children something that is good. You are worshiping God and that, to me, is heartwarming because we are all there . . . So to me, it's good. It seems like a *family time*.

One unique element of Muslim belief related to the practice of prayer that recurred in the AFF interviews is that united prayer, as a marital couple or as a family, was reported to be superior to personal prayer. This belief was referenced and explained by two Muslim husbands:

Orhan (Sunni husband): We believe that "together-prayer" has more rewards than just praying individually. So, this is one thing husband and wife can do together to increase their rewards . . . in the afterlife.

Hashim (Sunni husband): It is statutory in our family that if you pray by yourself, you get some [benefit], but if you pray *with your family*, you get more [benefit]. It's also social, you know, you feel more comfortable when you pray with your wife and when you pray with your children. It's [provides] a unity, you feel more comfortable when you pray together.

Few in the *American Families of Faith* project explained the whys behind shared couple prayer and faith with as much texture as Rehkah, a Muslim wife and mother, who said:

> Marriage is one of the most virtuous or most spiritual foundations in society. It is a very religious thing for me. And we think of it as one of the traditions of our Prophet, so it's a very spiritual thing. . . . We have a lot of traditions that say when a man and wife get *together*, [when] they marry, they have actually started a foundation. And both of their faiths become complete. For example, the worship that you used to do when you were single [is] so much more, worth more, after you are married. So [it] really increases the value of your faith, when you are married. We think of it as a way to progress spiritually. We become partners in growing religiously.

Having discussed the individual, couple, and family-level influence of prayer (*salat*), we now turn to a second and final Muslim family religious practice, the Ramadan fast.

The Month of the Ramadan Fast and Muslim Families

Ramadan refers to the ninth month of the Islamic lunar calendar. It is a time of fasting, one of the five pillars of Islam (the other four pillars include the declaration of faith, prayer, charity, and pilgrimage to Mecca; see Alaghafli et al., 2014). Muslims are to refrain from food, drink, or engaging in sexual relations during daylight hours. After sunset it is common to eat a small meal following the evening prayer. Later, many partake of a large meal, and some eat a third meal in the morning before sunrise. Some individuals are exempted from fasting including young children, menstruating women, the elderly, those traveling, and the afflicted. Children are introduced to fasting by incremental steps to ease them into the process. The Islamic calendar is lunar, and, therefore, annual events are not tied to any particular season, but change from year to year. This makes fasting (including abstaining from fluids) more difficult during summer months where the days are longer and hotter. Many practicing Muslims also abstain from many other pleasures during Ramadan to completely and symbolically break from the world. Some of these pleasures may include listening to music, applying bodily fragrances, and participating in any major activities of excitement (e.g., celebrations or parties).

No other topic seemed to excite quite as much enthusiasm among the Muslims interviewed for the AFF project as the month of fasting during Ramadan. It was not uncommon for parents, especially fathers, to discuss this religious practice in a passionate manner. A Sunni husband named Gulam said:

> The thing that we really enjoy and cherish is the month of Ramadan because we do so many things together as a family. We wake up in the middle of the night. We sit together, we eat together, and we pray together. [We] go to [the mosque] and bring food. And we get together as a family.

A Shia Muslim named Raghib reported:

> [Ramadan] is a very, very good experience for us. I think what fasting does is [that] it makes everything else so insignificant. Seeing the family, the marriage, human life—[these are] really the most important things in the world, because everything else means nothing, really. [During the year] we do get carried away with worldly things, the houses, the cars, and all of that, I think—[but Ramadan] really brings you right to the ground and [gets you] grounded with God.

A Sunni wife named Noreen expressed her feelings as follows:

> I think that religion affects our married life, because [on] this point we can agree: [the Ramadan fast is sacred]. We spend some time without

> arguing. For example, when we both fast, we do our activities together. We break the fast together [and] we wake up at midnight and eat before fasting. So we do these types of things together. . . . At this point we again agree and that's how religion is making our life, going together and growing together.

We conclude our discussion of Ramadan with the reflections of husband named Ismail who explained:

> Ramadan has been prescribed to us where every Muslim is supposed to [fast]. It's one of the five pillars of Islam. So . . . we get up early, very early in the morning [to] have a meal together, like a breakfast. We have a meal together, and then after the meal, we read Qu'ran, our scripture. And after we do that, it's time for prayer. We pray together . . . [then], in the evening [after sunset], which is the time of breaking [our] fast, again, the same thing happens as during the morning. We all come together as a family, and we eat together and we thank God together, we pray together. After [that] we break the fast. And then we do more prayers. So the whole month of Ramadan is a very unique experience. We do a lot less of the worldly things and a lot more of godly things than we normally do. . . . When you do those kinds of things together every day . . . it . . . bring[s] people together and it strengthens our beliefs and [our] family.

In the brief interview excerpts from Noreen (a Muslim mother) and Ismail (a Muslim father), we are presented with the word "together" 14 separate times, underscoring that Ramadan seems to hold a potent unifying function for some Muslim families. These cultural and religious minority families draw strength and cohesion from a unique facet of Islam that combines family and faith.

Conclusion

We have seen through the eyes of a small sample of 25 American Muslim families how the local Islamic community and various religious practices impact individuals and families. Muslims experience challenges in the United States, and many of these challenges are related to perceptions of non-Muslims regarding the treatment of women and violence in Islam. Most religious minorities face some level of perceived ostracism or lack of full acceptance, but many Muslims seem to experience even more challenges. In the eyes of those outside the faith, some challenges may be viewed as self-inflicted due to the literal separation of the sexes attached with stricter interpretations of *hijab*. Many Muslim women will not talk to, deal with, shake hands with, or mingle with men who are not related to them. This creates many practical and cultural challenges for those living in the United States. Most religious minority families have to deal with negative stereotypes, scheduling conflicts, or dietary rules (impacting school functions and work parties). In addition, like Orthodox Jewish families, Muslim families must also deal with fairly strict laws regarding gender issues such as modesty in dress and interaction with those of the other gender who are not family members.

This chapter has also helped illustrate how important the religious community is for religious minorities and their identity and well-being. Muslims rely on frequent interaction with other like-minded members of the Islamic community (*ummah*), and that interaction comes primarily during local Muslim community events and worship services at the mosque (*masjid*). Some Muslim participants stressed that the mosque is a place where unity of purpose and faith is fostered because, in both idealized belief and often in practice, class and racial divisions break down. Ideally, because the mosque is a place of equality, the poorest man may kneel and pray next to the wealthiest man.

Regarding religious observance in the home, prayer (*salat*) was frequently mentioned as both personally and relationally helpful. For many (if not most) of the Muslim families in the AFF project, fasting during Ramadan seemed to be the most salient religious practice. These religious practices, according to AFF Muslim participants, help unify families and create a bond between husbands and wives and between parents and children.

Chapter Summary Points

1. Islam is a sizeable global religion; approximately 20% of the world's population is Muslim.
2. The two major denominations of Islam are Sunni and Shia, and both rely on the Qur'an as their holy book.
3. Muslims in the United States account for about 1% of the population, but the number of Muslims may double over the next few decades.
4. Among the challenges facing modern Muslims are the sensationalism around the small minority of Muslims that are terrorists and the cultural treatment of women in some countries.

5. The use of the *hijab* is an Islamic practice that some find controversial; AFF Muslim participants reported both positive and negative ramifications of its use, such as establishing identity but also increasing ostracism.
6. AFF Muslims families often referenced the importance of the mosque in the religious development of their children and for their own benefit.
7. The two notable home-based rituals Muslim families reported were daily prayer and fasting during Ramadan.

Review Questions

1. How do historians believe Muslims first came to the United States?
2. What reasons did the AFF participants give for wearing the *hijab*?
3. What benefits did AFF participants attribute to mosque worship?
4. According to the responses from AFF Muslim families, how does daily prayer affect family life?
5. From what things do Muslims abstain during Ramadan, and what does this symbolically represent?

Notes

1. This chapter is authored with Trevan Hatch and Zahra Alghafli. Narrative excerpts are from the *American Families of Faith* research project, except where otherwise indicated.
2. We will not focus on the third dimension of *religious beliefs*, primarily because, while beliefs are extremely important in Christianity, they are less important in Islam and Judaism. We recommend Prothero (2010) as a valuable introductory resource on these traditions.

References

Agius, E., & Chircop, L. (Eds.). (1998). *Caring for future generations: Jewish, Christian, and Islamic perspectives.* Westport, CT: Praeger.

Alaghafli, Z., Hatch, T., & Marks, L. (2014a). Islam. In M. Coleman, & L. Ganong (Eds.), *The social history of the American family* (pp. 769–772). Thousand Oaks, CA: Sage.

Alghafli, Z., Hatch, T., & Marks, L. (2014b). Religion and relationships in Muslim families: A qualitative examination of devout married Muslim couples. *Religions, 5*, 814–833.

Canadian Islamic Congress (2002). Anti-Islam in the media 2002. Retrieved from http://www.canadianislamiccongress.com.

Diouf, S. (2013). *Servants of Allah: African Muslims enslaved in the Americas*. New York: New York University Press.

Dollahite, D. C., Marks, L. D., & Goodman, M. (2004). Religiosity and families: Relational and spiritual linkages in a diverse and dynamic cultural context. In M. J. Coleman & L. H. Ganong (Eds.), *The handbook of contemporary families* (pp. 411–431). Thousand Oaks, CA: Sage.

Haddad, Y. Y., Smith, J. I., & Moore, K. M. (2006). *Muslim women in America: The challenge of Islamic identity today*. New York: Oxford University Press.

Hatch, T. & Marks, L. (2014a). Bar mitzvahs and bat mitzvahs. In L. Ganong, M. Coleman, & J. G. Golson (Eds.), *The social history of the American family* (pp. 104–105). Thousand Oaks, CA: SAGE.

Hatch, T. & Marks, L. (2014b). Judaism and Orthodox Judaism. In L. Ganong, M. Coleman, & J. G. Golson (Eds.), *The social history of the American family* (pp. 781–784). Thousand Oaks, CA: SAGE.

Hatch, T. & Marks, L. (2014c). Passover. In L. Ganong, M. Coleman, & J. G. Golson (Eds.), *The social history of the American family* (pp. 1019–1021). Thousand Oaks, CA: Sage.

Howell, S. (2007). Mosques history. In Jocelyne Cesari (Ed.), *Encyclopedia of Islam in the United States* (pp. 432–434). Westport, CT: Greenwood Press.

Mahoney, A., Pargament, K. I., Tarakeshwar, N., & Swank, A. B. (2001). Religion in the home in the 1980s and 90s: A meta-analytic review and conceptual analyses of links between religion, marriage and parenting. *Journal of Family Psychology, 15*, 559–596.

Marks, L. D., & Dollahite, D. C. (2012). Don't forget home: The importance of sacred ritual in families. In J. Hoffman (Ed.), *Understanding religious rituals* (pp. 186–203). New York: Routledge.

Marks, L. D., Hatch, T., & Dollahite, D. C. (unpublished manuscript). Sacred practices and family processes in a Jewish context: *Shabbat* as the weekly family ritual par excellence.

Pew (April 30, 2013). The world's Muslims: Religion, politics and society. Pew Research Center. Retrieved from http://www.pewforum.org/2013/04/30/the-worlds-muslims-religion-politics-society-overview/.

Pew (January 6, 2016). A new estimate of the U.S. Muslim population. Pew Research Center. Retrieved from http://www.pewresearch.org/fact-tank/2016/01/06/a-new-estimate-of-the-u-s-muslim-population/.

Prothero, S. (2010). *God is not one*. New York: HarperOne.

White, S., & Mir, S. (2007). Head scarf. In J. Cesari (Ed.), *Encyclopedia of Islam in the United States* (pp. 279–283). Westport, CT: Greenwood Press.

9
Jewish Families in the United States[1]

As mentioned in chapter 8, the rich context of religious minority families offers the chance to highlight issues like identity formation in youth and emerging adults, the importance of social support from their religious community, and the unique challenges religious minorities face as they strive to live their religion. In this chapter we feature Judaism and the 30 Jewish families from the *American Families of Faith* project.

Jewish Family Life

The worldwide Jewish population as of 2010 was estimated by the Pew Research Center (2012) to be 13.85 million, or 0.2% of the world's population. Pew researchers also estimated that the United States contained the largest population of Jews in the world at 5.69 million (41.1%), followed by Israel at 5.61 million (40.5%). About 2% of Americans are Jewish. Due to a long-standing emphasis on the importance of knowledge and education, Jewish Americans are disproportionately involved in higher education and several influential fields in American society. Indeed, education is a major part of child-rearing and family life for most Jewish families.

Who Is a Jew? What Is Judaism?

Before discussing some of the features of American Jewish family life, it may be helpful to keep a broad definition of "Jews" and "Judaism" in mind while proceeding through this section. The term "Jew" (*Yehudi* in Hebrew) is derived from a biblical tribe named after Judah (*Yehudah* in Hebrew), who lived about 1,600 years BCE. Judah's 11 brothers also had tribes named after them. These 12 tribal families and their descendants, together, were called "Hebrews" or "Israelites" (named after Judah's father). Over a period of about 600 years, the tribe of Judah became the dominant tribe among the Israelites due to a combination of superior geographic location and greater fortune in surviving multiple invasions and deportations by neighboring nations. Thus, "Judah" eventually replaced, or was synonymous with, "Israel," and by 600 BCE, members of all 12 tribes of Israel were calling themselves "Jews."

The ancient Israelites, and later Jews, had a system of religious worship centered on their temple that involved prayer and many sacrificial and purification rituals. We call that ancient religious system "Judaism." It is the religion of the Jewish people (although contemporary Judaism is quite different in various ways from its ancient precursor, perhaps most importantly since ancient Judaism was based in worship at the Temple in Jerusalem). In other words, in the ancient world Jews were known as being an ethnic group *and* a religious group; therefore, one was also "Jewish" if he or she converted to the Jewish legal and religious system.

Today, as in the ancient world, one is "Jewish" either by lineage or by religion (or both). Not all Jews by lineage are adherents to the religion of Judaism, and not all religious Jews are of literal Jewish descent (e.g., converts to Judaism). Some lineal Jews, for example, may be Catholic, Protestant, or Buddhist in their religion (although many Orthodox Jews do not consider one who has adopted another religion to be Jewish). Further, Jews who are blood relatives of ancient Jews are found among many nations and ethnicities (e.g., French Jews, German Jews, Spanish Jews, etc.), while Jews by religion may be Asian, African, Hispanic, or even Persian or Arab. You can see how difficult it can be to discuss "Judaism," "Jews," or "Jewish history" because even the definitions of the terms are neither clear nor agreed upon by scholars or by all Jews themselves. In this chapter (and in our *American Families of Faith* project), we focus on families who *practice* the Jewish religion (including both Jews by lineage and a minority who are Jews by conversion).

Jews in the United States and Jewish U.S. Demographics

Just as there are various ways to be Christian (there are hundreds of Christian denominations; Prothero, 2010), Jews have developed several different ideas of what Judaism is or should be. Today, three main groups within Judaism have emerged out of the struggle to define Judaism: Conservative, Orthodox, and Reform. While there are other branches in Judaism (e.g., Reconstructionist), these three branches include the great majority of religious Jews. **Reform Judaism** first developed in Western Europe in the 19th century through the rationale that many Jewish practices and beliefs were outdated, superstitious, or unnecessary. Some Jewish thinkers proposed that the Jewish community should adjust and reinterpret Judaism to be more modern and useful. Reform Judaism quickly spread across Western Europe, and by the early 1820s, a Reform Synagogue was established in Charleston, South Carolina. Reform Jews currently comprise about 35% of the Jewish population in the United States, making it the largest Jewish group in America (Pew, 2013).

Orthodox Judaism emerged in response to Reform Judaism. Some Jews who rejected proposals for change argued that Judaism could not be reformed because it is a revealed religion (i.e., revealed by God); therefore, any attempt to reform Judaism was rejected by these more traditional, or "Orthodox," Jews. According to many Orthodox Jews, Reform Judaism is not considered authentic Judaism. Orthodox Jews constitute roughly 10% of the Jewish population in the United States—the smallest of the three major branches in America (Pew, 2013). However, nearly 20% of Jews that belong to a synagogue identify as Orthodox. The proportion of Jewish families that are Orthodox is currently increasing for at least two reasons: (1) Orthodox families tend to have significantly more children than Reform, Conservative, and non-religious Jewish families, and (2) there is a higher rate of intermarriage (marrying a non-Jewish spouse) among Conservative, Reform, and non-religious Jews, and only about one-third of children in intermarried families are raised Jewish. Thus, over time, the proportion of Jewish families who are Orthodox (more strictly observant of Jewish law) will likely continue to increase.

Conservative Judaism also emerged in relation to Orthodox Judaism and Reform Judaism. The Conservative movement flourished because it attracted Jews who viewed the Orthodox movement as too antiquated or unrealistic and who saw the Reform movement as too secular and non-observant. Conservative Judaism sought to *conserve* traditional Jewish practices and Jewish thought, like Orthodox Jews, while adapting to the ever-changing environment around them, like Reform Jews. Approximately 18% of American Jews are associated with the Conservative movement (Pew, 2013). It is important to know the basic distinctions between these three groups when examining American Jewish family life because significant differences are manifested between them. "Judaism" is not a single, uniform system of practices and beliefs. There is a wide spectrum of ideas regarding how Judaism should be lived among American Jews, and this is important to keep in mind while reading this chapter.

Based on a recent Pew (2013) survey, a large majority of Jews, even secular Jews, are proud to be Jewish and are involved in Judaism by attending local Jewish events, enrolling their kids in Hebrew school or Jewish day school, sending their kids to Jewish summer camps, or participating in Jewish holiday activities and traditions. We now survey three aspects of Jewish family life that highlight ways religion impacts Jewish individuals and families.

Challenges of Being a Religious Minority: Jewish Perspectives

Much has been written on anti-Semitism and the mistreatment of Jewish persons across time and history. The details of the Holocaust and the **pogroms**, among many possible examples of persecution of Jews, are horrific. These, however, are not our focus here. Instead, we turn our attention to challenges faced by contemporary Jewish families living in the United States. How are these families affected by their specific religious minority status in a country with an overwhelmingly Christian population (about 70% of Americans are Christian)? In our *American Families of Faith* data, one challenge repeatedly mentioned by Jewish mothers and fathers was that of observing **Shabbat** (the Sabbath) with family. *Shabbat*, however, was also mentioned as deeply meaningful by many families. We will discuss both the challenges and the benefits of *Shabbat* in this chapter.

The following three quotes, from three different Jewish families, illustrate some of the challenges of observing *Shabbat* in the home as a religious minority.

Ruth (Reform convert): The fact that we're not going on a weekly basis to services is something I'm trying to deal with, because it has a lot of implications. Friday nights are very hard. Saturday mornings aren't all that much easier, and the Rabbi has started a Saturday morning Sabbath service, to accommodate [some] families. . . . You know, the Friday nights are just impossible, with kids and their activities. But this concert was on the Sabbath, it was Friday night, and so we haven't made a rule in our family, we haven't said, "No outside activities on Fridays." And I don't know if we need to make that rule, and that's going to be a challenge for us, I think, to deal with. Because, if it's not Saturday night, if you say, "Okay, well fine, no Saturday morning," . . . then does that mean that they can't do soccer? Well yeah, it means they can't do soccer. So, what do you give up?

Rebecca (Reform mother): [Observing Sabbath] on a more regular basis is hard because the Friday nights, getting the kids there, there's football games and parties, and stuff they get invited to. We've tried to say, "Okay, if you don't go to synagogue on Friday night, then we're going to go on Saturday morning instead. This is what we do." We're going to give the kids that choice, if we don't go on Friday night, we go on Saturday morning. Well, [my husband's] a doctor, he's on-call many nights, we have Sunday school on Sunday morning, so Saturday morning is our only [free] day of the week . . . and most of the time, there's a baseball game or other kid's sports stuff on Saturday. Because we live in the world we live in, it's hard for us to really live Jewish as much as we would like to. We have to fight the calendar.

Melanie (Conservative mother): We had a big crisis that we had to confront, and that was whether or not we would let the kids play soccer on *Shabbat*, on Saturday morning.

Joshua (Conservative husband): Yeah, because all of [our daughter's] friends were playing soccer, so we let her do it for a few weekends, and we hated it, because it just stole the family away from us. And in the end we decided: *No, we weren't going to do it ever again.* And we've really held to that, not just with the children, but with ourselves as well. With very few exceptions, very rare exceptions. [*Shabbat*]'s the one time we're all together.

These interview excerpts—from Reform and Conservative families—capture the struggles faced when children's secular activities collide with the synagogue and *Shabbat* schedule. In these three families, we see slightly different perspectives on and responses to the constant cultural conflicts associated with Sabbath observance. Typically, Modern Orthodox families are more "strict" in their observance of *Shabbat*, and most would chose not to have their children involved in secular/sports activities on Friday evening or Saturday until after sundown. We now move from the challenge of conflicts associated with *Shabbat* to the topic of the religious community within Judaism.

Religious Community

Research shows that social support from a religious community provides families, including religious minority families, with many physical health, mental health, and relational health benefits (Koenig, King, & Carson, 2012; Koenig, McCullough, & Larson, 2001; Marks, 2005, 2006). For example, parents who scored higher on measures of religious involvement and perceived social support from their religious community reported more favorable parenting practices and lower hostility toward others, including their children (Strayhorn, Weidman, & Larson, 1990; Wilcox, 1998).

According to a study of 200 participants in 20 U.S. religions, social support from a religious community was a stronger predictor of family relationship satisfaction than was a religious belief in divine intervention (Abbott, Berry, & Meredith, 1990). One recent study that moved beyond the variable of frequency of religious attendance (Olson, Goddard, & Marshall, 2013) used a random sample of 1,204 young married participants and discovered that attendance at worship services was *not* positively associated with marital commitment. Rather, perceived *support* from one's religious community was positively related to marital commitment. In other words, it may be the case that strong social support from one's religious community is more important for marital and family relationship satisfaction than simply attending religious services, per se. To frame this differently, it is not just having a synagogue, mosque, or church to attend that seems to strengthen marriage; it appears to be the social, familial, and marital support received from friends in the faith community that matters more. Olson and colleagues' research suggests how significant a strong social support group may be for enhancing marriage and family relationships. With this research in mind, we will consider some aspects of American Jewish families, using additional data from the *American Families of Faith* project that highlight the importance of support from the local religious community, especially for religious minorities.

Unlike Jews in most parts of the United States, Christians likely have a support structure at school and work, where many (if not most) of their classmates and co-workers are at least nominal Christians. Their religious symbols and holidays are supported by the media and by advertisers through TV shows, commercials, concerts, light displays, and so forth. Jews, on the other hand, are typically more limited in religious social support from the surrounding community, which primarily comes through the synagogue or local Jewish Community Center (if they have one in their community, and many do not). In this context, consider the comment from a Reform Jewish man from a mid-sized southern city:

Jerry: [Our congregation] is really supportive and it helps us continue traditions where we might have a conflict between our various roles in the secular world and the religious world. Having a congregation to rely on helps us, and in many ways, enables us to do both things very well. It also creates a community where the kids feel like they belong to a group of people. We have very close friends from the synagogue who we engage with outside of the synagogue all the time. Our kids know that they're not the only Jews in [this city].

An Orthodox couple, William and Sheri, also explained that the local Jewish community is important to them because it functions as their extended family:

William: The synagogue is like an extended family. It's [a] nice place to go. Our daughter, most of her friends are at synagogue and she likes to go. Our son, most of his friends are not at synagogue and he does not like to go . . . so there's a social aspect.

Sheri: Observance is important to me but the sense of community and continuity is [also] great . . . the extended Jewish community has become our family. Because our families are spread out across the country, they [our friends from the synagogue] are our family.

A Jewish woman from California, Rebecca, explained what the support from her local Jewish community means to her and her family:

> Our synagogue is almost like a dysfunctional family. Most of the people in our synagogue are people whose paths we would never cross anywhere else. We run in different social circles, we are on different career paths, different aged kids, different schools. But, what we have in common with these people is what we share in the four walls of that building, and in thousands of years of Jewish tradition, and I can't explain why it clicks here better than anyplace else we've ever lived. . . . It is such a community.

Rebecca went on to share the following narrative that illustrated this sense of community:

> We had a real tragedy a few years ago in our synagogue where a family who w[ere] not even member[s] of [my particular] synagogue, but a Jewish family in town lost a child, and it was a horrific situation. People

> just showed up, came from out of the woodwork. It was a very painful situation to walk into. You feel like you are invading somebody's privacy, to go into their home at such a painful time when you don't even know these people. Yet they needed a Jewish community to help them pray and do what Jews do at this time, and people just showed up. . . . They brought food. They came night after night, bigger numbers every night. People just were there . . . because this is what Jews do for other Jews.
>
> (Hatch, 2015)

Comments from these Jewish parents illustrate why their community is so important to them and their families. They have access to a support group that understands their sensibilities, traditions, and struggles as Jews. In addition to general support from the community, research shows that shared experiences are also a crucial part of belonging to a community. Shared religious experiences are beneficial because they create common interests for couples, families, and the religious community.

Perhaps the best illustration of a shared cultural and religious community experience that impacts the family in a Jewish context is the tradition of bar/bat mitzvah. According to the latest Pew (2013) research on American Jews, nearly 60% of religiously involved Jews and nearly 30% of secular Jews had a bar/bat mitzvah ceremony.

> The term **bar/bat mitzvah** means "son/daughter of the commandment" and also refers to a series of Jewish rituals performed by adolescent males and females at ages 13 and 12, respectively, at their bar/bat mitzvah celebration (typically held at a synagogue). The millennia-old tradition of becoming bar/bat mitzvah consists of leading part of the worship service at the synagogue and reading the sacred texts in Hebrew in front of the assembly. These rituals signify that the community hereafter recognizes the adolescent as an adult. Many parents plan months in advance by hiring a teacher to get their child ready for the big day. For some families, the bar/bat mitzvah is similar to a high school graduation where photographers are hired to capture the event, invitations are issued to friends and family, and the adolescent receives gifts and monetary donations.

This rite of passage is typically a special event for the nuclear and extended family and the local Jewish community (Hatch & Marks, 2014). Although technically the bar/bat mitzvah ceremony is an achievement of the individual, the family and many from the community are often involved in the preparation of the event, as well as in the ceremony itself. The following comment from a Reform Jewish couple illustrates the importance of the shared religious experience that bar/bat mitzvah provides:

Susannah (wife): When my daughter had her bat mitzvah three years ago, this was something she wanted to do. So, when it came time for my son, I said, "You know, this is strictly your decision. You're doing the work. You've got to want to do this." And he said, "Yes, my religion is important to me." So, he did it. That's one thing I think we've given our children is a strong Jewish belief and they feel a part of the congregation.

Matthias (husband): The services, the bar and bat mitzvahs, those take a long commitment, a couple of years of study, weekly classes, things like that. And, it brought our children together, my daughter having done it before, helped my son learn the Hebrew, and things like that. It may be, to some extent, those events and the stuff associated with them . . . brought family into town, which is not something that happens [otherwise]. Our families don't get together that much, [but] that contributed to it.

To summarize our very brief discussion of Jewish families in a faith community context, we see that a synagogue can serve as an "extended family." This can be particularly important for Jewish families living in areas with a smaller Jewish population. Further, synagogue-based rituals including bar/bat mitzvah seem to unite biological and extended families for these life course events. As a result, the synagogue seems to have the power to both create a functional "extended family" for Jewish families as well as to unite and reunite literal extended family. Even so, as important as the synagogue and synagogue-based rituals and events (like bar/bat mitzvah celebrations) are for many Jewish families, the center of Judaism for many others is not the synagogue but the home, as discussed next.

Jewish Religious Observance in the Home

Cohen and Eisen (2000) in their classic book, *The Jew Within*, suggested that younger generations of Jews increasingly seem to be honoring their heritage and observing their religion in the home, with family. Jewish young adults, similar to young adults in general (Smith & Snell, 2009), appear to be moving away from the "organizations, institutions, and causes that used to anchor identity and shape behavior" for previous generations (Cohen & Eisen, 2000, p. 2).

Goldscheider (2004) similarly acknowledged that Jews generally appear to have become "less attached to religious activities and institutions" (p. 100). In many cases, however, the family seems to be filling some of the vacuum. Goldscheider (2004) argued that Judaism is not in decline, like many have suggested, but that Judaism is in transition or transformation. This transformation has consisted of a movement away from communal institutions and toward the family.

Cohen (1999) also posited that Jewish identity has undertaken salient transformations. He explained how Jewish cultural identities have transitioned through the 19th and 20th centuries from collective-based identity to individual-based identity (Cohen, 1999; Cohen & Eisen, 2000). Jews in North America, he argued, now feel free to incorporate into their individual and family lives only those aspects of Jewish culture and religion that are personally meaningful—and the retained aspects tend to be those more relevant to the family and the home (Cohen & Eisen, 2000). The following comments from *American Families of Faith* participants further illustrate what Cohen, Eisen, and Goldscheider have articulated about the significance of the transformation of American Judaism from the institution and synagogue to what some refer to as "home-based Judaism," where families live their religion in the home in ways that are meaningful to them.

Yigal (Orthodox father of two): There are so many reasons why we love our [family traditions]. Number one, we love it because we made it up and we both feel that Judaism . . . well, we don't believe that there was a tradition that was handed down in this kind of linear, ironclad way and that if you are part of the tradition you do what you are told and do exactly the things that the generation before you did. No! We believe that Judaism is a very fluid and dynamic thing that is constantly changing and has changed with different pressure[s] throughout history and that we have the power today to do with it as we will. Obviously it's based on certain principles and inspirations that we didn't just make up ourselves, but still we take it in directions that [we] decide to take it. But I also think [about] what are the beautiful characteristics of Judaism, and what are the things that I would want to have in my Judaism? Much more than a rigid observance of practices or doctrines, there would be a sense of love in the family—that the parents love and respect each other, and that parents love and respect the children, and the children love the parents, and that their Judaism is an expression of that.

Yigal went on to say:

> Sometimes you have parents that say, "This is what Judaism means, [so] you must do X." Even if the kids hate it, [the parents say], "To Hell with you, you must do it!" and that is the kind of Judaism that I grew up with. I disagree with the kind of Judaism where I just had to do certain things even if it made me miserable, you know—that we needed to do it because that is what you are "supposed to do." And that kind of slavish obedience to tradition is anathema to me. I loathe it! So because of that, the things that I loathe, I do the opposite. The things that are beautiful that the children and parents love and that we enjoy, we do it even if we aren't commanded to do, or even if we are commanded to do it. It injects our Judaism and our family with a sense of joy with the traditions, rather than the sense of obligation to follow traditions.

Earlier in our interview with his family, Yigal commented that he and his wife, Alissa, disagreed with a passage in the liturgy, and so they decided to not say it during the synagogue services. They essentially omitted it from their form of Judaism. Like Yigal's family, many religious people take what they believe they need (or want), based on their life's experiences, and discard what they do not find as helpful. Notice that Yigal referred to his religion as "my Judaism" and "our Judaism" several times. For his family, Judaism is special (in part) *because* it can be adapted. Indeed, for most contemporary Jews, "Judaism" presupposes change, adaptation, and even contradiction. However, Orthodox Judaism is less prone to value change and instead emphasizes adherence to tradition and more strict observance of Jewish law. This adaptive approach that most Jews bring to their observance of Judaism in the 21st century, as articulated by Yigal, reflects what sociologists like Cohen, Eisen, and Goldscheider have found in their research.

As previously mentioned, not all Jews appreciate or embrace flexible parameters of living their Judaism. Rabbi Jeffrey Salkin, for example, warned that observing only those aspects of one's religion that are meaningful at the time, or simply "following your bliss," is the "antithesis of living in covenant" (Kaplan, 2009, p. 60). Another American Jewish rabbi, Dana Kaplan, argued (2009) that the "New Supermarket Judaism" practiced by many Jews impedes experiencing religion the way "it was intended to be experienced." Rabbi Kaplan has explained:

> The plethora of choice is intoxicating, but ultimately unsatisfying. Approaching religion as one would a salad bar is unlikely to provide the

> person with the personal discipline necessary to experience religiosity as it was intended to be experienced. There is an intense spiritual satisfaction that is the result of self-sacrifice, and the perpetual "religious tourist" is unlikely to feel that sense of satisfaction since they have never made a commitment to sacrifice. Rather, they are constantly looking and evaluating and making temporary choices, only to reverse themselves and consider yet other options.
>
> (pp. 72–73)

Despite the pushback from some Jewish leaders and authors against those practicing a "cafeteria religion," it is likely that most American Jews, similar to people in other religions, will continue to approach Judaism in this "I'll take what I want" manner.

We now return our focus specifically to Jewish practice in a family context. Consider the three following AFF quotes from Reform, Conservative, and Orthodox Jewish families on the significance of the home in living as a Jew. A Reform convert confided:

Ruth: I feel I'm right now a little conflicted about the fact that we don't go to Friday night services. I know I have mentioned it several times in this interview. Because I'm hearing from the Rabbi that he really wants us to come more, and coming from a Catholic background, where you always went to church on Sunday, I mean that was not an optional thing. But in the Jewish community, the at-home participation in the Sabbath is equivalent to, not the same as going to synagogue, but that's the more important thing. If you had to only do one, you should light candles and say prayers at home.

A Conservative couple explained:

Interviewer: Is your religious life centered in your home and family or your synagogue?

Daniel: Home.

Wendy: Home. Home and family. The synagogue is an appendage. . . . I believe if there wasn't a synagogue . . . if, God forbid, there [was] like a Holocaust or something where we were forced to hide and practice Judaism, I would still figure out a way to get it done in the home.

Daniel: Well, in fact, you don't need a rabbi in Judaism for the religion to [continue] . . . In fact, so many times in the **pogroms**, they start

> with the rabbis—they kill the rabbis first. . . . And you know what? It still hasn't worked. And the reason is because it's kind of like the Second Amendment in the U.S. The reason that the U.S. will never be taken over is because every family has a gun. And so it's like every Jew, the religion or the culture of Judaism or the essence, the nugget of Judaism resides within every Jew in the home by and large, so it's very hard to extinguish that. The home is really . . . the center of the universe for us, for this particular Jewish family. We really enjoy [and] relish life in the synagogue, but if the synagogue went away, if we went into hiding, if we went into hibernation, if we had to disperse, we would be able to persevere [Judaism].

An Orthodox couple, when asked where their religious life was centered, responded:

Abram: I would say that, and I can only give this to you in a percentage, I would say that our religious life is centered in the home probably something like 60% [home and] 40% [synagogue] or 70%–30%.

Naomi: I think my percentage would be different, though. I think it would be more like 90% home. If you think about it, every major—with the exception of the High Holy Days—every major *mitzvah* [commandment] or every major holiday is done in the home. Fasts are at home. ***Pesach*** [**Passover**] is at home. ***Sukkot*** is at home. ***Shavuot*** is at home. All of these are family-based holidays. Yeah, lots of times you have guests or you are a guest among families in the community, but . . . you go to [synagogue], but when you're done with [synagogue], the celebration is at home.

Consistent with Naomi's report, many of the salient Jewish traditions practiced in the home are associated with the Sabbath and major holidays, like Passover. According to the Pew survey (2013), nearly half of Jews (45%) who have a Jewish spouse reported that they *always or usually* light ***Shabbat*** candles on Friday evenings. However, that percentage would likely be higher if the survey included additional Sabbath traditions in the home, such as special family meals.

Jewish participants in the *American Families of Faith* project mentioned practices associated with the Sabbath more than any other cultural or religious practice. Of the 30 Jewish families in the AFF sample, 28 (93%) discussed the Sabbath during the interview, and most mentioned it multiple times. More specifically, when asked, *"What practices or observances hold special meaning for you as a couple or family?"* 19 families (63%) immediately mentioned the *Shabbat*. The three main themes that emerged from the AFF project regarding the Sabbath were: 1) Sabbath traditions help form and maintain strong Jewish identity; 2) Sabbath facilitates peace and relaxation; and 3) Sabbath traditions unify the family (Hatch, 2015; Marks, Hatch, & Dollahite, under review). The following seven comments from Jewish mothers illustrate the dynamics for many families of observing *Shabbat* at home:

Wendy (Conservative): The kids know Friday night is *Shabbat*. They don't make plans. They know it's *Shabbat*. I'll pick them up from school [and] they'll be like "Tonight's *Shabbat*. Who's coming?" They're always asking. The older one said to me the other night, "I love *Shabbat*." . . . Everybody's together and we'll set the table and it's a nicer dinner. . . . We'll set the table, the kids, depending on who's coming, we'll put on nicer clothes, but we do the lights and the cooking.

Kristen (Reform): When our kids were younger we did *Shabbat* dinners every Friday night and it was really fun for all of us. . . . My daughter would run upstairs and put on her special *Shabbat* clothes and she and I would make *challah* (traditional Sabbath bread) together.

Melanie (Conservative): It's funny, there's all this stressful air before *Shabbat*, getting ready and all this, and then you light the candles. Everything does change. And you know the laws about *Shabbat*, you're not even supposed to be thinking anything stressful, let alone talking about anything stressful. It's like you leave all the stresses of the rest of the week behind . . . and the kids are always very excited about it. They know that no one's going anywhere, no one's answering the phone, no one's driving anywhere, that we're just going to be here as a family. . . . It's fun. We always change our clothes and put on nice clothes. . . . It's our moment. It's our evening and time to kind of . . . become a unit once again. We've all scattered and gone our separate ways during the week.

Esther (Orthodox): The special thing about *Shabbat* [is that] we always eat supper together, so at our house it's not so unique that we're all around the table. But I try to make special things for *Shabbat* that I know that the kids really like and they're looking forward to it.

Rachel (non-Orthodox but unspecified): Friday nights are big nights for us. [In the past], we took them to services every Friday night. We haven't really gone for the last year, but every Friday night, we [do] get out the Sabbath candles, and I light the candles, and say the prayer in

Hebrew, and I've got wine glasses, so we do grape juice in the wine glasses for the kids, and the boys know the prayer over the wine, and then they all do the prayer over the bread. . . . They know that Friday night is the Sabbath, and so that's our big deal . . . The kids love that. They love lighting the candles, and saying the prayers. They like drinking out of wine glasses. They think that's a big deal.

Simcha (Orthodox): [*Shabbat*] just makes us stop and rest. Normally during the week [we're] running around, whether it's work or errands or shopping. . . . This quiets us down. This gives us a rest. I mean we *can't* do anything. You can't go anywhere. I can't talk on the phone, it's not ringing. The TV is not on. It just, you know, you rest. You take naps, I go to classes. We just, we see friends, we talk. You know, we play, as a family we play games. Things like that.

Debbie (Conservative): [*Shabbat* gives us] a chance to breathe, to relax. We've had a busy week and here's our time to be together and we always take a deep breath before we do this and let all the thoughts, craziness and worries, and everything slip away. . . . I think that when we take the time out, when we light the candles Friday night, that's a time that I feel really close to them . . . When we sit across the table from each other, my husband and I, and the candles are lit, and you see the kids, there is something you get from that that is *so deep*. It's just a feeling that all is right in the world . . . it doesn't matter what else is going on. Right in that circle . . . it's awe-inspiring.

These mothers help convey, in richness and color, the active power associated with home-based Jewish practices for them, their husbands, and their children. These descriptions convey a family-unifying ideal. Our research demonstrates that the family ritual of *Shabbat* is a uniquely important (even central) element of what Judaism means to many observant families.

Conclusion

In this chapter we have shown, through the eyes of observant Jewish families, which aspects of Judaism seem to be most salient for families. We also caught a brief glimpse of the challenges and frustrations Jews experience as members of a minority religion in the United States. For example, several families reported that they felt forced to choose between: (a) observing the Sabbath (e.g., staying home with family and attending Sabbath synagogue services on Friday nights and Saturday mornings) *or* (b) being active in their non-Jewish community by participating in school dances, school plays, sporting events, work parties, and other community events that are usually scheduled on Friday nights and Saturdays.

We also learned in the chapter, as a natural transition from the section on "challenges," that the local Jewish community and synagogue are often very important for providing a strong social support structure. Members of the community enjoy a sense of belonging (Marks, Dollahite, & Barker, 2012). Their fellow adherents and like-minded friends reportedly serve as an "extended family." Many Jews in the United States do not live within driving distance from their parents, siblings, and extended family; therefore, their local Jewish community becomes their family and their social support group.

The final aspect of American Jewish families that we considered in this chapter deals with religious observance in the home. Although the religious community and synagogue serve a meaningful purpose and seem to foster a sense of identity and belonging, many Jews identify "home-based Judaism" as being more salient and meaningful for living as a Jew than "synagogue-based Judaism." *Shabbat* (Sabbath) is the most common Jewish observance in the home, and most Jews, even many non-observant Jews, observe some aspects of the Sabbath with family and friends. Sabbath activities may include family time, nice dinners, special food (e.g., challah), special clothing, dancing, music, and lighting candles. "Tradition," the word that brings to mind the classic film *Fiddler on the Roof*, is salient for many Jews, and Sabbath activities are often a vitally important vehicle to help Jewish families remember their traditions and disseminate them to the next generation.

Chapter Summary Points

1. Being a "Jew" can refer to either being of Israelite descent or a member of the Jewish faith.
2. There are three main groups within Judaism: Orthodox, Conservative, and Reform.
3. Observing *Shabbat* in the United States can be a challenge, given perennial conflicts with cultural, school, and business-related events.
4. The bar/bat mitzvah is an example of a sacred tradition that is a shared experience with the Jewish religious community.
5. Scholars note some trends that indicate a decline in synagogue-based Judaism, whereas other scholars explain this trend as a "transition or transformation" to more home-based observance.

6. While the current trend in Judaism appears to be moving away from institutional religion, some scholars contend that it is mirrored by a reactionary trend turning toward more home, family, and individually-based worship.
7. *Shabbat* is considered an important ritual by many Jewish families because of its identity-maintaining, peace-promoting, and family-unifying nature.

Review Questions

1. According to the text, what are some differences between the Reform, Orthodox, and Conservative branches of Judaism?
2. What are some benefits for families related to religious communities that are highlighted in the text?
3. What does the term bar/bat mitzvah mean? How does this translation of the term relate to the ritual of a bar/bat mitzvah?
4. What conclusions have Cohen and Eisen (2000) come to in their book?
5. What religious practice was discussed by 93% of Jewish participants in the AFF project? What themes have emerged from Jewish discussion of this ritual?

Note

1. This chapter is authored with Trevan Hatch.

References

Abbott, D. A., Berry, M., & Meredith, W. H. (1990). Religious belief and practice: A potential asset for helping families. *Family Relations, 39*, 443–448.

Cohen, S. M. (1999). Introduction. In S. M. Cohen, & G. Horencyzk (Eds.), *National variations in Jewish identity: Implications for Jewish education* (pp. 1–17). Albany, NY: State University of New York Press.

Cohen, S. M., & Eisen, A. M. (2000). *The Jew within: Self, family, and community in America*. Bloomington, IN: Indiana University Press.

Goldscheider, C. (2004). *Studying the Jewish future*. Seattle, WA: University of Washington Press.

Hatch, T. (2015). Mishpacha in the American Diaspora: An Exploratory Study of Highly Involved Jewish Families. Doctoral dissertation. Louisiana State University, Baton Rouge Louisiana.

Hatch, T., & Marks, L. (2014). Bar mitzvahs and bat mitzvahs. In L. Ganong, M. Coleman, & J. G. Golson (Eds.), *The social history of the American family* (pp. 104–105). Thousand Oaks, CA: Sage.

Kaplan, D. E. (2009). *Contemporary American Judaism: Transformation and renewal.* New York: Columbia University Press.

Koenig, H. G., King, D. E., & Carson, V. B. (2012). *Handbook of religion and health (2nd ed.).* New York: Oxford University Press.

Koenig, H. G., McCullough, M., & Larson, D. B. (2001). *Handbook of religion and health: A century of research reviewed.* New York: Oxford University Press.

Marks, L. D. (2005). Religion and bio-psycho-social health: A review and conceptual model. *Journal of Religion and Health, 44,* 173–186.

Marks, L. D. (2006). Religion and family relational health: An overview and conceptual model. *Journal of Religion and Health, 45,* 603–618.

Marks, L. D., Dollahite, D. C., & Barker, K. (2012). Don't forget home: The importance of sacred ritual in families. In J. Hoffman (Ed.), *Understanding religious rituals* (pp. 186–203). New York: Routledge.

Marks, L. D., Hatch, T. G., & Dollahite, D. C. (under review). Sacred practices and family processes in a Jewish context: Shabbat as the weekly family ritual par excellence. *Family Process.*

Olson, J. R., Goddard, H. W., & Marshall, J. P. (2013). Relations among risk, religiosity, and marital commitment. *Journal of Couple & Relationship Therapy, 12,* 235–254.

Pew (2012). "Nones" on the rise: One-in-five adults have no religious affiliation. Pew Research Center. Retrieved from http://www.pewforum.org/uploadedFiles/Topics/Religious_Affiliation/Unaffiliated/NonesOnTheRise-full.pdf.

Pew (October 1, 2013). A portrait of Jewish Americans. Pew Research Center. Retrieved from http://www.pewforum.org/2013/10/01/jewish-american-beliefs-attitudes-culture-survey/.

Prothero, S. (2010). *God is not one.* New York: HarperOne.

Smith, C., Snell, P. (2009). *Souls in transition: The religious and spiritual lives of emerging adults.* New York: Oxford University Press.

Strayhorn, J. M., Weidman, C. S., & Larson, D. (1990). A measure of religiousness, and its relation to parent and child mental health variables. *Journal of Community Psychology, 18,* 34–43.

Wilcox, W. B. (1998). Conservative Protestant childrearing: Authoritarian or authoritative? *American Sociological Review, 63,* 796–809.

Religion and Diverse Family Forms[1] 10

Some time ago, we observed that the research on religion and families had several pronounced limitations (Dollahite, Marks, & Goodman, 2004). One of these was a lack of racial and ethnic diversity in the families studied—indeed, almost all the families that had been studied were white. A second pronounced limitation was an almost exclusive focus on faiths within traditional Christianity. In our *American Families of Faith* project, we have worked to produce work that begins to fill the voids in these two areas. In terms of racial and ethnic diversity, about half of our sample of 200 families are racial or ethnic minorities. Additionally, about half of our sample falls outside of "traditional Christianity"—substantial portions of our families are from Jewish, Muslim, and "New Religious Traditions" within Christianity (e.g., Latter-day Saint/Mormon, Seventh-Day Adventist, Jehovah's Witness, or Christian Scientist).

A third limitation we noted a decade ago was that a significant majority of the studies that have been done primarily examine "two-parent, marriage-based families, a family form that has declined over the past 50 years" (Dollahite et al., 2004, p. 422). By comparison, there have been rather substantial increases in the numbers of cohabiting couples and same-sex couples, as well as "significant increases in the number of single-parent families, stepfamilies," and (particularly) families of divorce—however, the increasing prevalence of these diverse families has *not* been accompanied by increases in religion-family research on these family forms (Dollahite et al., 2004, p. 422). More specifically, as Rostosky and colleagues (2008) observed after reviewing the scant available literature, "virtually nothing is known about religious involvement in same-sex couples" (p. 389). Similarly, although many studies have illustrated that cohabiting couples tend be significantly less religious than married couples, little is known about the in-depth, religious processes in cohabiting families (Thornton, Axinn, & Hill, 1992). To restate, then, social science has offered very little in the way of empirical data when it comes to the religion-family connection in diverse family forms.

Due to our focus on strong marriages of 20 years or so, most of our own *American Families of Faith* work has not been helpful in filling the void related to diverse family forms. A small percentage of the strong, marriage-based families we interviewed were stepfamilies, but none were cohabiting, same-sex, single-parent, or currently divorced families. As a result, neither our *American Families of Faith* project (nor the broader social sciences) have had much light to shed on religion in diverse family forms until recently, when a landmark study on faith in children of divorced families was published.

Does the Shape of Families Shape Faith?

Given that our own research does not capture the important topic of how and why divorce relates to involvement in (or movement away from) faith, we reached out to some respected colleagues who have conducted rare, large-scale examinations into the topic of faith and families of divorce—and we asked them to collaborate with us on this chapter. Based on groundbreaking research and their important recent report, *Does the Shape of Families Shape Faith?*, we are pleased to have the expertise of Amy Ziettlow and Charles Stokes reflected here. Their project on faith and family diversity is especially relevant to an emerging adult audience because their project represents a major effort to examine and understand the religious and spiritual lives of young adults who have experienced parental divorce. In other words, the project literally gives a voice to emerging adults who have personally experienced the divorce of their parents—including a large number of you reading these lines in this book.

The Influence of Divorce and Religion on Emerging Adults

At least one-quarter of today's young adults in the United States are grown children of divorce (Denton, 2012). Further, about one million additional children in the United States each year experience the divorce of their parents. Even so, there has been little attention given to how experiencing a divorce and/or growing up in a divorced family might shape the religious identities and faith journeys of young people. How this generation approaches questions of moral and spiritual meaning, and the choices they make for themselves and their families with regard to religious identity and involvement, will undoubtedly influence broader trends in society and in faith communities themselves.

Through the *Does the Shape of Families Shape Faith?* project, we have learned that, compared to those who grew up in families in which parents stayed married, young adults who experienced their parents' divorce during childhood ("children of divorce") feel less religious on the whole and are less likely to be involved in the regular practice of a faith. In one national study, two-thirds of people from married-parent families, compared to just over half of children from divorced families, say they are "very religious" or "fairly religious." Likewise, more than one-third of people from married-parent families currently attend religious services almost every week compared to just a quarter of people from divorced families (Marquardt, 2005).

Yet this overall picture can mask important differences. Some from divorced families eventually become much more religious in the wake of their parents' divorce, while some become much less religiously involved or drop out of faith altogether. An additional note is that a minority (but still a significant portion) of young adults who are grown children of divorce report that they are *more* religious now than their parents ever were (Marquardt, 2005). Why? Seeing one's parents' divorce presents a *crisis*. A crisis, according to psychologist Erik Erikson, is a potentially life-altering choice point—a profound developmental challenge (Erikson & Erikson, 1997). Some come away from a given crisis stronger and more resilient than before, while some emerge with lasting harm and damage. Virtually all, however, are *changed* as a result of the crisis. For many, it appears, experiencing one's parents' divorce is not only a relational or family crisis, it is also a crisis of faith. Many children of divorce experience a decrease in, or even a full-blown shattering of, personal religious faith, while some turn toward faith and emerge with a deeper commitment to their religious life than before the divorce. The former experience of decreasing faith, disillusionment, or even devastation is the more common path among children of divorce and is captured in the narrative of Angie, a participant in our *American Families of Faith* project. She vividly recalled:

> When I was in [my former] church, I hit rock bottom when my parents divorced and then the minister was publicly humiliated because he was having affairs on his wife. That was my loss in trust, my trust was totally broken and my family life was shattered all at the same time. I had no

> idea where to go. . . . At that time I had hit rock bottom. I had God but I didn't have a faith.

Angie's "loss in trust" is similar to a "loss in faith" described in other qualitative work (Palkovitz & Palm, 1998). Angie left her denomination. Indeed, she left Christianity altogether and said (of her parents and her unfaithful minister), "I wondered, how can *these* people lead others?" Variations on Angie's story are not uncommon. As discussed previously, due to the reality that faith and family are closely tied together for many, a loss of faith in family relationships is often accompanied by a loss of faith in the Divine—or at least in organized religion—as well. Journalist Stephanie Staal (2000), author of *The Love They Lost*, wrote of her belief system shattering on what she called the "night of revelation" concerning her parent's divorce. She explained:

> The night when I learned of my mother's affair . . . in my mind . . . is that night of revelation when my family abruptly came undone, even though my mother didn't actually move out for another year. That night, in the span of minutes, my entire belief system was shattered. And sometimes when the phone rings late at night or someone walks into the room with a stricken look, I feel the same icy tingle I felt so many years ago, as if my body has programmed itself to receive the unexpected jolt. That's how deep the memory lies for me.
>
> (p. 59)

For some children of divorce, their interpretation of religious texts involving parents can shift as well based on experiencing the divorce of their parents. In the *Between Two Worlds* documentary film, a young man named Ben recites a poem he wrote about his father leaving his mother during his childhood entitled "The Postmodern Prodigal."

> He just had to get out, couldn't take it anymore
> He was finally going to see what this big world had in store
> Life so far had thrown him nothing but curves
> He was set to be out from under and get what he deserved
> Responsibility and restrictive curfews no more
> Time to sew a few oats, life so far a bore
> Taking only what was his he walked out the door
> He never looked back; never thought all he had left was more
> Now years later, his more meant much less

Could he ever go back?
Face to face he must confess
That he'd run away from life's best
He bought an empty dream
Sometimes the grass isn't as green as it seems
Would they have me back? He wondered aloud
My family I've abandoned and I've been chasing a cloud
I gave it all up, love, family, and grace
I don't deserve to have my kids see my guilty face
Please Lord help me if you can
Make a way for me, I've blown it
I'm the prodigal dad.[2]

Ben, the son of "the prodigal dad," now leads a ministry for children of divorce, but he spent many years as a non-practicing Christian with serious doubts about the trustworthiness of the Divine.

Scholars find that the greatest predictor of the religious lives of youth remains the religious lives of their parents, as shown in large-scale survey research (Bengtson, Putney, & Harris, 2013; Denton, 2012). In-depth interviews have revealed the same information; namely, that of all religious practices mentioned, the most important in the family context is to "practice what you preach," as we have discussed previously in this book.

> I hit rock bottom when my parents divorced. . . . That was my loss in trust, my trust was totally broken and my family life was shattered all at the same time. I had no idea where to go. . . . At that time I had hit rock bottom. I had God but I didn't have a faith.
>
> —Angie, a mother from *American Families of Faith*
>
> The night when I learned of my mother's affair . . . in my mind . . . is that night of revelation when my family abruptly came undone. . . . That night, in the span of minutes, my entire belief system was shattered.
>
> —Stephanie Staal, *The Love They Lost*

Parents also play a vital role in influencing children's religious lives after divorce, particularly in a culture in which church attendance and involvement are not as common as they were a generation ago (Dollahite et al., 2004; Uecker & Ellison, 2012). Recent research shows that divorced fathers are especially influential in whether their children will continue to have a life in the church—or whether the religious portion of the child's life will be collateral damage in the divorce (Marquardt, 2005).

It is also becoming clear that grown children of divorce are at the leading edge of an increasing number of the rising generation that has considered itself "spiritual but not religious." Yet they form a kind of *broken leading edge,* with spiritual stories quite often characterized by loss or suffering. Having turned to God for solace and hope, many think of themselves as spiritual persons, but they report more difficulty practicing a faith within religious institutions.

Some of their discomfort may lie with their earlier experiences in congregations. In a national study by Elizabeth Marquardt, out of those young adults who were regularly attending a church or synagogue at the time of their parents' divorce, two-thirds say that *not one person* from the clergy or the congregation reached out to them at that time, while only one-quarter remember either a member of the clergy or a person from the congregation doing so (Marquardt, 2005, p. 155). This failure looms large and potentially lasting. Our own finding from previous research is that faith communities can have a unique, supportive role during challenges and crises due to their close relationship with families. However, when one's faith community lets an individual or a family down, it can cause "deeper frustration and pain than failures by secular agencies and institutions" (Marks & Dollahite, 2001, p. 636). Phrased differently, it can hurt profoundly when "your" church lets you down.

If we dig deeper into the inner lives of children of divorce, we learn even more. Scholars observe that children of divorce experience a disruption of the "**domestic church**" of their home (Rubio Hanlon, 2014). If they become alienated from formal religious practice, they can experience what Annette Mahoney and her colleagues call a **second silent schism** in their lives—the first schism being the rupture of their parents' marriage, and the second being the rupture of the child's connection to a faith community and even to a life of faith itself (Mahoney, Warner, & Krumei, 2010a, 2010b).

When a marriage comes apart, a child's way of life is split in two, with consequences for the child's relationships with people within the family and beyond. Professor Julie Rubio Hanlon similarly wrote that children from fragmented families experience disruption of the "domestic church" of their home (Rubio Hanlon, 2014). Many persons of faith understand families as domestic churches because it is in the home that most children first engage in religious practices (Bourg, 2004; Marks & Dollahite, 2012). With their parents, many children pray at meals and/or bedtime, read stories, and ask questions about the nature of God and the meaning of life. In homes, most U.S. children celebrate religious holidays and participate in family traditions, including sacred traditions. The "saints" who first touch children's lives are those who care for them day in and day out, teaching them by example what it means to be a person of faith.

When divorce touches families, these practices can be more difficult to maintain, and children can also experience a rupture in their congregational lives. In fact, some studies show that family *practices* are even more closely linked to strong faith in adulthood than family structure, but intact families are more likely to have the stability necessary to keep these practices going (Day et al., 2009; Zhai et al., 2007). Along with feelings of brokenness and struggles with trust, the loss of a stable environment for religious practice may partially explain lower levels of connection to religious institutions and religious faith among young adults who do not grow up in intact families (Rubio Hanlon, 2014).

Divorced parents create two separate homes and, by extension, two separate "domestic churches," often marked by a distinctly different frequency and character of religious belief and practice. Marquardt notes in *Between Two Worlds* that "after the divorce it's no longer the parent's job to rub together the sharp edges of their two different worlds, instead the rough edges of their worlds rub together in only one place—the inner life of the child."[3] In summary, some of the empirical work reviewed indicates three painful breaks in many children's lives post-divorce: (1) a marriage splits, (2) a family divides, and (3) children find themselves alienated from congregations (Mahoney et al., 2010).

God Images and Parental Divorce

A substantial body of scholarship supports the idea that children's early images of God arise, at least in part, from their lived experience with their own parents, a kind of "spiritualization of attachment" (The Commission on Children at Risk, 2003, pp. 27–28). In chapter 7, we cited Robert Ingersoll's statement that "it is difficult for a child to find a father in God, unless he finds something of God in his father." When religious traditions teach that God is a perfect, loving parent—and many denominations do—they reinforce early God images that children might develop (Kiesling, 2011). So what happens to a child's concept of a protective father God if he does not even know his biological father? Or, what happens when a child *does* know her father, but there is so little of the "godly" in him that the parental example tends to dispel, rather than encourage, her faith in *anything* noble, whether human or Divine? As discussed previously in this chapter, it appears that divorce is significantly related with broken or decreased faith in many divorce-affected children. However, there are many others who make their way beyond marital failure and/or parental failure to eventually find their own strength and successes related to faith. One remarkable young father we (Loren and Dave) interviewed several years ago remains in our memory. Marty was a remarkably devoted father to his six children. At one point during his interview, he stated:

> Fatherhood is really, perhaps the greatest thing that I could attain to. If I'm president of the United States, if I'm a C.E.O. of a major corporation, or if I receive recognition in any particular endeavor, no matter what it may be, that will end. The time would come and I would be voted out of office, or I would resign or retire, or I would lose my position or whatever it may be . . . and yet I will *always* be the father of my children.

Marty went on to say:

> I remember when I (first got married) experiencing the joy of marriage, married life, and thinking, "Ah, this is real life. This is what it was all about." I had a lot of (interesting and enjoyable) experiences [before I got married], but being married now seemed like a higher level of life. You know, it seemed more complete. I thought, "This is what life's really about." But I remember after we had a child . . . looking back at everything before and saying, "No, no, no, marriage isn't the end of the road here. Having a child," I thought, "This is what life is really all about. This is the great experience in life."

Marty's almost effusive love of his six children, including his son with profound special needs, was evident throughout his interview. At the conclusion of his interview, Loren commented in an offhanded way, "You must have had a great father." Marty's countenance fell, and his exuberance vanished. He told us that he had a terrible relationship with his father—so bad that when Marty was in fifth grade, he started making a list. This list consisted of negative things his father did to him that Marty promised himself he would *never* do to his own children when he became a father. The list also contained positive things that Marty *wanted* his father to do that his father never seemed to do. Marty told us that by the time he started college, the list was over 100 items long. Then came Marty's point. Marty confided that, although he was now in his mid-40s, he still had the list. He kept it in his sock drawer so that each morning he could read a couple of lines from the list and recommit to be the faithful kind of father *he* had desperately wanted as a child.

Many individuals emerge from childhood with painful ruptures left by parental failures, or by the failure of their parents' marriage (or marriages), or both. Marty's narrative reminds us that there are some who respond to these crises with remarkable resilience. Even so, we need to know more about the influence these crises and events have on children's lives.

A Brief Note on Theories of Moral Development

In the field of children's moral and spiritual development, most of the notable resources were either written several decades ago, before divorce was widespread, or continue implicitly to assume that most children have an intact, married-parent family structure even though this is no longer the case.

The literature on children's moral and spiritual development gives virtually no attention to the question of family structure and how growing up in a different kind of family, such as a divorced family, might influence children's moral and spiritual development. Some of the primary authors on children's moral development include Jean Piaget, Erik Erikson, Lawrence Kohlberg, Robert Coles, and Carol Gilligan. The field of children's religious or spiritual development is more diffuse but includes Sigmund Freud, Carl Jung, James Fowler, and, again, Robert Coles—as well as other, less well-known scholars. The theorists of moral development are often required reading in degree programs that train professionals who work with children and young people. Yet in this field, with the exception of Robert Coles and Carol Gilligan, the major works are five or more decades old. Most were written when one could assume that most children grew up living with their married mother and father.

Even most contemporary authors who write on moral or spiritual issues seem to continue to assume that children have an intact family experience, often focusing instead on other sites of socialization such as schools, peer groups, or faith communities. Yet, while these latter sources of influence are certainly important, none are as primary and formative in a child's experience generally, or in their religious experience specifically, as the family (Bengtson et al., 2013). While it remains important to address the spiritual and religious needs of children and adults who were raised in a two-parent married household, it is becoming more important to also be sure to attend to the spiritual and religious needs of children and adults raised in other family forms.

Emerging Social Science on How the Decline of Marriage Impacts Faith Communities

In this section we consider four important and related bodies of research that each examine, or at least begin to examine, the connections between divorce and subsequent outcomes in children's religious lives and involvement. The four areas of interest that will be briefly reviewed are: (a) family structure and child well-being; (b) parental divorce and children's religious involvement; (c) the role of parents in children's religious lives; and (d) the role of faith communities in children's religious lives.

Family Structure and Child Well-Being

Given that about one million children in the United States each year experience the divorce of their parents, and that more than half of children born to women under age 30 are now born outside of marriage, the religious identities and experiences of young people growing up without two married parents is a pressing concern for the health and future of families and congregations. To summarize, more than half of all children will spend at least a portion of their lives in a divorced or single-parent family context—and in some geographic or inner-city areas, the figure is nearly 75% (Wilcox et al., 2011).

Most books and articles about children of divorce have tended to focus on the social or economic consequences of divorce, often showing the links between divorce and serious childhood problems such as poverty, dropping out of school, juvenile delinquency, early sexual activity, and teen pregnancy (Wilcox et al., 2011). For example, a major study by psychologist Mavis Hetherington examined more than 1,000 divorced families over three decades and found that only 10% of young people from *intact* families experience serious social and emotional problems. By contrast, about 20% of young adults from families that experienced one divorce report serious social and emotional problems—double the problem rate of children from intact families. Among children who experience multiple divorces, however, the rate of serious social and emotional problems nearly doubles again to 38%, a factor almost four times the rate of those from continuously intact families (Hetherington & Kelly, 2002, pp. 228, 269). Despite the relatively high prevalence of problems among those who have experienced multiple divorces, we underscore the reality that even in these difficult contexts, *most* of the children (62%) are resilient enough to escape without serious social or emotional problems.

There is, however, much more to learn beyond "symptoms lists" (Wallerstein, 1991, p. 353). Among clinician-researchers, Judith Wallerstein was a pioneer in examining the more subtle, psychological effects of divorce in children and young people. By getting to know a sample of children of divorce extremely well and returning again and again over the years to talk with them, Wallerstein painted a more detailed portrait of the way divorce shapes the inner lives of many children, whether or not they end up with severe, diagnosable symptoms. Based on a 25-year longitudinal study, Wallerstein, Lewis, and Blakeslee (2001) found that experiencing parental divorce during childhood can have a later, emerging "sleeper effect." They reported:

> Contrary to what we have long thought, the major impact of divorce does not occur during childhood or adolescence. Rather, it rises in adulthood as serious romantic relationships move center stage. When it comes time to choose a life mate and build a new family, the effects of divorce crescendo.
>
> (p. xxix)

For many children of divorce, it appears that the worst symptoms often appear when children of divorce leave home and attempt to form their own families, but do so with perhaps less ability to trust—and without an "up close" concept of what a lasting marriage looks like (Wallerstein et al., 2001). Indeed, divorce can impact relationships, and it can impact religious faith.

Parental Divorce and Children's Religious Involvement

As noted previously, we now know that when children of divorce reach adulthood, compared to those who grew up in intact families, they feel less religious on the whole and are less likely to be involved in the regular practice of a faith. One important study found that Catholic and mainline Protestant children of divorce are more than twice as likely to leave religious practice altogether and that conservative Protestants are more than three times as likely to do so than those from continuously married families (Lawton & Bures, 2001). In a new analysis of data from the General Social Survey, sociologists found that parental divorce most impacts the religious identity of the children involved—specifically, that children are likely to either leave faith community altogether or to switch denominations after experiencing the divorce (Uecker & Ellison, 2012).

A look at childhood involvement in faith communities turns up significant differences. Young people from intact families are much more likely to say that they attended religious services regularly as children, with almost three-quarters saying they attended every week or almost every week compared to just over half of children of divorce. People from divorced families are only half as likely as those from intact families to say that they attended religious services frequently throughout their childhood.

Can Faith Increase After Parental Divorce?

While we may be tempted to presume that divorce always has a negative effect on religious belief and practice, some from divorced families eventually become much *more* religious in the wake of their parents' divorce—especially when compared with their parents. Grown children of divorce are twice as likely as people from intact families to feel that they are *more* religious now than their mothers ever were. The same children (now adults) were also much more likely to feel that way about their fathers than their peers from intact families. As one evangelical pastor interviewed by University of Notre Dame sociologist Mary Ellen Konieczny observed, "Sometimes divorce is such a hard thing that they (the children of divorce) turn to God for help and healing" (Konieczny, 2010, pp. 14–15). Other growing children of divorce might turn to congregational life for help in coping with loneliness or suffering. For example, one participant in the *Does the Shape of Families Shape Faith?* study said that, as a teen, the church became his "home away from home" (Marquardt, 2005).

Some studies trace the different paths that children of divorce follow before and after their parents' divorce. Melinda Lundquist Denton (2012), analyzing data from the National Study of Youth and Religion, examined the religious starting points of youth in order to determine whether a parental breakup has different effects on youth depending on their religious experience prior to the breakup. She found that "the experience of parental breakup in adolescence triggers an increase in the odds of religious change, whether that change is a move toward or away from religion."[4] She continued:

> An interesting aspect of these findings, however, was that while a parental breakup was associated with religious change, the type of religious change was not always away from religion. Parental breakup was significantly associated with movement to religious profiles characterized by both more and less religious engagement.
>
> (p. 59)

Table 10.1 The Myth of the "Good Divorce" and Religious Involvement

Drawing on the writing of Constance Ahrons and others, some have presented the opinion that what harms children is not divorce per se, but the intense conflict that typically surrounds divorce. In an examination of children's religious involvement, sociologists found significant differences in religious experience when it came to those who reported they were raised in happy, intact marriages and those who reported their parents had a reasonably friendly or amicable divorce (Ellison et al., 2011). Key findings included:

1. The odds of religious attendance are more than twice as high for those raised in happy, intact marriages compared to those raised in amicable divorces.
2. Those raised in happy, intact marriages have the lowest levels of religious disinterest, compared to those raised in amicable divorces.
3. Those raised in happy, intact marriages are more likely to report an absence of negative experiences of God, compared to those raised in amicable divorces.
4. Those raised in happy, intact marriages are somewhat less likely than those raised in amicable divorces to identify as "neither religious nor spiritual."
5. At the same time, when it came to frequency of prayer activity, there were no observable differences when it came to family background.

—from Ellison et al., 2011

In another related study, Regnerus and Uecker explored the family contexts in which religious transformations occur. Using data from the National Longitudinal Study of Adolescent Health, they found that family structure is more significant for adolescents' religious decline than for religious growth (Regnerus & Uecker, 2006).

Consistent with the other studies mentioned, youth in single-parent families are more likely to report a decrease in church attendance and to say that their religious faith is less important when compared to those from intact, two-parent families. Adolescents in other diverse family forms are also more likely than their counterparts from intact families to show a decline in church attendance, but, at the same time, they are more likely to show an increase in private religiosity, such as frequency of personal prayer (Regnerus & Uecker, 2006).

While parental divorce might predict an adolescent's decision to abandon organized, institutional religion, it is more difficult to predict an increase in personal spirituality and individual-level religiosity. Thus, Regnerus and Uecker write:

> It may be helpful to think of positive religious transformations and conversions (involving sharp growth in religiosity) and religious apostasy

> (i.e., losing religion) as two separate entities, each with its own set of mechanisms and patterns. The presence of the one has little in common with the absence of the other.
>
> (p. 232)

Drawing on a study of 274 students at a Midwestern state university whose parents divorced within the past five years, psychologist Annette Mahoney and colleagues theorized that parental divorce can be a spiritual trauma (Mahoney et al., 2010). They suggest that parental divorce would be "experienced as a spiritual trauma depending on how much a child interprets parental divorce as threatening and damaging to the core spiritual values he or she holds" (2010b, p. 11). In particular, interpreting one's parents' divorce as a "sacred loss" or "desecration" intensifies the suffering felt by children of divorce because such an interpretation can "turn faith into an added source of suffering" (2010b, p. 2). The following three quotations from that study's participants are examples of such feelings:

> My family was very religious growing up and when the divorce happened, I lost that religious framework in my life. I saw my family as a sacred entity and then it was shattered.
>
> I felt the vows that they made before their families and God were violated and they now meant nothing.
>
> I am Catholic and I believe in God. I went through a divorce when I was 5 years old with my real dad and now I am going through another with my mom and stepfather at age 20. I believe God has a plan but it is hard to convince yourself [of] that [in the face of] such tragedy.
>
> (Warner, 2007; see also Warner, Mahoney, & Krumrei, 2009)

Overall, researchers found that college students who see their parents' divorce through a "negative spiritual lens" say that they felt greater distress (Mahoney et al., 2010b, p. 16).

While there are a diverse range of suggestions as to why the adult children of divorced parents are less likely to be involved in religious institutions than their peers from intact families, there is little doubt about the correlation. Much of the early research linking religious decline with divorce suggested that the erosion of religion as a source of normative authority undermined the institutional support for marriage. More recent work, however, such as that by sociologist Brad Wilcox, seems to point the arrow in the other direction. In other words, it appears that in significant measure, the decline of the institution of marriage—marked by widespread divorce, but also including increases in non-marital childbearing, cohabitation, and later ages at first marriage—has contributed to lower levels of religious affiliation and participation (Wilcox, 2007). In spite of this general decline, Dollahite, Hawkins, and Parr (2012) found that many religious couples seem to remain devoted to the institution of marriage despite the erosion of such devotion in contemporary society.

Role of Parents in Children's Religious Lives

As we have previously noted, the greatest predictor of the religious lives of youth is the religious lives of their parents (Smith & Denton, 2005). Sociologist Melinda Lundquist Denton has said, "Youth with highly religious parents are much more likely to be highly religious themselves, while youth whose parents are disengaged from religion are more likely to be disengaged as well" (Denton, 2012). Again and again, a marriage-based structure predicts higher levels of religious engagement by families across several studies (Denton, 2012; Myers, 1996; Regnerus & Uecker, 2006; Zhai et al., 2007).

Professor Denton continues, "Two-parent families may also be better able to support religious practices such as religious service attendance and engagement in a religious community" (also see, Day et al., 2009; Wilcox, 2006). Overall, the literature on family structure and religious socialization suggests that youth who live with two parents are more likely to identify as religious than youth who live in households with an alternative family structure—at least religious in terms of participation with a faith community. Denton partially attributed this drop to the ways a divorced parent may struggle logistically to maintain consistent attendance in worship or in activities of religious socialization for both the child and for herself or himself.

Parents play a vital role in influencing their children's religious lives after divorce, particularly in a culture in which congregational involvement or other forms of civic involvement are no longer as common as they once were. Sociologists Uecker and Ellison found that the role of parents appears to be both strong and growing in importance in determining the religiosity of children (Uecker & Ellison, 2012). Consistent with the findings of Denton presented earlier, Uecker and Ellison found that what seems to be most important is whether a child's parents identify as religious at all and whether the parents are religiously active and involved. The outcomes affected by parental divorce were most often children's leaving religion altogether or switching to another religion (Uecker & Ellison, 2012).

Sociologists Norval Glenn and Elizabeth Marquardt found that one reason adult children of divorce appear to be less religious overall is that they were less likely than those in intact families to recall finding sources of religious and spiritual guidance in their families. They were also less likely to say that their parents encouraged them to practice a religious faith. Just over half of children of divorce versus almost four-fifths of people from intact families agreed with the statement, "My mother encouraged me to practice a religious faith." That difference was even greater when it came to fathers, with about one-third of grown children of divorce saying their fathers encouraged them to practice a religious faith compared to about two-thirds of people from intact families (see Figure 10.1).

Glenn and Marquardt also found similar differences in the area of prayer. Far fewer than half of children of divorce but more than two-thirds of people from intact families agreed with the statement, "My mother taught me how to pray." Slightly more than one-third of children of divorce but more than half of people from intact families said that they often prayed with their mothers. Similarly, fewer than one-fifth of children of divorce but almost half of people from intact families said their fathers taught them how to pray, and fewer than one-fifth of grown children of divorce versus well over one-third of people from intact families said they often prayed with their fathers.

The national survey by Glenn and Marquardt also showed that children of divorce were about twice as likely to say that they doubted the sincerity of their parents' religious beliefs—a feeling that not only indicates the skepticism some have about their parents' religious beliefs but also hints at doubts many children of divorce have regarding their parents in general. Nineteen percent of children of divorce compared to 9% of their peers from intact families were skeptical of their mothers' religious beliefs, and 27% of children of divorce compared to 14% of people from intact families said the same thing about their fathers (see Figure 10.2).

Overall, in an analysis of the Glenn and Marquardt study, Professor Elisa Zhai and her colleagues found that the link between parental divorce and lower likelihood of the grown children being regular religious attenders was significantly explained by lower levels of the father's involvement in the religious lives of these children (Zhai et al., 2007). In at least one empirical study, there were hints that the relative lack of faith community involvement exhibited by children of divorce is not just about religious *activity* but also religious *identity*. In other words, divorce not only changed what many children *did* in terms of religious involvement; it also changed the ways they *thought* about and *saw* themselves.

Taken together, the findings outlined in this chapter highlight the powerful role that parents—including measurable influence from both mothers *and*

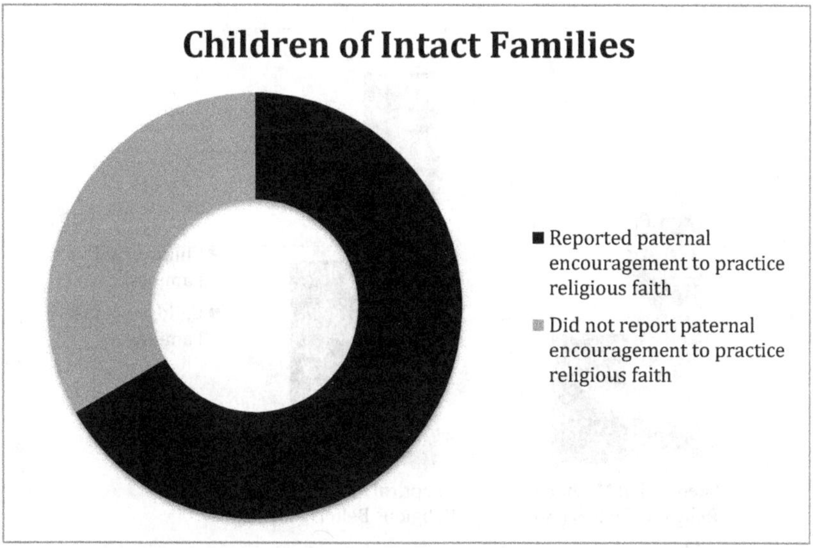

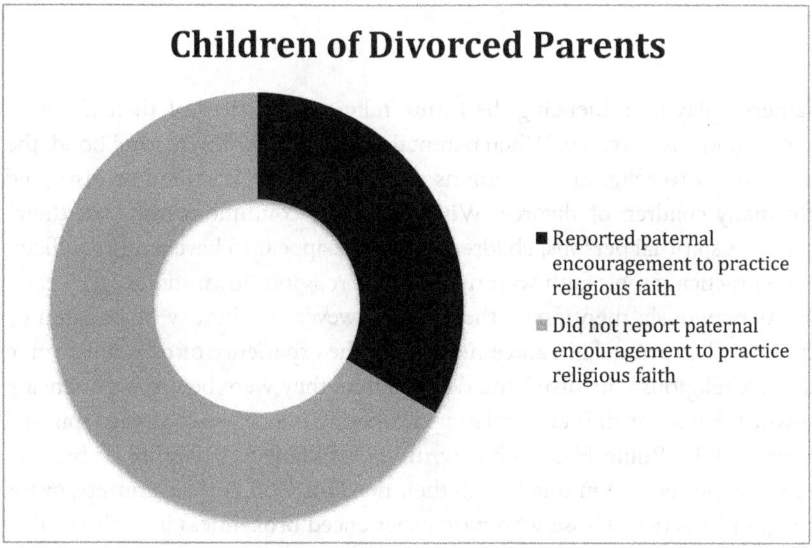

Figure 10.1 Children's Reports of Parents' Religious Encouragement

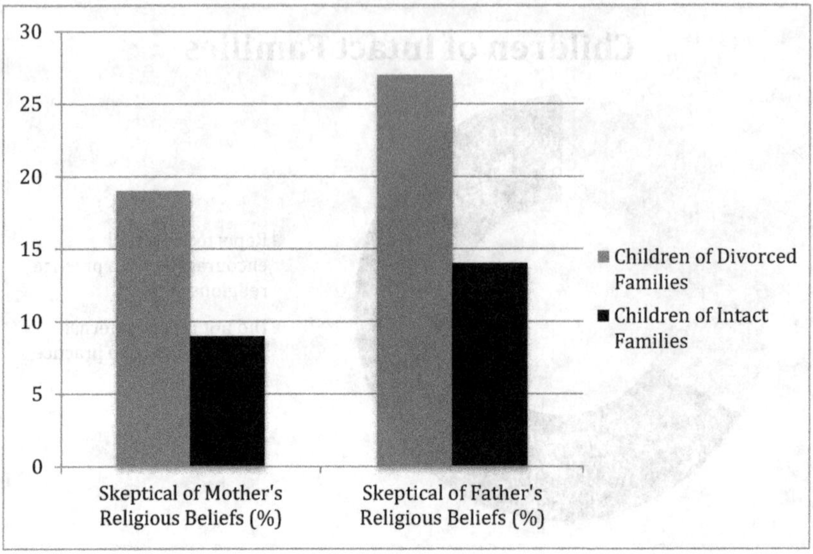

Figure 10.2 Children's Reports of Doubt of Sincerity of Parents' Religious Beliefs

fathers—play in influencing the future religious practices of their children, before and after divorce. When parental divorce breaks the marital bond, the attachment to religious institutions also seems to be fractured or disrupted for many children of divorce. While they may continue to think of themselves as spiritual persons, children of divorce appear to have a more difficult time practicing their faith within traditional religious institutions.

As previously mentioned, there are, however, a minority of children of divorce who turn to faith and emerge from the experience of parental divorce as *more* religiously involved and devoted than they were before experiencing divorce. For some, it seems, relational suffering is a pathway toward spiritual healing. Julie Rubio Hanlon has written that knowing suffering or brokenness can put people in touch with their need for God, for community, or for religious practice. Those who have experienced brokenness in their families of origin may have had early experiences of the imperfection and frailty of human beings. They may be open to the idea of a God who loves unconditionally, a faith community in which to seek meaning, or a religious practice that engages them with higher truths. We now turn to a brief discussion of faith communities and see that, unfortunately, these ideals are frequently unmet.

Role of Faith Communities in Children's Religious Lives

To this point in the chapter we have primarily focused on how divorce influences children's ongoing relationship with religion. We now take a closer look at another potential reason for the typical decline in religious involvement—the response (or lack of response) from the faith community itself. Sociologist Penny Edgell is among scholars who have pointed out that congregations are typically more welcoming of two-parent families, making it easier for such families to engage in congregational life in ways that single-parent and other diverse families might find less inviting or more difficult (Edgell, 2005).

Similarly, in his volume *Children of Divorce: The Loss of Family as the Loss of Being*, Andrew Root (2010) expresses the view that:

> The church might better serve the world and those millions of young people experiencing their parents' divorce if we could witness to the reality that divorce at its most primary level . . . is an act that leaves us [as children of divorce] feeling unreal, lost, as though the world is unreliable.
>
> (p. 139)

Root has further argued that the most important thing for the child to know is that the divorce was not his or her fault. Root further found that the most fundamental problem—and the greatest source of suffering—occurs at the level of children's being. Root argued that questions such as "Who am I?" take on a new and often confusing quality—now that the people who are responsible for bringing the child into being are no longer together.

Scholars like Julie Rubio Hanlon and Andrew Root, in separate studies and approaching the topic from different angles, both emphasized that faith community leaders can play a powerful role in honoring the lived experience and responding to the deep questions faced by children of divorce. Root (2010) concluded:

> The community of the church cannot eliminate the deep . . . fractures that occur when divorce strikes, but it can . . . stand with and for these children, bearing their brokenness. . . . You may have lost the union in the [family] community that created you, but you are secure in the [faith] community that knows a power that brings life out of death, a power in which isolation gives way to belonging.
>
> (p. 122)

Indeed, based on a large-scale study, sociologist Chris Ellison and his coauthors concluded that it appeared that those from divorced families are no less interested in finding meaning, truth, or a connection with God than their counterparts from intact marriages. However, those from divorced families do appear considerably more skeptical that established religious institutions or traditions can be helpful in that quest (Ellison et al., 2011). Perhaps their loss of trust in the institution of marriage and the loss of family traditions plays a role in their skepticism.

Similarly, leading marriage therapist and researcher Bill Doherty has noted the two-part reality that most emerging adults reportedly *want* a committed marriage relationship "someday" as much as previous generations but that they are more skeptical of whether this *can* actually happen than previous generations (Doherty, 2013). Children of divorce, in particular, find that they do not know how a long-term marriage functions, and they wonder if they can stay married.

These findings from Ellison and colleagues on one hand and Doherty on the other seem to reflect widespread longing for faith, for a sense of sacred meaning, and for high commitment marriage among emerging adults (including children of divorce)—but equally widespread is a sense of lingering doubt that such hopes are attainable based on the pain and disappointment that many have experienced in their families of origin. In connection with hopes and dreams related to both faith and future family relationships, faith communities *can*, at their best, provide space where married men and women—from newlyweds to those with young children to retired couples—can come to worship, serve, and have fellowship with each other. For a child of divorce, a faith community can provide positive models that allow them to see how the institution and covenant of marriage *can* work over a lifetime. Further, these positive examples of marriage with a faith community can be a vital element that gives them the confidence to choose to marry and stay married themselves. Faith communities can play a vital role in speaking hope to those grieving divorce and in modeling enduring relationships to children of divorce. Through story, mentoring, and (perhaps most importantly) genuine lived example, faith communities can create sacred space for children of divorce to hear and see how and why marriage matters.

Conclusion

In this chapter, we noted that a majority of the research on religion and families has addressed traditional families and that diverse family forms have largely been overlooked, including single-parent families, stepfamilies, same-sex families, and families of divorce. Using data and insights from the *Does the Shape of Families Shape Faith?* project, we were able to convey a novel portrait of families of divorce. In short, it appears that (like social science) many religions have not offered adequate attention to these families and their individual members. We have repeatedly observed that "a key challenge for [many] American churches in the 21st century will be to find a balance between supporting the standard of marriage-based families that is idealized . . . [while simultaneously and sensitively] addressing the pluralistic family realities that confront them" (Dollahite et al., 2004, p. 414; Marks, Dollahite, & Freeman, 2012, p. 188). The relational and spiritual futures and fates of many families (and some faith communities themselves) may rest, in some measure, in how well this is done in the years to come.

Chapter Summary Points

1. In an effort to fill gaps in social science research, the *American Families of Faith* research project has focused on collecting interview data from families of diverse ethnicities and different religions (including non-Christian religions).
2. Very little research has examined families of cohabiting couples, same-sex couples, single parents, or stepfamilies.
3. Research from the past decade has indicated that crisis in the family often leads to a crisis in faith for the children and that parental divorce often negatively impacts the religiosity of the children, although there are exceptions.
4. Much of the available literature about children's moral and spiritual development is inadequate because it does not address non-traditional families.
5. Divorce has been found to be influential on children even when they reach adulthood and begin their own families.
6. While faith communities tend to accept traditional families more readily, they can also provide divorced families with needed social support, guidance, and positive example.

Review Questions

1. What percentage of young adults who regularly attended services during their parents' divorce report that "not one member of the clergy or congregation reached out to them"?

2. What does "second silent schism" mean?
3. How do divorced parents affect a child's view of God, according to the text?
4. What explanation does Konieczny offer for children of divorce who say they are more religious than their parents?
5. What are some reasons the text cites for why adult children of divorce appear to be less religious?
6. According to Ellison et al. (2011), what are some similarities and differences between those from divorced and intact families with respect to religion?

Notes

1. This chapter is co-authored with Amy Ziettlow and Charles E. Stokes. Portions of this chapter are reprinted with permission from a report entitled, *Does the Shape of Families Shape Faith?* by Elizabeth Marquardt, Amy Ziettlow, and Charles E. Stokes. This was a Lilly Endowment–sponsored project, based at the Institute for American Values and developed in consultation with the University of Texas at Austin and the University of Chicago Divinity School.
2. From film version Marquardt et al. (2007), *Between Two Worlds*, Boyer Productions, Ltd., minutes 19:10–20:06. Last accessed March 4, 2015, at http://americanvalues.org/search/item.php?id=862.
3. From the *Between Two Worlds* film documentary.
4. Denton also categorized the five types of adolescent religiosity she found.

References

Bengtson, V. L., Putney, N. M., & Harris, J. (2013). *Families of faith*. New York: Oxford.

Bourg, F. C. (2004). *Where two or three are gathered: Christian families as domestic churches*. Notre Dame, IN: University of Notre Dame Press.

The Commission on Children at Risk (2003). *Hardwired to connect: The new scientific case for authoritative communities*. New York: Institute for American Values.

Day, R. D., Jones-Sappei, H., Price, J. L. S., Orthner, D. K., Hair, E. C., Moore, K. A., & Kaye, K. (2009). Family processes and adolescent religiosity and religious practice: View from the NLSY97. *Marriage and Family Review, 45*, 289–309.

Denton, M. L. (2012). Family structure, family disruption, and profiles of adolescent religiosity. *Journal for the Scientific Study of Religion, 51*, 42–64.

Doherty, W. J. (2013). *Take back your marriage (2nd ed.)*. New York: Guilford.

Dollahite, D. C., Hawkins, A. J., & Parr, M. R. (2012). Something more: The meanings of marriage for religious couples. *Marriage and Family Review, 48*, 339–362.

Dollahite, D. C., Marks, L. D., & Goodman, M. (2004). Religiosity and families: Relational and spiritual linkages in a diverse and dynamic cultural context. In M. J. Coleman, &

L. H. Ganong (Eds.), *The handbook of contemporary families* (pp. 411–431). Thousand Oaks, CA: Sage.

Edgell, P. (2005). *Religion and family in changing society*. Princeton, NJ: Princeton University.

Ellison, C. G., Walker, A. B., Glenn, N. D., & Marquardt, E. (2011). The effects of parental marital discord and divorce on the religious and spiritual lives of young adults. *Social Science Research, 40*, 538–551.

Erikson, E. H., & Erikson, J. M. (1997). *The life cycle completed*. New York: Norton.

Hetherington, E. M., & Kelly, J. (2002). *For better or for worse: Divorce reconsidered*. New York: W.W. Norton and Company.

Kiesling, C. (2011). An attachment theory approach to narrating the faith journey of children of parental divorce. *International Journal of Children's Spirituality, 16*, 301–313.

Konieczny, M. E. (2010). All of a sudden you don't fit: Clergy and congregational responses to divorce and marital conflict. Paper presented at the Society for the Scientific Study of Religion and Religious Research Association Annual Meeting, Baltimore, MD.

Lawton, L. E., & Bures, R. (2001). Parental divorce and the "switching" of religious identity. *Journal for the Scientific Study of Religion, 40*, 99–111.

Mahoney, A., Warner, H., & Krumei, E. (2010a). Broken vows and the next generation: Recognizing and helping when parental divorce is a spiritual trauma. *Counseling and Spirituality, 29*, 99–126 [French language version].

Mahoney, A., Warner, H., & Krumei, E. (2010b). Broken vows and the next generation: Recognizing and helping when parental divorce is a spiritual trauma. [English language version]. Retrieved from http://www.ncbi.nlm.nih.gov/pmc/articles/PMC4478045/#R37.

Marks, L. D., & Dollahite, D. C. (2001). Religion, relationships, and responsible fathering in Latter-day Saint families of children with special needs. *Journal of Social and Personal Relationships, 18*, 625–650.

Marks, L. D., & Dollahite, D. C. (2012). "Don't forget home": The importance of sacred ritual in families. In J. Hoffman (Ed.), *Understanding religious ritual: Theoretical approaches and innovations* (pp. 186–203). New York: Routledge.

Marks, L. D., Dollahite, D. C., & Freeman, J. J. (2012). Faith and prayer in family life. In A. J. Hawkins, D. C. Dollahite, & T. W. Draper (Eds.), *Successful marriages and family life* (pp. 185–195). Provo, UT: BYU Studies.

Marquardt, E. (2005). *Between two worlds: The inner lives of children of divorce*. New York: Crown.

Myers, S. M. (1996). An interactive model of religiosity inheritance: The importance of family context. *American Sociological Review, 61*, 858–866.

Palkovitz, R. & Palm, G. (1998). Fatherhood and faith in formation: The developmental effects of fathering on religiosity, morals, and values. *The Journal of Men's Studies, 7*, 33–52.

Regnerus, M. D., & Uecker, J. E. (2006). Finding faith, losing faith: The prevalence and context of religious transformation during adolescence. *Review of Religious Research, 47*, 217–237.

Root, A. (2010). *Children of divorce: The loss of family as the loss of being*. Grand Rapids, MI: Baker Academic.

Rostosky, S. S., Riggle, E. D. B., Brodnicki, C., & Olson, C. (2008). An exploration of lived religion in same-sex couples from Judeo-Christian traditions. *Family Process, 47*, 389–403.

Rubio Hanlon, J. (2014). Ministering to the unaffiliated: A challenge for the church. In Karlijn Demasure (Ed.), *Family's many faces: La famille as pluriel* (pp. 113–130). Walpole, MA: Peeters.

Smith, C., & Denton, M. L. (2005). *Soul searching: The religious and spiritual lives of American teenagers*. New York: Oxford.

Staal, S. (2000). *The love they lost: Living with the legacy of our parent's divorce*. New York: Delta.

Thornton, A., Axinn, W. G., & Hill, D. H. (1992). Reciprocal effects of religiosity, cohabitation, and marriage. *American Journal of Sociology, 98*, 628–651.

Uecker, J. E., & Ellison, C. G. (2012). Parental religious characteristics, parental divorce, and the religious lives of young adults. *Journal for the Scientific Study of Religion, 51*, 777–794.

Wallerstein, J. S. (1991). The long-term effects of divorce on children: A review. *Journal of the American Academy of Child Adolescent Psychiatry, 30*, 349–360.

Wallerstein, J. S., Lewis, J., & Blakeslee, S. (2001). *The unexpected legacy of divorce: A 25 year landmark study*. New York: Hyperion.

Warner, H. L. (2007). Understanding Parental Divorce from a Religious and Spiritual Framework: Religious Coping Theory and Post-Divorce Adjustment. Unpublished manuscript based on preliminary examination. Bowling Green State University.

Warner, H. L., Mahoney, A., & Krumrei, E. J. (2009). When parents break sacred vows: The role of spiritual appraisals, coping, and struggles for young adults' adjustment to parental divorce. *Psychology of Religion and Spirituality, 1*, 233–248.

Wilcox, W. B. (2006). Family. In H. R. Ebaugh (Ed.), *Handbook of religion and social institutions* (pp. 97–120). New York: Springer.

Wilcox, W. B. (2007). As the family goes. *First Things* (May 2007). Retrieved from http://www.firstthings.com/article/2007/04/as-the-family-goes.

Wilcox, W. B., et al. (2011). *Why marriage matters: Thirty conclusions from the social sciences*. New York: Institute for American Values.

Zhai, J. E., Ellison, C. G., Glenn, N. D., & Marquardt, E. (2007). Parental divorce and religious involvement among young adults. *Sociology of Religion, 68*, 125–144.

11 How Religion Influences Coping with Stress and Challenges in Families[1]

In three short words, psychiatrist M. Scott Peck tells us in his book *The Road Less Traveled*, "Life is difficult" (Peck, 1978). However, Dr. Peck also shares that once we accept that life is fraught with difficulties, that fact no longer incapacitates us. Our longtime friend and colleague, Professor Jeff Hill, begins his family studies classes by reminding his students of two truths: (1) "Life is hard," but (2) "We can do hard things." He should know; several years ago during mid-life, he lost his beloved wife to cancer. Jeff is now a co-parent in a large, blended family and is remarried to Tammy, who lost her first spouse as well. Their shared life is full of stressors and challenges, but Jeff still ends his e-mails with the signature: "Life is wonderful." We continue to be inspired by his optimism, strength, and profound faith.

One key finding of our *American Families of Faith* research project is that (instead of being defeated by challenges) strong families find ways to effectively cope with and *grow closer* through stressful situations. Interestingly, six decades ago, Jeff Hill's uncle, family sociologist Reuben Hill, began to conceptually and empirically examine why some families succumb to crisis as a result of a stressful situation, while other families remain resilient. While stress can lead to crisis, crisis can also lead to familial resilience and the ability of the family to better cope with future stressors. Different families obviously have different strengths and weaknesses. Hill (1958) referred to family strengths and assets as resources. In the context of this book on religion and families, we note that for families that identify as highly religious (including most of those in the *American Families of Faith* project), their religion is a multi-faceted resource that can help through providing meaning (e.g., through spiritual beliefs), coping behaviors (e.g., through sacred personal and familial rituals), and social support (e.g., through local faith community). In those families, couples, and individuals for whom religion is central, turning to religion is a frequent collective response to a stressful situation. We next examine religious coping in more detail.

Religious Coping

Religious coping has been defined as a partnered, sacred search for significance alongside a higher power and during a time of stress (Pargament & Raiya, 2007). Sacred can reference a higher power or God (Pargament & Mahoney, 2002), or sacred can describe the transition of an experience from ordinary to holy (Burr, Marks, & Day, 2012). Either way, religious coping is a partnered response to stress, and God is often the partner of choice.

For those for whom religion is central or important, religious coping is most likely to come to the forefront of coping processes during situations that are perceived as extreme, threatening, and uncontrollable (Pargament, 1997). For example, following the devastating 9/11 terrorist attacks, one study asked 1,900 Americans about their coping responses and found that over 90% of them had turned to religion as a way to cope (Silver et al., 2004). In addition, religious coping as a coping mechanism is more common among certain groups and in specific contexts (Spilka, Shaver, & Kirkpatrick, 1985). For example, research has consistently found that religious coping is more common among poorer families, African-American families, and older families (Koenig, King, & Carson, 2012). Further, those with limited resources (e.g., money and social support) are more likely to consider the sacred in their perception of the stressor event, perhaps because they have relatively few alternative resources to draw upon (Pargament & Raiya, 2007). Also, predictably, religious coping is more common for those families highly involved in religious contexts and faith communities (Pargament, 1997). As with psychological coping in general, religious coping can be expressed in various ways and can be either positive or negative.

Variations of Religious Coping

Religious coping has been separated into three distinctive approaches: (1) the **self-directing approach**, where families recognize the existence of God or a higher power but choose not to involve the Divine in coping with the stressor; (2) the **deferring approach**, in which the family "passes the burden" to God and the entire coping responsibility is deferred to the Divine; and (3) the **collaborative approach**, wherein the coping responsibility is shared between the family and their God (Pargament, 1997). To highlight these different approaches with an example, let's consider a child committing a serious crime as the stressor event. If the family chooses to place the child in a reformative intervention without praying to (e.g., consulting) God in the decision, then they are taking a *self-directed* approach. If the family decides *not* to personally intervene in the criminal behavior of the child, but instead ask God to deal with the situation, they are taking a *deferring* approach (e.g., "We'll leave it all in God's hands."). Finally, if the family seeks divine guidance and then uses that guidance to inform their decision to take reformative action, they are taking a *collaborative* religious coping approach (e.g., "With God's help, we can get this child back on track."). Beyond these three approaches, there exist positive and negative variations of religious coping.

Just as non-religious coping is not always positive and effective at minimizing or eliminating the stressor, religious coping is not always a healthy response to stress. Furthermore, researchers have been challenged with overly simplistic definitions and measurements of religious coping. As a solution to the oversimplified measures of religiosity, Dr. Kenneth Pargament and colleagues sought to develop a better way to measure religious coping for people experiencing stress (Pargament, 1997; Pargament, Koenig, & Perez, 2000). Their efforts led to a detailed, 105-item instrument that identified both positive and negative religious coping responses (Pargament et al., 2000).

During a stressful situation, positive religious coping has been associated with a secure attachment to God, a belief that life has meaning, and a spiritual connection with close family and friends (Pargament & Raiya, 2007). Positive religious coping may appear in the form of someone reappraising a situation from a religious perspective or collaborating with his or her God to seek a solution for the stressor event.

By way of contrast, negative religious coping has been associated with a detachment from one's God, feelings that one has been abandoned by God, and avoiding one's religious institution or congregation (Pargament & Raiya, 2007). An individual may exhibit aspects of negative religious coping if he or she believes that God has allowed the stressor to be experienced as a form of punishment.

Scores of studies have associated positive religious coping with better mental health (Koenig et al., 2012; Tarakeshwar & Pargament, 2001), but negative religious coping has repeatedly been correlated with poorer mental and physical health outcomes (Cole, 2005; Pargament et al., 2001; Pargament & Raiya, 2007). Further, these findings have been validated in studies with varying religious groups, cultures, and ethnicities. In addition, in these different groups, research has consistently found that prayer is the most frequently practiced form of religious coping in response to stress (Bänziger, Uden, & Janssen, 2008; Koenig et al., 2012; Taylor, Chatters, & Levin, 2004). As Ken Pargament, a leading psychologist of religious coping, has observed, "Although religion is often a source of help and integration, certain religious expressions appear to be part of the problem rather than part of the solution when it comes to coping" (Pargament et al., 1998, p. 88). The take-home message is that not all religious coping is created equal.

Prayer as a Coping Mechanism

Pioneering psychologist of religion William James (1902) believed that prayer is "the soul and essence of religion" (p. 365). More than a century later, over 75% of U.S. adults pray daily or weekly, and although people pray for many reasons (e.g., thanksgiving, understanding, praise), studies of religious coping have typically explored **petitionary prayer** (e.g., Pew Forum, 2008). Petitionary prayers make a request and place an emphasis on outcome (Bänziger et al., 2008). Petitionary prayers are often thought of as impulsive cries for help, in at least partial contrast to rote prayers that are "memorized." Further, petitionary prayers are often the result of stressors, with the prayer calling on God to alter the impact of the stressor. Although little research has examined the use of prayer as a coping mechanism in families, information gleaned from research on individual prayer can inform our understanding regarding families.

One study found that prayer is most often used as a source of coping for health-related issues (Koenig et al., 2012). While this may also hold true for families, as recognized by the numerous prayer studies on caregivers for sick family members (Johnson, Elbert-Avila, & Tulsky, 2005), family dynamics can create unique stressors beyond health that may evoke a need to pray. For example, many minority families utilize prayer to cope with structural and blatant racism in the workplace and other settings (Hayward & Krause, 2015; Marks et al., 2006; Shorter-Gooden, 2004). The prayers of a family may be framed in any of the three religious coping approaches (i.e., self-directing, deferring, or collaborative), but when used as a deferring or collaborative approach, prayer has been found to ease the anxiety and depression associated with stress (Koenig et al., 2012; Wong-McDonald & Gorsuch, 2000).

Several additional prayer studies have found prayer to be a useful coping mechanism for challenges that arise in parent-child or husband-wife relationships (Brown et al., 2011). Many of these studies address **intercessory prayer**, or praying on behalf of someone else. Instead of seeking a personal outcome in relation to a personal stressor, those that say intercessory prayers are asking God or a higher power to heal, bless, or help someone else (Krause, 2010). Nearly 98% of praying Americans report that they pray for others, and these other-oriented prayers are most often on behalf of their family members (Gallup & Lindsay, 1999). When studying intercessory prayer as a coping mechanism, the research focus is typically on the impact experienced by the person *doing* the praying, not the person being prayed for.

Let's consider a couple scenarios. A mother is concerned about the behavior of her son; he has been fighting at school, and she fears that his actions will land him in a detention center. The mother has reached her breaking point, and all she can do is pray for her son to change his rebellious ways. In another home, a husband is dealing with the stress of having a cancer-stricken wife. The husband fears that his wife may not be able to overcome the illness, and he prays relentlessly for her health. In both instances, it is possible that the family member offering the prayers feels strengthened in his or her personal coping efforts. It is also possible that neither the rebellious son nor the cancer-stricken wife may gain any benefit from the prayers offered on their behalf. While research has found that intercessory prayers can have a positive impact on physical and psychological well-being when those being prayed for are aware of the prayers (Krause, 2010), frequently the prayers have a calming effect that lessen the perceived severity of the stressor for the person praying (Schafer, 2013). In the aforementioned scenarios the stressors were likely thought to be beyond the unaided control of the praying family member. The praying mother and husband recognized the limited control they had in the outcomes of the family situations and therefore turned to a higher power to "give it up to God" (Marks et al., 2005). By transferring the locus of responsibility, or passing the burden, intercessory prayers align with the deferring religious coping approach and may relieve psychological distress for the individual who is praying, whether or not the intercessory prayer for intervention is "answered" (Bänziger et al., 2008; Marks, 2008).

To this point in the chapter, we have discussed religious coping generally, and the most prevalent kind of religious coping, prayer, in more detail. Having provided an outline of what religious coping involves, we now turn to our *American Families of Faith* data to illustrate and capture some examples of religious coping from mothers, fathers, and families in the real world.

Religion and Coping as Described by *American Families of Faith*

When asked how he and his family handle the challenges of life, a Christian father named Ernie told us:

> I really believe that, no matter what it is, that God will give me the strength to endure it, or I'll grow from it, no matter what it is. And it will just be an opportunity for me to grow. . . . He gives *us* the strength to endure.

Ernie mentioned that God "gives me strength" in his personal life, but Ernie's concluding statement that "he gives *us* the strength to endure" moves his discussion of coping from the individual level to the family level. An African-American mother named Elizabeth also discussed strength at the family level. She explained her perspective:

> A family who believes [and] has [a] good foundation, [they] are going to be able to weather storms real good. . . . Having a strong, faith-based family will help you through a lot. Knowing God and having something that you believe in will help you to get through. . . . [It is important to] put God first, in everything that you do, and to trust Him, in every situation. Always call upon Him . . . because, if you put Him first, in everything that you do, then you always know, you can always turn to Him in times of trouble.

A Latino Catholic father similarly reflected:

> What we've been through this past year would put a strain on any marriage but we have [been reminded] that our family is the most important thing to us and that we're in this together. . . Our faith is all involved with that.

Tara, an African-American Baptist mother, stated:

> As I grow closer to God and more involved in faith—I mean, you're always going to have struggles—but [I] learn how to handle them better and life becomes easier to cope with.
>
> (Marks et al., 2012)

Each of these participants report that "God," "faith," or both of these provided strength to handle the varied and unpredictable challenges of life.

However, they tell us little about *how* their faith serves as a resource. We next examine two themes—(1) religious beliefs and coping and (2) religious practices and coping—in order to examine in more depth how and why these two dimensions of religion have been valuable coping resources that have helped our AFF participants cope with life issues such as the death of family members, sudden and chronic health problems, financial problems, conflict, and daily life challenges.

Theme 1: Religious Beliefs and Coping

Religious beliefs were foundational for how most (but not all) *American Families of Faith* participants framed their perceptions of life challenges. A variety of beliefs were repeatedly referred to by these couples—beliefs that reportedly helped them better cope with the hardships of life. Central concepts that linked coping and religious beliefs included the following four sub-themes: (1) the importance of having similar beliefs in marriage, (2) keeping a long-term perspective, (3) challenges are needed in life, and (4) challenges can bring people closer to God.

Sub-Theme 1: The Importance of Having Similar Beliefs in Marriage

One concept that emerged repeatedly was that sharing similar belief systems and values enabled these couples to approach difficulties through a united bond. A mother named Vickie spoke of the powerful influence that shared beliefs had in her marriage. She explained:

> We are more united in our marriage because we both . . . [have] the same faith and same beliefs. We see things more in the same light so we work together. We have the same values and the same goals that we're striving for in our marriage and as parents. . . . I know that's been a big influence on our marriage.

Similarly, a Catholic husband and father named Jed stated:

> There [were] several years that were very hard, and I guess that is [like] any other couple, but I think one of the things that has kept us together is the fact that we are thinking on the same plane.

Other couples expressed that having similar beliefs and values not only helped them resolve conflict but also minimized conflict because they already agreed on many major life issues—so when there was conflict, it was often limited to less important issues.

Sub-Theme 2: Keeping a Long-Term Perspective

Many of our AFF couples shared their belief that their "long-term perspective" increased their commitment to their marriage. This belief was also repeatedly mentioned as helpful in coping with difficult challenges. A belief that marriage is meant to last seemed to minimize or at least ameliorate day-to-day difficulties the couples experienced, both by way of impact as well as number. Linda, a Latter-day Saint, explained how her commitment to their "eternal family" and marriage helped her through the pain of delivering a stillborn child:

> Our . . . child was stillborn. That was difficult. That was very difficult. And if we didn't have the commitment we have, to the eternal family, I think it would have been very hard for me. . . . It was a crazy time for me. But I think it was my commitment to Jonathan and our eternal commitment—and our spiritual commitment to each other that . . . helped me make it through that.

Sub-Theme 3: Challenges Are Needed in Life

Another belief that framed the way that many AFF families seemed to cope with adversity was a belief that challenges and adversity are an important part of life that provides opportunities for personal growth and that challenges can draw people nearer to God and each other. Sophie, a Presbyterian wife and mother, asserted, "[Our belief in God has] given the marriage more strength, [and has] given me more strength within the marriage when we hit difficult times."

Many individuals who spoke about the challenges in their lives mentioned the hand of God in orchestrating those challenges or allowing them to happen because they served a needful purpose. Thomas, a Presbyterian husband and father, said, "I believe that God orders our lives so that we wind up coming around to what he wants us to do. I think he uses crises in our lives to bring us to stronger faith."

Others also spoke of an opposing force that caused adversity but believed that adversity served a higher purpose. Although they believed this opposition and the associated challenges were also a normal and needful part of life, they attributed the source of the challenges to a contrary force and not to God. Lee, a non-denominational Christian husband and father, said:

> I know that there's a force that's working against love, peace, and harmony, when I look at my religious faith and belief. And like "in sickness and in health" . . . sometimes this world will test that for us. [Life] has a way of testing if you mean[t] what you said [in your marriage vows]. . . . You said it, but now that you're confronted with it, are you really going to live up to it? Are you going to hold [true to] your sacred vows?

For wives and husbands like Sophie, Thomas, and Lee, the belief that adversities are not only inevitable but also often needful and purposeful, no matter the source, reportedly helped some couples cope more effectively with the challenges they faced.

Sub-Theme 4: Challenges Can Bring People Closer to God

AFF couples often seemed to engage in the process of "sanctifying" their challenges and adversity by seeing a divine purpose or reason for them. Whether or not they believed God "sent" specific challenges or crises, many couples believed that God actively played a role in helping them *cope* with their challenges. Indeed, many couples believed that God was not only willing but anxious to help them with their challenges.

Many participants described their belief that marriage (and the human experience in general) was beyond their own ability to deal with successfully. Several "knew" that they needed God to help negotiate and cope with the challenges. Some described this power as grace, as did Karen, a Catholic, who explained:

> Grace is a word [we use] when we talk about sacraments. It's God's hand in things, God's helping hand, [as He's] helping you along. And so I think when you talk [about] marriage, I don't know how people stay together without faith because it's too hard . . . on a human level to just keep a relationship going. So that's what I mean. You have to have something bigger than you.

Although Karen's explanation is quite general, many participants offered specific examples of how divine help made a difference in their lives. In speaking of raising a child with special needs, Krista, a non-denominational Christian mother, stated:

> You can go much further than what you think you can go. You can do much more than what you think you can do. It was a challenge, but in the midst of all the ups and downs, there was still joy and there was still love. [The challenge] really did teach me a lot of things in a logical way—how life truly is, and how through all of that, you can live above your circumstances, if you truly depend upon God, [and] truly trust God for everything.

Similarly, Yuusif, a Muslim husband, described how he has felt a divine influence working out things in ways that were beyond his own capacity. He reported:

> I have been up against obstacles and difficulties where I tried every possible logical thing, and I said, you know, there's nothing more we can do. And then suddenly something changed and it was done. And right away [I] knew that it was not in my capacity [and that God helped].

Some couples spoke of how God's interventions helped them deal with conflict. Charles, an Orthodox Christian husband, described his experience as follows:

> God does act in your lives and show you things so that you see things differently. And you're given strength to do things, you're given more strength than you had before and you're given more charity and you just don't see things the same way. You see things in His light and not in your own. And that allows you to do what you have to do.

Another couple, Lin (husband) and Zhen (wife), struggled for nine years and finally "accepted God" following a harrowing experience in their marital life. They explained, "We together first believed in God because of the adversity in May of 1995, [when] we lost our first child. We were baptized together for the same reason." Life course theory posits that transitions in life are windows of time when other accompanying changes are more probable (Hareven, 2000). Indeed, the death of a child has led more than one religious person *away* from faith. However, in Lin and Zhen's case the result was the reverse. As Lin reported, "The desperation of a man is the beginning of [knowing] God." They explained that now they sincerely try to convey the love of God to others. When Lin and Zhen converted, they changed their views from believing that "there is no God" to believing that God lives and that "God is love" (Lu et al., 2013).

For these individuals and couples—and many others like them—a belief in God's enabling hand seemed to lead to a sanctified perspective of coping with challenges in their lives. We now turn from the coping resource of religious beliefs to that of religious practices.

Theme 2: Religious Practices and Coping

AFF couples and families mentioned several religious practices that helped them cope, including: (1) prayer, (2) scripture study, (3) religious rituals, and (4) repentance and forgiveness. Each of these practices are discussed and illustrated next as sub-themes.

Sub-Theme 1: Prayer

Prayer was the most frequent response when couples were asked what religious practices helped them cope with challenges. Frank, a Catholic husband, explained:

> Prayer certainly is helpful. I think trying to find some outlet, not only a spiritual outlet in terms of trying to realize our way and control over it, and so many factors that make things stressful. . . . There are things I don't directly have control over. [I am] trying to give that up, [to] let God come in, [and] let Him work those things out and let me realize I'm just a piece in the puzzle.

Frank described prayer as a process through which he worked through challenges and sought release from the stress of trying to do it on his own. Rebecca, a Latter-day Saint wife, explained how God not only gives perspective but actively helps as a result of her petitional prayers. She said:

> I find that I can get very tired and cranky, but when I take time to say a prayer, or to think about spiritual things, or to go to a meeting, I think that influence of . . . [God's] Spirit, then calms me and helps me to be patient in situations where maybe I normally wouldn't be able to.

Although nearly all of the participants spoke positively about prayer as a helpful resource in coping, a handful of participants felt differently. One couple in particular felt that petitional prayer (asking God for help) was *not* helpful. Saul, a Reform Jewish husband, explained his belief, "I mean, if all you had to do was pray and God did whatever you said, then God would be like a puppet on a string. Right?" Saul insisted that prayer was sometimes useless because you can't pray to change things that had already happened and that coping has to do with doing the best we can in a situation instead of trying to change it.

Although Saul was one of the only people to say petitional prayer does not lead to help, he was not alone in believing that at times we simply must do the best we can in hard situations. Several individuals and couples believed that God would not necessarily help by changing your situation directly, but most seemed to believe God could help you make it through, especially if help was sought through prayer.

Sub-Theme 2: Scripture Study

Another religious practice reportedly used to cope with challenges was scripture study or reading sacred texts. Ibrahim, a Muslim husband and father, explained his view that the scriptures provide help when times are positive or negative. He said:

> There are times where, you know, you're not very happy with what's going on. And then you turn to Allah and you seek guidance. So it's like, always that feedback, when you're not sure of what's going on, and you're distressed, and you're looking for guidance. Whether it's marriage or any other aspect of life, the Muslims tend to look at the scripture and say, "What am I supposed to do? How am I supposed to react? What has God prescribed for me under these circumstances?" We try to look for guidance, so I think . . . it has [an] effect when times are good and when times are bad.

Scripture study seemed to be a way for several participants to find specific direction in how to cope or handle challenges, but this practice also seemed to be a way that some participants connected with God. Georgia, a Baptist wife, explained, "I have to really get down with the Lord. I have to go search the scriptures and find a verse that relates, something for me to hold onto throughout the day." Scripture study was also seen by some as an important practice to help with marital conflict. Jenny, another Baptist wife, described this in general terms when she said:

> Like all marriages, we have our ups and downs and our differences and disagreements, and I think being able to go back to the word and [to] read scripture and [to see] what scripture says about it helps. That is my roadmap for my life and for my marriage.

Many of our AFF couples seemed to use the scriptures somewhat like some less religious couples might use self-help books. More specifically, many believed that the answers to daily challenges and conflicts lay in putting into practice the principles their holy writ contained.

Sub-Theme 3: Religious Rituals

Many couples spoke of the strength, comfort, and direction they found in religious rituals when they were faced with life challenges. Some rituals were tied to regular worship activities. Shantelle, a Latter-day Saint wife and mother, spoke of the peace that came from attending the temple, a special building for rituals and worship. She reflected:

> When you go in [the temple], at least for me, it makes me feel more calm and I relax about the cares that I have in the world, including relationship issues. And it humbles me and makes me a little more open, I guess, to resolving issues or figuring things out together.

Frank, a Catholic husband and father, similarly explained how the rituals of his worship were a resource to him:

> What the church offers in terms of those tools that God has given it to help strengthen us: the Eucharist, the Sacrament of Reconciliation, those things. When I'm really in personal stress, I can think of times where [during] the most challenging times, I'll go before God and the blessed sacrament, and just pour my heart out, and the answers flow back. So, yes, that's where I turn.

Another coping resource for individuals and couples was family-based rituals prescribed or encouraged by their religion. Although these rituals were not used only in times of crisis, they often provided a foundation or a structure to help deal with challenges or even prevent challenges from arising. Kent, a Mormon father, felt that their weekly ritual of Family Home Evening (the practice of dedicating one night a week for religious family activities) was an important part of helping his family live more happily. He said:

> Family Home Evening is very important. We've noticed that when we don't do that, there's been a few times in our marriage where that slips a little bit and you can tell. A few more problems [start] going on, things aren't as happy as they were.

Recent research from our project indicates that in addition to the power of Family Home Evening for Mormon families like Kent's, similar unifying family benefits are attributed to *Shabbat* family rituals by Jewish families and the Ramadan fast by Muslim families (Alghafli et al., forthcoming; Marks et al., forthcoming A, forthcoming B).

Sub-Theme 4: Repentance and Forgiveness

Couples from almost every faith tradition spoke of two principles in practice that helped them deal with conflict: repentance and forgiveness. Many of these couples spoke of the helpful and healing nature of these practices and the central role they played in coping with, facing, and resolving the stressor of conflict in marriage. Some spoke of repentance and forgiveness as situation specific, and others spoke of these processes as a part of their weekly worship practices. Alvin, a Presbyterian husband and father, described forgiveness in his marriage in these terms:

> I think the Christian emphasis on forgiveness has played a big role when we're going through hard times. [We believe that] one can be forgiven and we can move on—and that's a very fundamental part of the Christian faith.

Repentance and forgiveness rarely came easily to couples and individuals. Karen, a Catholic wife and mother, shared her struggle to forgive as she explained, "You understand it humanly . . . that you're called to [forgive] sometimes, [but] that's not easy and almost takes supernatural powers." Similarly, Neal, an Orthodox Christian husband, spoke of their family ritual of asking forgiveness of one another on the way to communion each week. He shared, "There are some weeks when I want to turn around and say, 'No! Not this week! Sorry! No! Not after what you did this week!' " The couple laughed about this and admitted that while they knew that repentance and forgiveness were both essential to resolve conflict in their marriage, they sometimes struggled to give and ask for it. This topic will be discussed at length in chapter 12.

> I love you even more today than I did yesterday. That is because yesterday you really ticked me off.
>
> —anonymous

Conclusion

In this chapter we examined and discussed several ways that religious families seem to access resources from their faith to help them cope with the stresses and challenges of life. When stressors enter into the life of one or more in the family, the family can either succumb to the stressor in such a way as to produce a crisis, or they can employ various coping techniques and actually grow and become more resilient. To restate a point made at the outset of the chapter, the *American Families of Faith* project has found that "strong" families are not families without problems (there are no such families). Instead, a defining feature of strong families is their ability to find ways to *unify* during difficult times.

While also employing resources common to more secularly oriented families, strong families of faith tend to rely on other religious means of coping, especially when the problems are perceived as extreme or highly difficult. Religious coping refers to efforts to involve God to find positive meaning in the challenges—but religious coping often involves seeking means by which to overcome challenges as well.

Religious coping can be divided into three categories. When couples or families simply acknowledge the presence of a higher power but do not explicitly involve that higher power to cope with the stressor, the coping is referred to as "self-directed." When the family chooses to approach the stressor by passing the problem on to God, it is referred to as "deferring." Finally, when couples or families involve God while also taking other initiatives to deal with a stressor, it is referred to as "collaborative." As with more secular means of coping, religious coping can lead to positive or negative outcomes. Religious coping can lead to increased stress and difficulty—or to a reduction of stress and an increase in family-level resiliency and unity.

In this chapter we focused on knowledge gained regarding religious coping from available social science research including the *American Families of Faith* research project. Families in the AFF research project spoke of how three aspects of their religious faith influence their family: beliefs, practices, and community. In this chapter, we focused on two of these aspects in relation to religious coping: beliefs and practices. There were four specific aspects of belief that the families in the AFF project employed to better cope with stressors: (a) the benefit received through shared beliefs, (b) the belief that marriage is meant to last and that all problems must be seen through a long-term perspective, (c) the belief that challenges are a necessary and (at times) even helpful part of life, and (d) the belief that challenges are meant to bring us closer to God. Further, we saw how religious couples employ four specific behaviors as part of their religious coping: prayer (especially petitional prayer), scripture study, religious rituals, and the centrality of repentance/forgiveness.

These religious beliefs and practices reportedly provided additional resources by which families can cope with the challenges they face. The families who were part of the AFF project not only spoke of leaning on their sacred beliefs and practices often, they also referenced and related the benefits they perceived from doing so. By understanding religious coping better, we are enabled to see how religious families differ in dealing with the stressors that are part of everyday life for all families.

Chapter Summary Points

1. Religion is often used as both an individual-level and family-level coping tool to deal with the difficulties in life.
2. Religious coping tends to be more frequently employed by minority families and families with limited resources.
3. Three approaches to religious coping include self-directing, deferring, and collaborative approaches.
4. Religious coping can be positive or negative depending on factors including perceptions of God, self, and others—and also perceptions regarding the challenges being faced.
5. Prayer is the form of religious coping most practiced in response to stress, including stress associated with health-related issues.
6. Beliefs can be helpful in the coping process, especially when the beliefs are shared within the family, when they provide a long-term perspective, when they help put the challenge into perspective, and when they bring the family "closer to each other" and to God.

7. Religious practices, such as prayer, scripture study, and religious rituals, are often invoked and involved in religious coping.

Review Questions

1. How does the text define religious coping?
2. Among which groups of people is religious coping more common?
3. What are three approaches to religious coping? Explain them in your own words.
4. Imagine a family is faced with unexpected unemployment and the resulting financial strain. What would the family do if they chose to take a self-directed approach to religious coping? What about with the deferring and collaborative approaches?
5. According to the text, what are some differences between positive and negative forms of religious coping? What is the difference in their outcomes?
6. What did William James say is the "soul and essence of religion"?
7. What is petitionary prayer?

Note

1. We co-authored this chapter with Antonius Skipper and Mike Goodman. Portions of this chapter are reprinted or adapted with permission from M. A. Goodman, D. C. Dollahite, L. D. Marks, & E. Layton (2013), Religious faith and transformational processes in marriage, *Family Relations, 62*, 808–823.

References

Alghafli, Z., Marks, L. D., & Hatch, T. G. (under review). A qualitative study of Ramadan: A month of fasting, family, and faith.

Bänziger, S. J., Uden, M. V., & Janssen, J. (2008). Praying and coping: The relation between varieties of praying and religious coping styles. *Mental Health, Religion and Culture, 11*, 101–118.

Brown, T., Lu, Y., Marks, L. D., & Dollahite, D. C. (2011). Meaning making across three dimensions of religious experience: A qualitative exploration. *Counselling and Spirituality, 30*, 11–36.

Burr, W. R., Marks, L. D., & Day, R. D. (2012). *Sacred matters: Religion and spirituality in families*. New York: Routledge.

Cole, B. S. (2005). Spiritually-focused psychotherapy for people diagnosed with cancer: A pilot outcome study. *Mental Health, Religion and Culture*, 8(3), 217–226.

Gallup, G., & Lindsay, D. M. (1999). *Surveying the religious landscape: Trends in U.S. beliefs*. Harrisburg, PA: Morehouse Publishing.

Hareven, T. K. (2000). *Families, history, and social change*. Boulder, CO: Westview.
Hayward, R. D., & Krause, N. (2015). Religion and strategies for coping with racial discrimination among African Americans and Caribbean Blacks. *International Journal of Stress Management, 22*, 70–91.
Hill, R. (1958). Generic features of families under stress. *Social Casework, 49*, 139–150.
James, W. (1902). *The varieties of religious experience*. New York, NY: Random House.
Johnson, K. S., Elbert-Avila, K. I., & Tulsky, J. A. (2005). The influence of spiritual beliefs and practices on the treatment preferences of African Americans: A review of the literature. *Journal of the American Geriatrics Society, 53*, 711–719.
Koenig, H. G., King, D. E., & Carson, V. B. (2012). *Handbook of religion and health*. New York, NY: Oxford University Press.
Krause, N. (2010). The social milieu of the church and religious coping responses: A longitudinal investigation of older Whites and older Blacks. *International Journal for the Psychology of Religion, 20*, 109–129.
Lu, Y., Marks, L. D., Nesteruk, O., Goodman, M., & Apavaloaie, L. (2013). Faith, conversion, and challenge: A qualitative study of Chinese immigrant Christian marriages. *Journal of Comparative Family Studies, 44*, 227–247.
Marks, L. D. (2008). Prayer and marital intervention: Asking for divine help . . . or professional trouble? *Journal of Social and Clinical Psychology, 27*, 678–685.
Marks, L. D., Hatch, T. G., Dollahite, D. C., Goodman, M., & Phillips, T. (under review). "The Family that prays and plays together stays together": Qualitative reports on Mormon Family Home Evening as a weekly ritual.
Marks, L. D., Hatch, T. G., & Dollahite, D. C. (under review). Sacred practices and family processes in a Jewish context: Shabbat as the weekly family ritual par excellence.
Marks, L. D., Hopkins, K., Nesteruk, O., Chaney, C., & Baumgartner, J. (2012). A qualitative exploration of why faith matters in African-American marriages and families. *Journal of Comparative Family Studies, 43*, 695–714.
Marks, L. D., Nesteruk, O., Hopkins-Williams, K., & Davis, T. (2006). Stressors in African American marriages and families: A qualitative exploration. *Stress, Trauma, and Crisis, 9*, 203–225.
Marks, L. D., Nesteruk, O., Swanson, M., Garrison, M.E.B., & Davis, T. (2005). Religion and health among African Americans: A qualitative examination. *Research on Aging, 27*, 447–474.
Pargament, K. I. (1997). *The psychology of religion and coping: Theory, research, and practice*. New York, NY: The Guilford Press.
Pargament, K. I., Koenig, H. G., & Perez, L. (2000). The many methods of religious coping: Development and initial validation of the RCOPE. *Journal of Clinical Psychology, 56*, 519–543.
Pargament, K. I., Koenig, H. G., Tarakeshwar, N., & Hahn, J. (2001). Religious struggle as a predictor of mortality among medically ill elderly patients: A 2-year longitudinal study. *Archives of Internal Medicine, 161*(15), 1881–1885.
Pargament, K. I., & Mahoney, A. (2002). Spirituality: The discovery and conservation of the sacred. In C. R. Snyder, & S. J. Lopez (Eds.), *Handbook of positive psychology* (pp. 646–659). New York, NY: Oxford University Press.
Pargament, K. I., & Raiya, H. A. (2007). A decade of research on the psychology of religion and coping: Things we assumed and lessons we learned. *Psyke & Logos, 28*, 742–766.

Pargament, K. I., Smith, B. W., Koenig, H. G., & Perez, L. (1998). Patterns of positive and negative religious coping with major life stressors. *Journal for the Scientific Study of Religion, 37*, 710–724.

Peck, M. S. (1978). *The road less traveled: A new psychology of love, traditional values and spiritual growth*. New York: Simon and Schuster.

Pew (February, 2008). U.S. religious landscape survey. Pew Research Center. Retrieved from http://www.pewforum.org/files/2013/05/report-religious-landscape-study-full.pdf.

Schafer, M. H. (2013). Close ties, intercessory prayer, and optimism among American adults: Locating God in the social support network. *Journal for the Scientific Study of Religion, 52*, 35–56.

Shorter-Gooden, K. (2004). Multiple resistance strategies: How African American Women cope with racism and sexism. *Journal of Black Psychology, 30*, 406–425.

Silver, R. C., Poulin, M., Holman, E. A., McIntosh, D. N., Gil-Rivas, V., & Pizarro, J. (2004). Exploring the myths of coping with a national trauma: A longitudinal study of responses to the September 11th terrorist attacks. *Journal of Aggression, Maltreatment, & Trauma, 9*, 129–141.

Spilka, B., Shaver, P., & Kirkpatrick, L. (1985). General attribution theory for the psychology of religion: The influence of event-character on attributions to God. *Journal for the Scientific Study of Religion, 22*, 326–339.

Tarakeshwar, N., & Pargament, K. I. (2001). Religious coping in families of children with autism. *Focus on Autism & Other Developmental Disabilities, 16*, 247–260.

Taylor, R. J., Chatters, L. M., & Levin, J. (2004). *Religion in the lives of African Americans: Social, psychological, and health perspectives*. Thousand Oaks, CA: Sage.

Wong-McDonald, A., & Gorsuch, R. L. (2000). Surrender to God: An additional coping style? *Journal of Psychology and Theology, 25*, 149–161.

Forgiveness, Faith, and Families[1] 12

Robert Quillen, a mid-20th-century journalist, observed, "A happy marriage is the union of two good forgivers." As we will see in this chapter, the research on forgiveness, faith, and families seems to indicate that there is more than a little truth in this statement.

Forgiveness: An Introduction and Definition

What is forgiveness, and how does it relate to families? One of the better social science definitions, as offered by Denham and colleagues (2005), begins, "Forgiveness is a transformation of one's affect, cognitive judgments, and motivations toward an offender" (p. 129). How is this done? The authors explain that the transformation called forgiveness begins when the victimized individual assesses the harm done to him or her and (1) "makes an assessment of the harm done and acknowledges the perpetrator's responsibility" but (2) "voluntarily chooses to cancel the debt, giving up the need for revenge, punishments, or restitution" and then, finally, (3) "one removes oneself from the negative emotions directly related to the transgression" (p. 129).

There are several parts of this definition that are helpful. It includes the idea of a transformation, and it includes three components of changes—changes in thinking, emotion, and motivation (see also, Fincham, Davila, & Beach, 2007). As the negative emotion is checked and subsides, forgivers continue to recognize that a wrong existed, but there are changes in their thinking so the continuing poison and pain from the wrong that was done to them do not continue to be a part of their present and future life. To illustrate these processes, we share the following story from one of our sources.

The Year of Forgiveness

My wife's sister went through a phase of drug abuse and landed in trouble with the law. We were in graduate school at the time and had no money, but upon promise of repayment we borrowed a couple thousand dollars for a bail bond. The repayments did not come and, for years, we carried the twin burdens of resentment and financial debt. Every month during our [marital] budget meeting, the debt and resentment were both there with us. . . . I was reading in the Old Testament one day, where God commands Israel to forgive all debts during the seventh (Sabbatical) year. This sunk into my heart and I presented the idea to my wife, who told me she had been having similar thoughts. She was tired of being angry with her sister and having that point of tension (the unpaid debt) at the center of every conversation they had. We wrote a letter forgiving the debt in full, promising not to raise the issue again. The sense of healing was almost immediate. My only regret was that we didn't do it years earlier.

—author's name withheld

Forgiveness in Family Relationships

Forgiveness is relevant for most human relationships, but it is widely recognized that it is particularly important in family life. In fact, some have suggested it is the most important factor in whether families are successful (Fenell, 1993). Religious involvement facilitates forgiveness.

To summarize an important principle, *forgiveness helps families find successes and avoid failures, and the lack of forgiveness is damaging in families.* To paraphrase a related quote, "When you get bitten by a rattlesnake, you have two choices: You can scream in pain until you die or you can get the poison out." The scholarly literature is not the source of the principle and practice of forgiveness; the roots of the idea are embedded in the traditions of the world religions. The word "forgive" appears 43 times in the New Testament. Most of the time it is about God forgiving sins, but 11 times it is about humans forgiving each other. We see three themes in these references: (1) God can and will forgive sins, (2) humans ought to forgive others as many times as they are offended, and (3) humans will only be forgiven by God if *they* are forgiving. In the Lord's Prayer or "Our Father" held sacred by many Christians, Jesus's model of how to pray includes the phrase: "Forgive us our debts *as* we forgive our debtors" (Matthew 6:12, KJV, emphasis added). The pivotal and conditional phrase "*as* we forgive out debtors" seems to reference at least two aspects of forgiveness—the timing and the degree. Is one's offering of forgiveness mercifully quick or painfully slow? Is it provisional, constrained, and insincere—or pure and complete? Indeed, a rephrasing of the forgiveness phrase of the Lord's Prayer might well read: "Our Father which art in Heaven . . . Please do *not* forgive me in full, *until* I have forgiven in full." This emphasis on cleansing one's own heart first is illustrated in the following narrative from a father and husband we interviewed in the *American Families of Faith* project. Joseph, a father from Pennsylvania, said:

> We're people, we screw up . . . but as we invite God into our life and He forgives us of our sins and as we present ourselves to Him, He changes us and makes us more like Him and . . . the desires of our hearts change and we develop friendship with God. . . . The whole meaning of life is to get to know God and to become like Him and to do the same sorts of things that He is invested in. And I'm sure that I fall way short and still have a lot that I don't see and mess up on but . . . [because I'm] a Dad (and having had kids), you see your kids make efforts to please you and to do what you want and to imitate you, you don't get upset that they didn't do better. It's just amazing that they even want to try, you know? So rather than focus on the shortcomings, it's just about trying to relate to God and to get to know Him better.

Another father we interviewed, Jake, spent some time in prison early in his marital life. He used that time to reflect on his poor decisions. His post-prison life involved a legitimate job, turning to faith, and becoming the father and husband he believes God wants him to be. Discussing God, this father stated:

> He's just waiting there with loving arms, and says, "Come on, I understand. I understand what you're going through, because I've been there." . . . And I believe that's what people need to know. And God is not . . . sitting there with a black robe, pounding his gavel, but He's there with open arms, just waiting to take you in.

For both of these fathers, their conceptualizations of God, their sense of connection to Him, and their desire "to relate to God and to get to know Him better" are evident. The assurance of Jake, who had made serious mistakes and been incarcerated, was that God is "there with open arms, just waiting to take you in." These beliefs in a God who willingly forgives reportedly instilled a desire in Joseph to both seek and to offer forgiveness, especially to his own children.

Forgiveness is a central and important idea in Christianity, and the refusal to forgive is a serious wrong. Indeed, forgiveness is an important theme in many world religions. For example, the Qu'ran reads, "He who forgiveth, and is reconciled unto his enemy, shall receive his reward from God" (Sura 42:40). A passage from Mormon scripture similarly reads:

> Wherefore, I say unto you, that ye ought to forgive one another; for he that forgiveth not his brother his trespasses standeth condemned before the Lord; for there remaineth in him the greater sin. I, the Lord, will forgive whom I will forgive, but of you it is required to forgive all men.
> (Doctrine and Covenants 64:9–10)

> You shall blot [any offenses against you] out of your mind and not bear a grudge. For as long as one nurses a grievance and keeps it in mind, one may . . . take vengeance. The Torah therefore emphatically warns us not to take a grudge. . . . This is the right principle. It alone makes civilized life and social interaction possible.
> —Jewish philosopher Maimonides, *Mishneh Torah*

One of the reasons we believe the principle of forgiveness is true and powerful in families is because of comments made by people we have interviewed about the role of forgiveness in their lives. For example, one individual explained:

> The presence and absence of forgiveness has been a powerful part of my life and it has made an important difference in my own family and in my extended family. I watched resentments continue for decades among some of my uncles and watched it destroy their relationships and add to the hurt in the lives of many around them. Their inability to forgive began early in their lives with childish things, and [the failure to forgive] continued as adults with more substantial things, and it lasted until they were all in their graves. As their resentments toward each other festered and grew, it got so they would not attend family gatherings if they learned a certain brother would be there.

Another reason we believe forgiveness has an influence on family successes and failures is because we have observed forgiveness (or the lack of it) in a variety of families of faith including abundant examples in counseling and educational settings. In sum, we have observed over the decades that willingness to forgive has made an important difference in families we love, know, and work with—including our own. We have watched some who have been unwilling to forgive others for small indiscretions and some who have found it in their hearts to forgive major offenses. Some of these situations, for good or ill, have influenced more than one generation. As we have watched forgiveness for both small and major offenses, we have seen the healing balm dissipate negative emotions and help families move on with kindness and compassion. The following two examples illustrate these observations, although perhaps at different levels of intensity. One Christian father explained, in connection with everyday frustrations in his marriage, that he frequently reminds himself of this:

> One of the basic teachings of the Savior is forgiveness, so . . . if you want to be forgiven, the Bible teaches that you need to forgive other people. And obviously we're imperfect and we want to be forgiven, and so I think both of us bring that idea or that principle into our marriage relationship and we see that we have to be willing to forgive the other person and . . . that influences our ability to maybe forgive a little bit sooner than we normally would have.

Another related example applies the same principle to a significant betrayal of trust—infidelity. One person related the following:

> [Our neighbor's] husband [had an affair that] led to a pregnancy. When the wife learned of the affair, she was hurt and furious, and considered divorce. In the next several months they decided to try to re-create the kind of marriage they had wanted. It was difficult, but she was forgiving and he was repentant, and they worked hard at their marriage. It is now about 15 years after this situation, and they have become a loving and effective family, and have found many successes they probably would not have found without forgiveness.

Whether the balm of forgiveness is applied to mundane, everyday hurts or to piercing wounds like infidelity (see DiBlasio, 2000; Mamalakis, 2001), it reportedly has the power to promote healing in the lives of individuals and families. Narratives like these seem to capture and reflect the essence of Jean Paul Richter's observation that "humanity is never so beautiful as when praying for forgiveness, or else forgiving another." We now transition to several important forgiveness-related findings from social science research.

Forgiveness: A Review of Social Science Research

The scholarly study of forgiveness has created a number of new and important insights about the principle of forgiveness and the processes behind it. This body of research provides information about the nature of forgiveness, how it ought to be defined, and how it can be observed and measured. It also provides new and persuasive evidence of the validity and importance of the principle and how it can help families. Some of the research even outlines ideas and steps for helping people increase their ability and inclination to be forgiving. One reality that scholars have documented is that forgiveness tends to be a *process*, not an event.

Forgiveness Is a Process, Not an Event

There is accumulating evidence that forgiveness is qualitatively different for the minor slights, forgetfulness, hurts, and misunderstandings that are a part of everyday interaction, as opposed to serious breaches in relationships such as abuse, betrayal, and infidelity. Forgiveness can be accomplished quickly and easily in long-term and committed relationships when the offenses are about minor conflicts and everyday hurts (Fincham, Beach, & Davila, 2004), but the process typically becomes more complex and involved as the seriousness of the misbehaviors, offenses, or violations increases.

Several scholars have argued that there are stages in the forgiveness process. Apparently, when many people say, "I forgive you," this declaration may be more of a decision to try to forgive rather than a culmination of the process. Indeed, incompletely resolved feelings of anger or resentment about the transgression often intrude later, can resurface in the relationship, and take longer to completely resolve (Fincham, 2000; Fincham, Hall, & Beach, 2005).

One model of forgiveness, developed by Gordon and Baucom (1998), suggests that there is an impact stage, a definition stage, and a "moving on" stage. One of the important findings from a series of studies using their model (Gordon & Baucom, 1998, 2003; Gordon, Baucom, & Snyder, 2005; Gordon et al., 2009) is that as people move through the stages, they deal with the negative dimension of forgiveness (i.e., forgiving the wrong done) early in the process but deal with the positive dimension of restoring positive affect (i.e., respect, trust, fondness) later or perhaps never.

Consistent with Gordon and Baucom's work, Enright's (2001) model also emphasizes that forgiveness is more of a process than an event. Enright views forgiveness as a journey through four phases: an uncovering phase, a decision phase, a work phase, and a deepening phase. This model has also received some empirical support (Enright & Fitzgibbons, 2000). Sometimes the stages in these models overlap and are dealt with in different orders, but the models that have suggested stages are helpful because they divide the rather complex processes of forgiveness into more manageable parts.

> Atonement is the ultimate expression of freedom because it brings together the two mental acts—repentance and forgiveness—that have the power to break the iron grip of the past.
>
> —Rabbi Jonathan Sacks, *Not In God's Name*

Ways Forgiveness Is Helpful

There are a number of different research questions that have been addressed in the literature, and reviews by Enright and North (1998), Fincham et al. (2004), Fincham, Hall, and Beach (2006), and Worthington (2005) chronicle the progress. One intriguing area of research has examined the effects of forgiveness on the *forgiver*. More specifically, this area has focused on effects of offering forgiveness on physical, mental, relational, and spiritual health (Harris & Thoresen, 2005). In the early days of forgiveness research, claims about positive benefits outweighed supporting data. Thus far, however, no studies have found harmful effects, and several have documented beneficial effects. For example, Toussaint et al. (2001) found from a national survey that forgiveness was associated with fewer negative health symptoms in a sample of elderly people. This is an area where additional research is needed because no "direct" evidence indicates that "unforgiveness is related to [poorer] long-term health or disease." However, this "lack of direct evidence is not surprising, given that the notion of unforgiveness and the means to measure it are fairly recent developments" (Harris & Thoresen, 2005, p. 322).

A number of studies have focused on the relationships between forgiveness and marital processes. Fincham and Beach (2002) and Finchman et al. (2004, 2006, 2007) have repeatedly reviewed this literature, and the cumulative findings are consistent and persuasive. The family-related research in this area has focused mostly on relational outcomes such as marital quality, marital satisfaction, level of happiness, and marital adjustment, but the research also examines connections with other aspects of marital relationships such as conflict, hostility, aggression, communication, retaliatory and conciliatory responses, emotional and intellectual intimacy, trust, and commitment. None of the studies found unexpected or negative relationships between forgiveness and desirable aspects of marriage, and many of them found relationships that were encouraging. For example, Fenell (1993) found that spouses report that the ability to ask for and offer forgiveness is viewed as one of the most important factors contributing to marital longevity and marital satisfaction. These findings—particularly those involving the ultimate importance of offering sincere apologies, seeking forgiveness (and some might say "repenting of wrongs")—have potent implications in marriage. Perhaps it is just as important to seek forgiveness as it is to offer it.

Gordon and colleagues (2005) note that many marital therapists view forgiveness as a vital part of the healing process necessary to overcome profound marital threats such as infidelity, and Fincham, Hall, and Beach (2006) conclude it is also important in healing relatively minor but damaging "everyday relational harms" (p. 415). Marital researcher and therapist Bill Doherty has repeatedly identified the mundane wear and tear of everyday living as *the* greatest threat to many marriages (Doherty, 2000; Doherty & Carlson, 2004). It seems likely that the capacity to both forgive and ask for forgiveness for the "everyday relational harms" in marriage may be an important asset in overcoming the threat of everyday living that tends to pull marriages apart. Indeed, Gordon and colleagues (2009) undertook a review of the research a few years after their previously mentioned study and summarized that "the association between forgiveness and relationship functioning has been well documented" (p. 2). More specifically, greater forgiveness has been associated with higher levels of dyadic adjustment (Gordon & Baucom, 2003; Paleari, Regalia, & Fincham, 2005), greater empathy (McCullough et al., 1998), more positive communication patterns and less psychological aggression (Fincham & Beach, 2002), and greater intimacy and closeness in the relationship (Finkel et al., 2002; Gordon & Baucom, 2003). The Gordon et al. (2009) review further noted, based on studies from three different research teams (Fincham & Beach, 2002; Finkel et al., 2002; Gordon & Baucom, 2003), that "lower levels of forgiveness are associated with poorer relational adjustment, intimacy, and closeness, and higher levels of psychological aggression" (Gordon et al., 2009, p. 2).

In their review of social science research on forgiveness in families, Battle and Miller (2005) drew the following conclusion:

> Individuals with higher levels of dispositional forgiveness—that is, those who have a greater tendency to forgive those close to them after transgressions—are more likely to experience higher quality relationships . . . in their families.
>
> (p. 232)

Research has continued to provide new insights about the effects of forgiveness on family processes. Maio et al. (2008) found, using longitudinal data, that children tended to model the forgiveness-related behavior of parents and that forgiveness had a variety of positive effects, including greater expressiveness and cohesion, emotional stability, agreeableness, and extraversion and less conflict. Gordon et al. (2009) similarly found that forgiveness was related to marital satisfaction and children's perceptions of the quality of marital functioning. Future research on issues such as these will undoubtedly add many more insights about the results of forgiveness.

Ways Forgiveness Can Be Harmful

The scholarly study of forgiveness has almost exclusively emphasized its beneficial effects, but there is some evidence that there are circumstances where it can also be harmful. For example, Murphy (2002) suggested forgiveness may have some long-term costs. In another study, McNulty (2008) has suggested, "There are a number of reasons to expect that the frequency of partners' transgressions should moderate the effects of forgiveness. For instance, forgiveness may remove the accountability necessary to motivate changes in the transgressing partner" (p. 171). McNulty also goes on to explain that removing accountability "may allow more frequent problems to worsen over time. Further, forgivers faced with numerous transgressions may feel frustrated or betrayed in a manner that is qualitatively different than in those with relatively few partner transgressions to forgive" (pp. 171–172).

McNulty studied these issues with longitudinal data and found some replicated correlations between forgiveness and (positive) marital outcomes, but some novel (negative) interactions also appeared. When spouses were rarely negative, forgiveness was positively related to satisfaction and to a lower severity of problems, but both of these relationships became inverse when spouses were frequently verbally negative. These findings suggest that there may be some circumstances where forgiveness may not be wise, or that (at least) the timing may be important.

> Forgiveness is an absolute necessity for continued human existence . . . but almost always we should not forget that there were atrocities, because if we do, we are then likely to repeat those atrocities. . . . [They] will return to haunt us.
>
> —Bishop Desmond Tutu (1998, p. xiii)

Reasons Forgiveness Is Helpful

The religious literatures encourage forgiveness, and the scholarly literature documents that relationships exist between forgiveness and a number of variables, but these two bodies of literature are limited in the information they provide about *why* forgiveness helps. Our observations and interviews suggest that forgiveness is important because of what happens inside people (and in their relationships) when there are wrongs or offenses that are forgiven—or not forgiven. When we feel wronged, there apparently are a number of negative emotions and motivations that tend to build up and be retained, sometimes for long periods of time. Some of these emotions are resentment, frustration, and anger. Some of the motivations often include finding ways to retaliate or get even.

If we retain feelings and motivations of resentment, especially if they become intense, they have a number of predictable and undesirable effects. Our minds and hearts increasingly become cankered with negative affect, and this tends to color our perceptions. This leads us to attribute more evil and aggressiveness to the intentions of others than may actually exist, a tendency psychologists refer to as "hostile attribution bias" or "**negative sentiment override**" (Gottman & Silver, 2015). Also, we tend to find ourselves motivated to act in retaliatory ways, even though we may usually be loving and kind. An added negative side effect is that we often find ourselves transferring anger and resentment to other relationships and being mean and vicious to the very people we love the most (Warner, 2001). It is difficult to neatly "contain the poison" in one area of our lives without damaging other domains and relationships. The result is often that negative emotions that are retained lead us to be more unloving than we would otherwise be. Conversely, when we forgive, we lose a host of negative phenomena that interfere with our desires to be loving, and we have an increased capacity to be loving and kind rather than mean, vindictive, and unkind.

> He who has not forgiven an enemy has never yet tasted one of the most sublime enjoyments of life.
>
> —Johann Kaspar Lavater
>
> The quality of mercy is not strained.
> It droppeth as the gentle rain from heaven
> Upon the place beneath. It is twice blessed:
> It blesseth him that gives and him that takes.
>
> —William Shakespeare, *The Merchant of Venice*

Cheong and DiBlasio (2007) have argued that it is important to view forgiveness as salient in families because the offering is a vital part of what it means to love others. It helps us be accepting, kind, understanding, and helpful rather than rejecting, condemning, and hurtful. Our aim is that these beginning ideas (about how and why forgiveness helps) will contribute to future work examining these processes. However, these ideas also are only a beginning; there is a need for future scholarship that will provide more insights.

Applications

An increasing number of programs have been developed to help people learn how to be forgiving and to help them forgive. There have been family life education programs (Al-Mabuk & Enright, 1995; Burchard et al., 2003; Ripley & Worthington, 2002) and therapeutic programs (Al-Mabuk & Downs, 1996; Coyle & Enright, 1997; DiBlasio, 1998; Freedman & Enright, 1996; Gordon, Baucom, & Snyder, 2000; Worthington, 1998). The effectiveness of many of these programs has been studied empirically, and the results have shown discernible improvements in forgiveness and marital and family outcomes. Even so, Fincham and colleagues (2006) have reviewed this research and argue that the research about these programs is limited because it only deals, so far, with modest and short-term parts of the forgiving process. Again, more is needed.

Conclusion

In this chapter, forgiveness was identified as a leading example of a social science research domain where work from both sacred and academic sources can be integrated to enhance conceptual and practical understanding of a given family-related issue. The chapter discussed the idea that forgiveness helps families find successes and avoid failures and that a lack of forgiveness is damaging to both individuals and families. We addressed the emergence of a growing scholarly literature about the nature and measurement of forgiveness that beneficially augments scriptural and sacred treatments of the concept and noted that the scholarly work is beginning to examine ways forgiveness relates to marital and family phenomena. This research was reviewed, evaluated, and summarized, and some new ideas were introduced regarding how and why forgiving helps families.

We conclude by calling for a careful and multi-faceted examination of forgiveness from diverse secular and sacred perspectives as a model for what we hope to see in the future. When other significant issues including sacrificing, loving others, and coping with undesirable behavior in families receive the level of thoughtful attention from sacred and secular perspectives that forgiveness has, we believe that the results will be synergistic—and that these efforts can benefit both academic and applied family professionals in ways that will matter to real families in the real world.

Chapter Summary Points

1. Forgiveness has been defined as "transformation of one's affect, cognitive judgments, and motivations toward an offender"; it also may involve assessing harm, choosing to cancel a "debt," and removing negative emotions.
2. Children tend to follow the pattern of forgiveness (or lack of forgiveness) demonstrated and modeled by their parents.
3. Forgiveness can be harmful in families under some circumstances.
4. While forgiveness is an important process, many people agree that it is important not to forget in order to prevent similar things from happening again.

Review Questions

1. What are the three stages of forgiveness identified by Denham and colleagues?
2. According to Enright (2001), what four phases constitute the journey of forgiveness?
3. There is a difference among scholars about the definition of forgiveness. Which definition do you prefer and why?

4. What are some of the effects of forgiveness on the forgiver?
5. What did Fenell find to be the most important factors in predicting marital longevity and satisfaction?
6. Can forgiveness be harmful? If so, how?

Note

1. Portions of this chapter are reprinted and/or adapted with permission from W. Burr, L. Marks, & R. Day (2012), Forgiveness, in *Sacred Matters: Religion and Spirituality in Families*, Routledge.

References

Al-Mabuk, R. H., & Downs, W. R. (1996). Forgiveness therapy with parents of adolescent suicide victims. *Journal of Family Psychotherapy, 7*, 21–39.

Al-Mabuk, R. H., & Enright, R. D. (1995). Forgiveness education with parentally love-deprived late adolescents. *Journal of Moral Education, 24*, 427–444.

Battle, C. L., & Miller, I. W. (2005). Families and forgiveness. In E. L. Worthington (Ed.), *Handbook of forgiveness* (pp. 227–243). New York: Routledge.

Burchard, G. A., Yarhouse, M. A., Kilian, M. K., Worthington, E. L., Berry, J. W., & Canter, D. E. (2003). A study of two marital enrichment programs and couples' quality of life. *Journal of Psychology and Theology, 31*, 240–252.

Cheong, R. K., & DiBlasio, F. A. (2007). Christ-like love and forgiveness: A biblical foundation for counseling practice. *Journal of Psychology & Christianity, 26*, 14–25.

Coyle, C. T., & Enright, R. D. (1997). Forgiveness intervention with postabortion men. *Journal of Consulting and Clinical Psychology, 65*, 1042–1046.

Denham, S. A., Neal, K., Wilson, B. J., Pickering, S., & Boyatzis, C. J. (2005). Emotional development and forgiveness in children: Emerging evidence. In E. L. Worthington (Ed.), *Handbook of forgiveness* (pp. 127–142). New York: Routledge.

DiBlasio, F. A. (1998). The use of a decision-based forgiveness intervention within intergenerational family therapy. *Journal of Family Therapy, 20*, 77–94.

DiBlasio, F. A. (2000). Decision-based forgiveness treatment in cases of marital infidelity. *Psychotherapy, 37*, 149–158.

Doherty, W. J. (2000). *Take back your marriage*. New York: Guilford.

Doherty, W. J., & Carlson, B. (2004). *Putting family first*. New York: Owl Books.

Enright, R. D. (2001). *Forgiveness is a choice: A step-by-step process for resolving anger and restoring hope*. Washington, DC: APA Life Tools.

Enright, R. D., & Fitzgibbons, R. P. (2000). *Helping clients forgive: An empirical guide for resolving anger and restoring hope*. Washington, DC: American Psychological Association.

Enright, R. D., & North, J. (Eds.) (1998). *Exploring forgiveness*. Madison, WI: University of Wisconsin Press.

Fenell, D. (1993). Characteristics of long-term first marriages. *Journal of Mental Health Counseling, 15*, 446–460.

Fincham, F. D. (2000). The kiss of the porcupines: From attributing responsibility to forgiving. *Personal Relationships, 7*, 1–23.

Fincham, F. D., & Beach, S. R. H. (2002). Forgiveness in marriage: Implications for psychological aggression and constructive communication. *Personal Relationships, 9*, 239–251.

Fincham, F. D., Beach, S. R. H., & Davila, J. (2004). Forgiveness and conflict resolution in marriage. *Journal of Family Psychology, 18*, 72–81.

Fincham, F. D., Davila, J., & Beach, S. R. H. (2007). Longitudinal relations between forgiveness and conflict resolution in marriage. *Journal of Family Psychology, 21*, 542–545.

Fincham, F. D., Hall, J., & Beach, S. R. H. (2005). Till lack of forgiveness doth us part: Forgiveness and marriage. In E. L. Worthington (Ed.), *Handbook of forgiveness* (pp. 207–225). New York, NY: Routledge.

Fincham, F. D., Hall, J., & Beach, S. R. H. (2006). Forgiveness in marriage: Current status and future directions. *Family Relations, 55*, 415–427.

Finkel, E. J., Rusbult, C. E., Kumashiro, M., & Hannon, P. A. (2002). Dealing with betrayal in close relationships: Does commitment promote forgiveness? *Journal of Personality and Social Psychology, 82*, 956–974.

Freedman, S. R., & Enright, R. D. (1996). Forgiveness as an intervention goal with incest survivors. *Journal of Consulting and Clinical Psychology, 64*, 983–992.

Gordon, K. C., & Baucom, D. H. (1998). Understanding betrayals in marriage: A synthesized model of forgiveness. *Family Process, 37*, 425–449.

Gordon, K. C., & Baucom, D. H. (2003). Forgiveness and marriage: Preliminary support for a measure based on a model of recovery from a marital betrayal. *American Journal of Family Therapy, 31*, 179–199.

Gordon, K. C., Baucom, D. H., & Snyder, D. K. (2000). The use of forgiveness in marital therapy. In M. E. McCullough, K. I. Pargament, & C. E. Thoresen (Eds.), *Forgiveness: Theory, research, and practice* (pp. 203–227). New York: Guilford Press.

Gordon, K. C., Baucom, D. H., & Snyder, D. K. (2005). Forgiveness in couples: Divorce, infidelity and couples therapy. In E. L. Worthington (Ed.), *Handbook of forgiveness* (pp. 407–422). New York, NY: Routledge.

Gordon, K. C., Hughes, F. M., Tomcik, N. D., Dixon, L. J., & Litzinger, S. C. (2009). Widening spheres of impact: The role of forgiveness in marital and family functioning. *Journal of Family Psychology, 23*, 1–13.

Gottman, J. M., & Silver, N. (2015). *Seven principles for making marriage work*. New York: Harmony.

Harris, A. H. S., & Thoresen, C. E. (2005). Forgiveness, unforgiveness, health and disease. In E. L. Worthington (Ed.), *Handbook of forgiveness* (pp. 321–333). New York, NY: Routledge.

Maio, G. R., Thomas, G., Fincham, F. D., & Carnelley, K. B. (2008). Unraveling the role of forgiveness in family relationships. *Journal of Personality and Social Psychology, 94*, 307–319.

Mamalakis, P. M. (2001). Painting a bigger picture: Forgiveness therapy with pre-marital infidelity: A case study. *Journal of Family Psychotherapy, 12*, 39–54.

McCullough, M. E., Sandage, S. J., Brown, S. W., Rachal, K. C., Worthington, E. L., & Hight, T. L. (1998). Interpersonal forgiving in close relationships: II. Theoretical elaboration and measurement. *Journal of Personality and Social Psychology, 75*, 1586–1603.

McNulty, J. K. (2008). Forgiveness in marriage: Putting the benefits into context. *Journal of Family Psychology, 22*, 171–175.

Murphy, J. G. (2002). Forgiveness in counseling: A philosophical perspective. In S. Lamb, & J. G. Murphy (Eds.), *Before forgiving: Cautionary views of forgiveness in psychotherapy* (pp. 41–53). London: Oxford University Press.

Paleari, F. G., Regalia, C., & Fincham, F. D. (2005). Marital quality, forgiveness, empathy, and rumination: A longitudinal analysis. *Personality and Social Psychology Bulletin, 31*, 368–378.

Ripley, J. S., & Worthington, E. L. (2002). Hope-focused and forgiveness-based group interventions to promote marital enrichment. *Journal of Counseling and Development, 80*, 452–463.

Toussaint, L. L., Williams, D. R., Musick, M. A., & Everson, S. A. (2001). Forgiveness and health: Age differences in a U.S. probability sample. *Journal of Adult Development, 8*, 249–257.

Tutu, D. (1998). Without forgiveness there is no future. In R. D. Enright, & J. North (Eds.), *Exploring forgiveness* (pp. xiii—xiv). Madison, WI: The University of Wisconsin Press.

Warner, C. T. (2001). *Bonds that make us free: Healing our relationships, coming to ourselves*. Salt Lake City, UT: Shadow Mountain.

Worthington, E. L. (1998). An empathy-humility-commitment model of forgiveness applied within family dyads. *Journal of Family Therapy, 20*, 59–76.

Worthington, E. L. (2005). *Handbook of forgiveness*. New York: Routledge.

13 What We Have Learned and What We Hope You Will Take with You

We began this book by explaining our reasons for writing the book, including our own life-changing experiences during emerging adulthood, as well as our personal and professional interest and investment in young adults who are faced with many of life's most important decisions. In the spirit of a highlight film, in our last chapter, we will review several of the most important issues and findings we have discussed throughout *Religion and Families*. We do so hoping this will help you as you consider what you might take with you from your study of this book.

Chapter 1: Why Religion Matters to You Right Now and in Your Future Family

Without an expansive vision of the horizon, our perceptions are likely to be severely flawed. This matters because when you wrestle with and think deeply about the BIG questions (questions about Being, Intimacy, and God), your vision and perception of your personal "life horizon" can be expanded, extended, and clarified. We discussed what Aristotle called the Terrifying Questions (e.g., "Is this life all there is?"), but with respect to emerging adulthood, we think these should be called the "Terrific Questions" because these are the deep, meaningful, and thought-provoking questions that require us to really ponder what Robert Emmons (1999) calls the psychology of ultimate concerns.

As William James (1902/1997) teaches us, *perceptions matter profoundly.* When we believe or perceive so deeply that these beliefs or perceptions become *real* to us, these beliefs and perceptions then begin to cause real effects. This matters because what James called authentic, "unmistakable religious spirit" is transformed into observable action. This matters in both our own personal and family lives, but it also matters immensely in our efforts to understand human behavior in the world around us—especially the behavior of deeply religious persons and families.

On this note, Burr, Marks, and Day (2012) emphasized that *it is what we do as a result of perceptions, ideals, and beliefs about the sacred that determines whether the sacred is helpful or harmful in families.* This matters because regardless of what we *claim* to believe, it is our action and behavior that most define us individually, as well as our relationships with our family members. Accordingly, we offer the principle of lived invitation: *Our behavior is permission to others to behave similarly . . . but it is more than that. It is an invitation to do so.* Our decisions yield influence on the lives of countless others—providing all the more reason for each of us to truly ponder the BIG questions.

Chapter 2: What in the World Is Religion?

There have been many definitions of "religion," but a three-dimensional definition/conceptualization of religion involving (1) beliefs, (2) practices, and (3) community is helpful in better understanding how religion influences individual, marital, and family well-being.

For most of the 20th century, the BAD/RAP (**B**ogus **A**nd **D**angerous/**R**eligion **A**s **P**sychopathology) hypotheses portrayed religion as a childish fantasy harmful to mental health, and a small but vocal group of so-called New Atheists continue to rail against religion with downright religious fervor (Prothero, 2010). However, Rodney Stark's (1971) finding that religious involvement related to *lower* levels of mental illness opened a new and more empirical chapter in the study of religion and well-being. Subsequent research on religious involvement has generally been correlated with positive outcomes, although there are negative evidences as well. While the state of the science on religion and individual/family outcomes has progressed markedly over the past 100 years (especially the past 20), the empirical research addressing religion and family has many limitations, including a lack of depth, difficulty in measuring religion with validity, and limited participation in "family" research.

Chapter 3: Does Religion Matter to Families?

Based on a large and growing body of research demonstrating significant influence of religious beliefs, practices, and communities on marriage and family life, it is now clear that any scholarly dialogue on family issues that does not include thoughtful and challenging discussion of the influence of religion on family relationships is significantly limited. Similarly, a religious dialogue that does not include information on contemporary religious families is not likely to be particularly pragmatic or relevant to human beings.

Indeed, "a substantial minority" of people reportedly hold religion as "the single most important influence in [life]" (Miller & Thoresen, 2003, p. 25). Many disciplines (secular or sacred, social science or theological), many persons (individuals and families), and many situations (including those of the "helpers" and the "helped") can be benefitted by additional knowledge regarding the religion-family connection. The quality and strength of the religion-family knowledge base will be expanded as religion-family research moves beyond recurring correlations to examine the important whys (meanings) and hows (processes) that are at work (Marks, 2006; Marks & Dollahite, 2011). Such efforts can allow us to see how religion can be a potent influence for bad *or* for good, depending on how family members believe, interpret, experience, and act out their religion (Burr et al., 2012).

Existing empirical studies examining individuals have found that: (1) religious practices are typically correlated with decreased alcohol and substance abuse, improved addiction recovery outcomes, and decreases in alcohol-related domestic violence; (2) religious beliefs are correlated with increased mental health and greater optimism; and (3) active involvement in a religious community has been correlated with benefits including lower rates of cancer, increased life expectancy, more healthy relationships, and greater social support. While these outcomes are technically "individual" in nature, some reflection will show that each of these issues (e.g., alcohol/drug abuse, domestic violence, mental health, physical health, longevity, and social support) have potent direct and indirect influence at both the family and societal level as well (Stark, 2012). Many of these particularly impact marriage.

Chapter 4: Why Does Religion Matter in Marriage?

Available research that focuses on the religion and marriage connection has demonstrated that same-faith marriages are significantly more stable than inter-faith marriages. In fact, in some religions, the divorce rate doubles or even triples in inter-faith marriages (Lehrer, 2009). Further, multiple studies across time have repeatedly correlated (shared) religiosity with increased marital satisfaction, increased commitment, and fidelity (Mahoney, 2010; Mahoney et al., 2001; Marks & Dollahite, 2011). Exceptions and problems have been noted, however, when husbands' mental health is poor (Sullivan,

2001), when religious beliefs differ significantly (Curtis & Ellison, 2002), when religious beliefs (e.g., tolerance of abuse) contribute to the ongoing victimization of battered women, and when religion contributes to struggles (Dollahite, Marks, & Pearl, unpublished manuscript). It is also important to note that local faith communities tend to provide various kinds of support for many married couples who are actively involved—however, faith communities tend to be less helpful and supportive to those in non-traditional/non-marital families (Dollahite, Marks, & Goodman, 2004).

Recent qualitative research indicates that the strongest marriages are often between two people who not only share the same denomination but also share the same level of commitment to their religion, or feel they are "equally yoked" or "on the same page." Qualitative research from the national *American Families of Faith* project further found that even among the strongest marriages the couples faced difficult challenges and conflicts, especially in their early years of marriage. Many couples reported that a shared family vision, often derived from religious beliefs, was central to their marriage.

Chapter 5: The Influence of Religious Beliefs in Marriage

The connection between religious beliefs and marriage was discussed at length with the help of qualitative data from the *American Families of Faith* project. Focused attention was given to themes including the unifying influence of pro-marriage beliefs, the stabilizing influence of anti-divorce beliefs, the importance of shared spiritual beliefs in marriage, and faith in God as a marital support. We also illustrated how religious beliefs can be a source of *harm* in marriages and families. Three specific and documented harms include: (a) excessively rigid anti-divorce beliefs that delay or prevent divorce when it is probably necessary, (b) concerns over "male headship" and submission of wives as taught in the writings of the Christian apostle Paul (concerns were expressed by women and men), and (c) family conflict and tension due to divergent religious beliefs (both within and across generations).

On one hand, religiously based, pro-marriage beliefs can encourage a sense of greater commitment to marriage and a sense of greater accountability before God to be a good spouse—while shared spiritual beliefs and a unified "family vision" lie at the heart of many strong marriages and families. On the other hand, religious beliefs can also be harmful in families. For example, a strong aversion to divorce can be damaging in situations where divorce may be warranted; religious beliefs may be applied and interpreted in ways that are sexist or abusive; and conflict or tension in marriage or across generations can arise due to differing beliefs. Family professionals who are aware of the help and harm that can result from religious beliefs, and who are sensitive to and respectful of the religious beliefs of those they serve, are likely to be more effective (whether the professional shares the same beliefs or not).

Chapter 6: Parenting in Faith—What Research Has Found

Previous research and the *American Families of Faith* project both capture largely positive but sometimes negative connections between religion and parenting. Lived parental example is of foundational importance in the religion-family connection as reflected in our principle of lived invitation: "Our behavior is permission to others to behave similarly, but it is more than that—it is an *invitation* to do so." This seems to hold particularly true in the context of parent-child relationships.

Additionally, the power of example seems to be most effective when accompanied by warm relationships. Large-scale research indicates that religious beliefs are most likely to be transmitted between parents and children when there is a strong and nurturing relationship between the parent and child (Bengtson, Putney, & Harris, 2013). Even so, "walking the walk" is not the whole story. Religious practices—including conversations about faith—often have positive influences on parent-child relationships and faith development. In other words, "talking the talk" in a way that respects the agency, opinions, and desires of children and youth also matters greatly.

Chapter 7: Parenting and *American Families of Faith*

Research from several sources has indicated that parents are a primary factor (and typically *the* primary factor) in their children's religious and spiritual lives—and this influence often remains into adulthood. Although it is probable that children will stay in their parents' religious denomination, almost half do not remain affiliated with their parents' faith. A strong predictor is whether a close relationship existed between the parents and child—another predictor is whether parents remain together or divorce (chapter 10).

Research and conceptual work both indicate that the charge to "practice what you preach" is an important and powerful call for religious parents to remember and live. In addition, it is important for religious parents to learn how to talk about religious matters with their children—especially teenaged and young adult children—in ways that promote strong families and strong faith. The best way to "talk" is often to *listen.*

Chapter 8: Muslim Families in the United States

Chapter 8 was the first of three chapters that addressed and presented some of the challenges that accompany religion and family life for those who fall outside the white, Christian, traditional, marriage-based family population. We were offered the opportunity to see through the eyes of a sample of 25 American Muslim families how the local Islamic community and various religious practices impact these individuals and families.

Some Muslim participants stressed that the mosque is a place where unity of purpose and faith is fostered. We saw the importance of the religious community because Muslims rely on frequent interaction with other like-minded Muslims. In the United States such interaction comes primarily during local Muslim community events and worship services at the mosque.

Regarding religious observance in the home, prayer (*salat*) was frequently mentioned as both personally and relationally helpful. For many (if not most) of the Muslim families interviewed in the AFF project, fasting during the month of Ramadan was reported to be the most salient religious practice pertaining to family life. The religious practices of prayer (*salat*) and Ramadan reportedly helped unify families and strengthened bonds between husbands and wives and between parents and children.

Chapter 9: Jewish Families in the United States

From in-depth interviews with 30 Jewish families with varying degrees and styles of religious observance, we learned about aspects of Judaism that were most salient for many of them. We also caught a glimpse of the challenges and frustrations that Jewish families experience as members of a minority religion in the United States. Several families reported that they felt forced to choose between observing the Sabbath (e.g., staying home with family and attending Sabbath synagogue services on Friday nights and Saturday mornings) *or* being active in their non-Jewish community by participating in school dances, school plays, sporting events, work parties, and other community events that are often scheduled on Friday nights and Saturdays.

Although the religious community and synagogue serve a meaningful purpose and seem to foster a sense of identity and belonging, many Jewish family members identified "home-based Judaism" as being even more meaningful for living as a Jewish American than "synagogue-based Judaism." *Shabbat* (Sabbath) is the most common Jewish observance in the home, and most Jews observe some aspects of the Sabbath with family and friends. Sabbath activities may include family time, nice dinners, special food (e.g., challah), special clothing, dancing, music, and lighting candles. *Shabbat* was discussed by 93% of Jewish participants in the AFF project and is considered an important ritual by many Jewish families because of its identity-maintaining, peace-promoting, and family-unifying nature.

Chapter 10: Religion and Diverse Family Forms

Very little research has examined families of cohabiting couples, same-sex couples, single parents, or stepfamilies. However, scholars have observed that religious congregations are typically more welcoming of two-parent families, making it easier for such families to engage in congregational life in ways that single-parent and other diverse families might find less inviting or more difficult (Edgell, 2005).

In chapter 10, through data from the *Does the Shape of Families Shape Faith?* project and other sources, we reported that divorce leaves many children feeling lost and "as though the world is unreliable" (Root, 2010, p. 139). By and large, most faith communities have not responded well to the related needs and crises of divorced persons and their children.

Research reflects a widespread longing for faith, for a sense of sacred meaning, and for high commitment marriages among emerging adults (including children of divorce)—but equally widespread is a sense of lingering doubt that such hopes are attainable, based on the pain and disappointment that many have experienced in their families of origin.

Through story, mentoring, and (perhaps most importantly) genuine lived example, faith communities can create sacred space for children of divorce to hear and see how and why marriage matters. We have observed that "a key challenge for [many] American churches in the 21st century will be to find a balance between supporting the standard of marriage-based families that is idealized . . .

[while simultaneously and sensitively] addressing the pluralistic family realities that confront them" (Dollahite et al., 2004). The relational and spiritual futures of many families (and some faith communities themselves) may rest, in some measure, in how well this is done in the years to come. Following three chapters on minority and diverse religious families, we turned to two chapters on religion and family processes, *coping* (chapter 11) and *forgiving* (chapter 12).

Chapter 11: How Religion Influences Coping with Stress and Challenges in Families

Research has demonstrated that a defining feature of strong families is their ability to find ways to *unify* during difficult times. While also employing processes and resources common to more secularly oriented families, strong families of faith tend to rely on other religious means of coping, especially when the problems are perceived as extreme or highly difficult. Religious coping refers to efforts to involve God to find positive meaning in the challenges—but religious coping often involves seeking means by which to overcome challenges as well.

We explained that religious coping can be divided into three categories: self-directed, deferring, and collaborative. As with more secular means of coping, religious coping can lead to positive or negative outcomes. Religious coping can lead to increased stress and difficulty—or to a reduction of stress and an increase in family-level resiliency and unity.

American Families of Faith project participants discussed the benefits they received through shared beliefs as they dealt with life's challenges. Specifically, they addressed the belief that marriage is meant to last and that problems should be seen through a long-term perspective; the belief that challenges are a necessary and (at times) even helpful part of life; and the belief that challenges are meant to bring us closer to God. Further, we saw how religious couples employ four specific behaviors as part of their religious coping: prayer (especially petitional prayer), scripture study, religious rituals, and the centrality of repentance / forgiveness.

These religious beliefs and practices reportedly provided additional resources by which families can cope with the challenges they face. The families who were part of the AFF project not only spoke of leaning on their sacred beliefs and practices often; they also referenced and related the benefits they perceived from doing so. By understanding religious coping better, we are able to see how religious families differ in dealing with the stressors that are part of everyday life for all families.

Chapter 12: Forgiveness, Faith, and Families

A variety of scholars have demonstrated that forgiveness helps families resolve relational divides and that the lack of forgiveness is damaging in families. Forgiveness is needed for both major and minor relational harms and hurts. On the "minor" note, marital researcher and therapist Bill Doherty has repeatedly identified the mundane wear and tear of everyday living as *the* greatest threat to many marriages (Doherty, 2000; Doherty & Carlson, 2004). It seems likely that the capacity to both forgive and ask for forgiveness for the "everyday relational harms" in marriage may be an important asset in overcoming the threat of everyday living that tends to pull marriages apart. In many cases, religious involvement facilitates forgiveness.

Battle and Miller (2005) concluded that "those who have a greater tendency to forgive those close to them after transgressions—are more likely to experience higher quality relationships . . . in their families" (p. 232). Similarly, Cheong and DiBlasio (2007) stated that it is important to view forgiveness as salient in families because the offering is a vital part of what it means to love others. Burr and colleagues (2012) indicated that forgiving helps us be accepting, kind, understanding, and helpful rather than rejecting, condemning, and hurtful. Indeed, we concluded the main body of this book with a chapter on forgiveness because of its pervasive and indispensable power and influence for good in families—religious or not. We now conclude with three take-home messages.

Three Take-Home Messages from the *Religion and Families* Book

There are many research-based ideas about the nexus of religion and family life that we have strived to convey to you in this work. From all of these, however, there are three focal points from the empirical research, including our nearly two decades of work on the *American Families of Faith* project, that we encourage you to consider carefully: (1) significant commitment matters, (2) shared faith matters, and (3) synergy among dimensions of religion matters.

Significant Commitment Matters (The "Threshold Effect")

At the individual level, literally hundreds of studies have linked religious involvement with better mental health, elevated levels of physical health (including substantially lower cancer rates), and years of additional longevity (Koenig, King, & Carson, 2012; Koenig, McCullough, & Larson, 2001). Research also indicates that a number of positive correlates of religious involvement are evident not only in later life but as early as adolescence and emerging adulthood (Smith & Denton, 2005; Smith & Snell, 2009). Many of these influences are so substantial that they impact not only individual but also family life.

At the marital and family level, several positive correlations have been observed and documented as well, including increased marital stability, marital quality, and marital satisfaction (Mahoney, 2010; Marks & Dollahite, 2011), as well as benefits to parent-child relationships (Bengtson, Putney, & Harris, 2013; King, 2003; Marks, 2006; Wilcox, 2004). However (and this is the take-home message), a close and comprehensive look at the empirical research reveals that the greatest personal and familial benefits seem to accompany fairly *high* levels of religious involvement. Those persons with significant commitment to their faith seem to attain a "threshold" where measurable benefits are discernible and often substantive, while nominal faith community members or occasional attendees do not. This pattern emerges in studies of adolescents and emerging adults where the religiously "Devoted" reap significantly greater benefits compared to other less engaged groups (Smith & Denton 2005; Smith & Snell, 2009). As Smith and Denton (2005) concluded in arguably the most comprehensive study to date on U.S. teens and religion:

> A modest amount of religion . . . does not appear to make a consistent difference in the lives of U.S. teenagers. *It is only the more serious religious teens, the Regulars and the Devoteds, whose outcomes are more consistently and significantly more positive than those of their entirely religiously Disengaged peers.* (p. 233, emphasis added)

A similar pattern holds in later adulthood for longevity (Hummer et al., 1999) and cancer rates (Enstrom, 1998; Koenig et al., 2001)—those who cross the threshold to relatively high levels of religious involvement and commitment tend to reap the greater rewards. Indeed, high investment in religious commitment seems to yield significantly, even disproportionately, higher returns (Stark & Finke, 2000). When we focus our attention on the family domain, however, there is a very important provision for claiming these higher returns, as we discuss in our two final take-home messages.

Shared Faith Matters

A close look at the several positive correlations that have been discovered at the nexus of religion and marriage, including increased marital stability, marital quality, and marital satisfaction, reveals that there typically seem to be two requirements for maximum benefit: (1) a relatively high level of involvement and/or commitment and (2) a *shared* faith between spouses. However, a high level of religious commitment (typically associated with several benefits) can cease to be a benefit and can become a liability in a marriage where faith is not shared among the spouses.

Research indicates that core religious differences tend to spill over and exacerbate conflict in many other areas, including but not limited to child-rearing practices, division of housework, and spousal roles (Curtis & Ellison, 2002). As repeatedly noted, divorce rates increase dramatically (sometimes two- or three-fold) in inter-faith marriages (Lehrer, 2009)—and there are many reasons for this, although they vary somewhat by faith (see Dollahite & Marks, 2006).

Further, repeated analyses of data from our *American Families of Faith* project indicate that wives and husbands, mothers and fathers, including some who have experienced inter-faith marriage and divorce personally, emphasized the vital importance of not only sharing the same faith, but "being on the same page," being "equally yoked," and "sharing a vision" of family and faith. For example, even if spouses share a denomination (e.g., both are Catholic or Methodist or Reform Jewish) but have very differing degrees of belief, level of religious commitment, and/or desired amounts of religious participation and sacrifice, significant marital difficulties can ensue. It is difficult to overstate the emphasis placed on this latter point by the AFF women and men who represent 8,000 years of collective marital experience.

Synergy among Dimensions of Religion Matters

Throughout this book, we have addressed the three dimensions of religious belief, practice, and community in our definition of religion. We have shown that social scientific research demonstrates how each of these dimensions impact marriage and family relationships. On their own, each of these dimensions has the power to influence relationships for good or bad. But we have learned that a harmonious synergy between these three dimensions and relationships has the greatest power to matter. Family members who consciously consider and discuss how their religious beliefs, practices, and community can work together for the good of their marriage and family relationships are likely to discover ways to increase harmony between these dimensions. This is particularly important in the increasingly individualistic and secular culture in which contemporary couples and families find themselves.

Conclusion

In conclusion, we believe that the social scientific evidence demonstrates that for religion to be most likely to benefit marriage and family relationships, people should: (a) live their faith seriously (significant commitment matters); (b) live their faith in harmony with loved ones (shared faith matters); and (c) harmoniously combine religious beliefs, practices, and community (synergy among dimensions matters).

May you be blessed in your own journey of finding the best ways of living your faith in your marriage and family life. May you find joy in working together with your loved ones to discover the ways that religious beliefs, sacred practices, and a faith community might be a blessing to each of your family members at various points in your development. In other words, may God bless you and keep you and your family.

References

Battle, C. L., & Miller, I. W. (2005). Families and forgiveness. In E. L. Worthington (Ed.), *Handbook of forgiveness* (pp. 227–243). New York, NY: Routledge.

Bengtson, V. L., Putney, N. M., & Harris, J. (2013). *Families of faith*. New York: Oxford.

Burr, W. R., Marks, L. D., & Day, R. (2012). *Sacred matters: Religion and spirituality in families*. New York: Routledge.

Cheong, R. K., & DiBlasio, F. A. (2007). Christ-like love and forgiveness: A biblical foundation for counseling practice. *Journal of Psychology & Christianity, 26*, 14–25.

Curtis, K. T., & Ellison, C. G. (2002). Religious heterogamy and marital conflict. *Journal of Family Issues, 23*, 551–576.

Doherty, W. J. (2000). *Take back your marriage*. New York: Guilford.

Doherty, W. J., & Carlson, B. (2004). *Putting family first*. New York: Owl Books.

Dollahite, D. C., & Marks, L. D. (2006). Family and community nurturing spirituality in Latter-day Saint children and youth. In K. Yust, A. N. Johnson, S. E. Sasso, & E. C. Roehlkepartain (Eds.), *Religious perspectives on spirituality in childhood and adolescence* (pp. 394–408). Lanham, MD: Rowman & Littlefield.

Dollahite, D. C., Marks, L. D., & Goodman, M. (2004). Religiosity and families: Relational and spiritual linkages in a diverse and dynamic cultural context. In M. Coleman, & L. H. Ganong (Eds.), *The handbook of contemporary families* (pp. 411–431). Thousand Oaks, CA: Sage.

Dollahite, D., Marks, L. D., & Pearl, K. (unpublished manuscript). *Relational Struggles in Religious Families: How the Fire of Faith Sometimes Burns*.

Edgell, P. (2005). *Religion and family in changing society*. Princeton, NJ: Princeton University.

Emmons, R. (1999). *The psychology of ultimate concerns*. New York: Guilford.

Enstrom, J. E. (1998). Health practices and cancer mortality among active California Mormons. In J. T. Duke (Ed.), *Latter-day Saint social life: Social research on the LDS Church and its members* (pp. 441–460). Salt Lake City: Bookcraft.

Hummer, R., Rogers, R., Nam, C., & Ellison, C. G. (1999). Religious involvement and U.S. adult mortality. *Demography, 36*, 273–285.

James, W. (1902/1997). *The varieties of religious experience: A study in human nature.* New York: Longmans, Green.

King, V. (2003). The influence of religion on father's relationships with their children. *Journal of Marriage and the Family, 65*, 382–395.

Koenig, H. G., King, D. E., & Carson, V. B. (2012). *Handbook of religion and health (2nd ed.).* New York: Oxford University Press.

Koenig, H. G., McCullough, M. E., & Larson, D. B. (2001). *Handbook of religion and health.* New York: Oxford University Press.

Lehrer, E. L. (2009). *Religion, economics, and demography: The effects of religion on education, work, and the family.* New York: Routledge.

Mahoney, A. (2010). Religion in the home 1999 to 2009: A relational spirituality perspective. *Journal of Marriage and Family, 72*, 805–827.

Mahoney, A., Pargament, K. I., Tarakeshwar, N., & Swank, A. B. (2001). Religion in the home in the 1980s and 90s: A meta-analytic review and conceptual analyses of links between religion, marriage and parenting. *Journal of Family Psychology, 15*, 559–596.

Marks, L. D. (2006). Religion and family relational health: An overview and conceptual model. *Journal of Religion and Health, 45*, 603–618.

Marks, L. D., & Dollahite, D. C. (2011). Mining the meanings from psychology of religion's correlation mountain. *Journal of Psychology of Religion and Spirituality, 3*, 181–193.

Miller, W. R., & Thoresen, C. E. (2003). Spirituality, religion, and health: An emerging research field. *American Psychologist, 58*, 24–35.

Prothero, S. (2010). *God is not one.* New York: HarperOne.

Root, A. (2010). *Children of divorce: The loss of family as the loss of being.* Grand Rapids, MI: Baker Academic.

Smith, C., & Denton, M. L. (2005). *Soul searching: The religious and spiritual lives of American teenagers.* New York: Oxford.

Smith, C., & Snell, P. (2009). *Souls in transitions: The religious and spiritual lives of emerging adults.* New York: Oxford.

Stark, R. (1971). Psychopathology and religious commitment. *Review of Religious Research, 12*, 165–176.

Stark, R. (2012). *America's blessings.* West Conshohocken, PA: Templeton Press.

Stark, R., & Finke, R. (2000). *Acts of faith: Explaining the human side of religion.* Berkeley, CA: University of California Press.

Sullivan, K. T. (2001). Understanding the relationship between religiosity and marriage: An investigation of the immediate and longitudinal effects of religiosity on newlywed couples. *Journal of Family Psychology, 15*, 610–626.

Wilcox, W. B. (2004). *Soft patriarchs, new men: How Christianity shapes fathers and husbands.* Chicago: University of Chicago Press.

Glossary

bachelor mindset—a term used to reflect male difficulty in shifting from "me first" to "we first" thinking after marriage.

BAD/RAP definition of religion—acronym for the **B**ogus **A**nd **D**angerous/**R**eligion **A**s **P**sychopathology) hypotheses where religion is conceptualized and/or characterized as bogus (childish fantasy, false), as dangerous ("a poison," "opiate of the masses"), and as "psychopathology" (mental illness).

bar/bat mitzvah—literally means "son/daughter of the commandment" and also refers to a series of Jewish observances performed by adolescent males and females at ages 13 and 12, respectively.

behavior-belief congruence—practicing what you preach.

BIG questions—acronym for **B**eing, **I**ntimacy, and **G**od questions, including "Who am I?" "Where am I going?" and "What is my relationship to God?"

collaborative approach—a type of religious coping wherein the coping individual or family shares responsibility with their God or higher power.

Conservative Judaism—a branch of Judaism that tends to view the Orthodox movement as too antiquated or unrealistic and the Reform movement as too secular and non-observant; approximately 18% of American Jews are associated with the Conservative movement.

Conservative Protestant—conservative denominations typically include Assemblies of God, Southern Baptists, Independent Baptists, many Black Protestant churches, Churches of God in Christ, non-denominational churches, and Pentecostal denominations, among others, including most evangelicals and fundamentalists in the United States; they comprise about 30% of the U.S. population.

crisis—as defined by psychologist Erik Erikson, a crisis does not mean a disaster; it means the decisive moment, a turning point, a crucial time.

deferring approach—a religious coping strategy in which individuals or families pass the burden and the entire coping responsibility to God.

dogma—a belief or set of beliefs that is accepted by the members of a group without being questioned or doubted.

domestic church—the religious beliefs, practices, traditions, and patterns that take place within the family home.

equally yoked (see also, *matched-level marriage*)—a Christian phrase often meaning a marriage involving two persons of the same faith (and sharing a similar level of commitment to and involvement in the faith).

exemplar—a noteworthy model, a fine example, a prototypical case; in the *American Families of Faith* project we sought to interview exemplar families.

Family Home Evening—a Latter-day Saint (LDS, Mormon) practice of gathering as a family on Monday evening for spiritual instruction, recreation, and planning.

generalizable (generalizability)—a trait sought for within social science research that allows for a small sample to represent the larger population because it reflects similar characteristics.

Hasidic Judaism—founded in the 18th century in Eastern Europe by Rabbi Yisroel ben Eliezer (also called the Baal Shem Tov); a group within Ultra-Orthodox Judaism that has elements of mysticism and that focuses on creating a personal, loving relationship with God.

high-tension religions (also called *high-demand*)—religions that require significant investments of time, energy, and money; often, these religions also conflict with several elements of contemporary culture.

hijab—Arabic term meaning (a) "curtain" that usually refers to the head covering, although the extension of *hijab* might include a full body covering and a veil (*niqab*) that completely covers the face; (b) a broader principle that references a general separation of males and females in Islam.

intercessory prayer—a prayer to God on behalf of someone else; this type of prayer often asks God to heal, bless, comfort, strengthen, or help another.

inter-faith marriage—a marriage between two people of different religions or denominations.

Mainline Protestant—mainline churches include the "Seven Sisters of American Protestantism"—the Methodist, Lutheran, Presbyterian, Episcopal, American Baptist, Church of Christ, and Disciples of Christ denominations—and tend to share a liberal approach to social issues. They comprise about 15% of the U.S. population.

male headship—the idea of male headship comes from a few New Testament biblical verses, including Ephesians 5:21–33, which includes the phrase "husband is the head of the wife," and Colossians 3:18–4:1, which calls for wives to be subordinate to husbands and includes the idea that husbands have a stewardship to provide spiritual leadership in marriage and family life; Christians debate the meaning of these verses. Those with a complementarian perspective take a more traditional view and those with an egalitarian perspective take a more progressive view.

marital stability—refers to the ability of the relationship to endure; often synonymous with avoiding divorce.

matched-level marriage (see also, *equally yoked*)—a Christian phrase often meaning a marriage involving two persons of the same faith (and sharing a similar level of commitment to and involvement in the faith).

Modern Orthodox Judaism—a movement within Orthodox Judaism that attempts to synthesize Jewish values and the observance of Jewish law with the secular, modern world.

mosque (*masjid* in Arabic)—a place of worship for followers of Islam; masjid means "place of prostration."

Muhammad—beginning at age 40 Muhammad reported that he received several revelations from the heavenly messenger Gabriel that were later transcribed and combined in one volume known as the Qu'ran (Koran), and he founded Islam in the seventh century CE.

Nation of Islam—a faction of Islam created in the U.S. during the 20th century that focuses on improving the spiritual, social, and economic status of African-Americans.

negative sentiment override—a failure for one partner to give the other the benefit of the doubt so that a neutral or positive communication sent by one partner is interpreted by the other partner as negative.

New Christian Religious Traditions—This designation typically includes denominations founded since 1800. The most prominent of these include, in order of membership, Seventh-Day Adventists (SDA), the Church of Jesus Christ of Latter-day Saints (also called LDS or Mormon), Jehovah's Witnesses, and Christian Scientists.

novena—a series of prayers that are said for nine straight days, usually as a prayer of petition but sometimes as a prayer of thanksgiving.

Orthodox Judaism—a branch of Judaism that rejected (Reform Jewish) proposals for change and argued that Judaism could not be reformed because it is a revealed religion; Orthodox Jews constitute roughly 10%

of the Jewish population in the United States but constitute nearly 20% of Jews who belong to a synagogue.

parent-centered conversations—an approach to parent-child interaction similar to lecturing or moralizing that tends to feature one or more of the following four (negative) characteristics: (a) parents talk too much, (b) parents' talk is unsolicited or unwanted, (c) parents give demands without explanation, and/or (d) conversation is too restrictive for the adolescents.

Passover—see *Pesach*.

Pesach—literally "to pass over," or Passover in English, this is perhaps the most commonly observed Jewish holiday; it takes place in the spring in remembrance of God passing over Jewish homes in Egypt when He was slaying every firstborn in the region as a punishment to the Egyptians for not freeing the Jews (led by Moses) from bondage.

petitionary prayer—involves a request and often places an emphasis on a specific outcome, including calling on God to positively alter the impact of a given stressor.

pogroms—attacks on Jewish communities (most notably, but not exclusively, during the 19th- and 20th-century Russian Empire); these persecutions involved looting, murder, and rape.

principle of lived invitation—"Our behavior is permission to others to behave similarly . . . but it is more than that. It is an *invitation* to do so."

Qu'ran (Koran)—the holy book of Islam that includes revelations revealed by God, communicated through the angel Gabriel to Muhammad, transmitted orally by Muhammad to his followers, and then written down after the death of the Prophet.

Ramadan—the ritual month of fasting in Islam in which faithful followers do not eat, drink, or have sexual relations during the daylight hours.

Reform Judaism—a branch of Judaism first developed in Western Europe in the 19th century through the rationale that many Jewish practices and beliefs were outdated, superstitious, or unnecessary; the leaders of this movement believed that Judaism should be adjusted and reinterpreted to be more modern and useful, and Reform Jews now comprise about 35% of the Jewish population in the United States.

religion—defined in this text as comprising three dimensions: (1) religious beliefs, (2) sacred religious practices, and (3) a faith community consisting of believers with whom religious worship, practice, and service takes place.

religious beliefs, dimension of—personal, internal beliefs, framings, meanings, and perspectives that are sacred in nature.

religious community, dimension of—support, involvement, and relationships grounded in one's congregation or religious group.

religious practices, dimension of—include outward, observable expressions of faith such as prayer, scripture study, rituals, traditions, or less overtly sacred practices or abstentions that are religiously grounded.

religious refugee—a sociological term referring to an individual who believes in God but who has lost faith in organized religion, often due to a breach in faith attributed to religious congregants or leadership.

religious transmission—the transfer of religious beliefs, values, and practices from the parents' generation to the children's generation.

salat—Arabic word meaning connection; also, daily prayer; one of the five pillars of Islam.

second silent schism—the break (schism) between members of a family and their faith community that may follow a divorce (the first schism).

self-directing approach—a form of religious coping where families recognize the existence of God or a higher power but choose not to involve the higher power in coping with the stressor.

Shabbat—the Jewish Sabbath, a day of worship, rest, and spiritual enrichment; *Shabbat* is observed from just before sunset on Friday evening until just after sunset on Saturday evening.

Shavuot—the Jewish Festival of Weeks, held seven weeks from Passover; on this day, Jews celebrate the reception of the Torah on Mount Sinai.

Shia—one of the two main branches of Islam; rejects the first three Sunni caliphs and regards Ali, the fourth caliph, as Muhammad's first true successor; accounts for approximately 15%–20% of all Muslim believers, found mostly in Iran, Oman, Bahrain, and a minority in Iraq.

social capital—the value assigned to social networks and how, through the norm of reciprocity, individuals help each other.

spirituality—a term that covers a broad range of applications but generally refers to the sense of connection and desire to connect to a transcendent something outside oneself, such as God or nature.

Sukkot—meaning "booths" or "tabernacles," *Sukkot* is a fall holiday when Jews commemorate their ancestors who wandered in the wilderness for 40 years with Moses by constructing temporary dwellings in yards or synagogue parking lots, taking meals in them, and perhaps sleeping in them.

Sunni—one of the two main branches of Islam, commonly described as orthodox, and differing from Shia in its understanding of the Sunna and in its acceptance of the first three caliphs; accounts for approximately 80%–85% of all Muslim believers.

temporal compartmentalizing—confining the practice of religion to a certain time, space, or setting, with little or no religious practice demonstrated outside that context.

Thomas Theorem—early 20th-century sociologist W. I. Thomas posited that "a situation perceived as real is real in its consequences."

three-fold cord—a biblical concept that includes God, wife, and husband as three woven cords in a marital rope that "is not easily broken" (see Ecclesiastes 4:12; Mark 10:8; Matthew 19:5).

time affair—unduly heavy involvement by a spouse in any outside-of-marriage activity.

time horizon—the imagined but influential assumption regarding how much time we have until we reach the edge of our own life's horizon (i.e., death).

Umma—Arabic word referring to the unity of the global community of Muslims.

Yom Kippur (Day of Atonement)—a profoundly solemn holy day in Judaism on which adherents refrain from eating and other pleasures and repent for the previous year's sins.

youth-centered conversations—an approach to parent-child interaction that tends to feature one or more of the following five (positive) characteristics: (a) adolescent talks more and parents listen, (b) adolescent seeks and receives understanding from parents, (c) religion is related to adolescent's life, (d) conversation is open, and (e) parent-adolescent relationship is nurtured.

zakat—Arabic term meaning "almsgiving"; one of the five pillars of Islam that is designed to take care of the poor and foster empathy; it is designated that a person should pay at least 2.5% of personal wealth for this purpose.

Author Index

Subject Index